Living
WITH
Grief

AT WORK, AT SCHOOL, AT WORSHIP

Living With Grief:
At Work, At School, At Worship

Edited by Joyce D. Davidson
and Kenneth J. Doka

**HOSPICE FOUNDATION
OF AMERICA**

Ordering information:

Bookstores and individuals may order additional copies from
Brunner/Mazel
A Member of the Taylor & Francis Group
47 Runway Road
Levittown, PA 19057

To order by phone, call toll-free: 1-800-821-8312
or send orders on a 24-hour telefax: 1-215-269-0363
Orders can be placed via e-mail: bkorders@taylorandfrancis.com

For bulk quantity orders, call Hospice Foundation of America
at 1-800-854-3402

or write:
Hospice Foundation of America
2001 S St. NW #300
Washington DC 20009
www.hospicefoundation.org
hfa@hospicefoundation.org

Hospice Foundation of America staff assistance:
Lisa McGahey Veglahn, Linda Iekel, Michon Lartigue,
Chris Procunier, and Jon Radulovic

Library of Congress Cataloging-In-Print data available upon request

ISBN: 1-58391-006-9

*To Pat, who has shown me what
excellence and love commingled
look like in end-of-life care.*

—JD

To Curt Boyer

1951–1999

*Who in his rich, but all too brief,
time touched many with his life,
his death, and his music.*

—KD

Contents

Foreword
Jack D. Gordon ....*ix*

Acknowledgments ....*xi*

Introduction: *Where We Grieve*
Kenneth J. Doka *1*

1. A Primer on Loss and Grief
   Kenneth J. Doka *5*

I. Living With Grief: At Work...............................*13*

2. Grief in the Workplace:
   Supporting the Grieving Employee
   Marcia E. Lattanzi-Licht *17*

3. Grief in the Law Enforcement Workplace:
   The Police Experience
   Michael Kirby *29*

4. Grief at Work: New Challenges and
   New Opportunities
   Robert Zucker *45*

   Programs That Work:
   Starbucks Coffee Company...*61*

5. Death in the Military Workplace
   Bonnie Carroll *63*

6. AIDS in the Workplace
   Veronica Ryan Coleman..*73*

7. When Caregivers Grieve
   Paul R. Brenner *81*

Practical Suggestions: At Work...............................*89*

II.   Living With Grief: At School 93

8.   The Grieving Child in the School
     Environment
     Jennie D. Matthews...95

9.   School as a Resource for HIV-Affected
     Children and Youth
     Carol Levine and Azadeh Khalili 115

     Programs That Work:
     Calvary Hospital...129

10. The Grieving College Student
     Robert L. Wrenn 131

Practical Suggestions: At School 143

III.   Living With Grief: At Worship 147

11. Ministry at the End of Life
     Marilyn Barney...149

12. Ritual Responses to Death
     Paul E. Irion...157

     Programs That Work:
     Evergreen Community Hospice.........................167

13. The Religious Community in Times of Loss:
     Strong, Loving, and Wise
     Patrick M. Del Zoppo.......................................169

Practical Suggestions: At Worship.......................185

IV.   Living With Grief: At Home 187

14. Caregiving Communities
     Myra MacPherson 189

15. Giving and Receiving Help During Later Life
     Spousal Bereavement
     Dale A. Lund...203

16. If I Am not for Myself: Caring for Yourself
     as a Caregiver for Those Who Grieve
     James E. Miller 213

Resource Organizations 225

References...237

Foreword

Jack D. Gordon, President
Hospice Foundation of America

One of the central tenets of hospice is that the unit of care is not just the patient, but also the patient's family, and that family is defined to be whomever the patient decides. (This is also one of the fundamental differences between hospice care and other forms of medical care). In a very real sense in our society, the workplace has become a kind of extended family. Businesses have responded to the changing needs of American families by adding programs that reflect this connection between work and life, such as flexible work schedules, onsite childcare, and support for employees caring for aging parents or other loved ones. It follows, then, that grief and bereavement issues affect a workplace as well.

This is why Hospice Foundation of America undertakes the 1999 *Living With Grief* teleconference on grief in the workplace, as well as the other places of our lives, of which this volume is the companion piece.

Why is it that the effects of a death in the workplace mirror the effects of a death in the family? For many years the diagnosis of a chronic or life-threatening illness meant that a person would almost inevitably leave work. Now there are more options. There has been a change in philosophy, too—one that stresses that even in the midst of illness it is important to continue to live life as normally as possible. For many people, that includes maintaining a connection to their work environments, schools, and places of worship.

Yet the nuclear family has become smaller as grown children often live far from aging parents. And caring for a loved one who is ill while juggling a full-time job is a daunting task. Guilt feelings arising out of such conditions, or grief resulting from impending loss, can result in diminished ability to effectively accomplish workplace tasks. It is not uncommon for these dynamics to affect co-workers, thereby inserting a weakened link in the work team. In similar ways, relationships in schools or faith communities can be strained as well.

As the illness progresses or after the patient dies, employees will continue to go to work. And they will be grieving their loss. Grief is not contained by time or place. Loved ones will grieve not only at home but also at work, school, or worship. How well organizations respond to the grieving persons in their midst will either complicate or facilitate their grief. The sensitivity of persons within these environments, especially those in leadership roles, as well as the flexibility and support of organizational policies, can therefore have profound effects on the course of the grieving experience. And the better the organizations respond, the more rapidly they can become completely focused on their missions, as work teams return to cohesiveness.

Hospices can help. Under Medicare law, bereavement services are provided to the families of hospice patients for up to a year after death. Because of that mission, hospices have developed a unique expertise in the care of the bereaved. Hospices bring their decades of experience and extensive knowledge of the nature of the bereavement process to work, school, and faith communities. Such assistance not only supports family members in their grief but also empowers them to take more significant roles in the care of the dying loved one. By lessening the stress or conflict between their work and school roles and their family responsibilities and by strengthening the support from their faith communities, hospices can provide critical support to both family members and dying patients. Organizations are a major beneficiary of this valuable hospice activity. And these activities help hospices by broadening their mission as well as sources of referral and support.

It is my hope that the lessons learned from this book will help hospices to truly become a central resource in their communities, by reaching out to people in all places of their lives—at work, at school, at worship. It is also my hope that the issues raised here will lead to the extension of hospice care to a wider number of people, as well as exert a humane influence on both the workplace and the health-care system.

Acknowledgments

A delightful task in editing or writing a book is to thank all those who make the effort both possible and meaningful. It seems suitable to begin with Jack Gordon, the President of the Hospice Foundation of America. His vision continues to frame both the teleconference and the book that accompanies it, as his gentle wisdom quietly guides the process.

This vision also becomes a reality through the hard work of so many at the Hospice Foundation, both in the Washington, DC and Miami Beach offices: David Abrams, Sophie Viteri Berman, Linda Iekel, Kim Knight, Michon Lartigue, Maria Prado, Chris Procunier, Jon Radulovic, Johana Silva, and Lisa McGahey Veglahn—all have helped, each in his or her way.

Individually, we would like to acknowledge those who have supported us in our work:

JD: First and foremost, I want to thank Ken Doka—still mentor, now colleague and friend. I am daily cognizant of and grateful for his invaluable contribution to my work in this field.

To my colleagues at Hospice of New York. You exemplify Henry David Thoreau's statement: "To affect the quality of the day—that is the highest of arts." I am honored to be in the company of such remarkable people.

Of course, thank you to my husband Rex, who continues to be supportive and cheerful and has never even hinted that it bothered him when I was chained to the computer on weekends.

And especially to the patients and families who have so bravely and graciously permitted me to share exquisitely tender, painful moments in their lives—what a privilege and sacred trust you bestow!

KD: It is always a pleasure to work with my co-editor, Joyce Davidson. I still want to identify her as my student and research assistant. But she is long past that point now—making her own mark in the field. A special thanks to Chris Procunier, who has become a valuable contributor to the process.

My school, The College of New Rochelle, continues to offer a strong, supportive, and stimulating environment. President Steve

Sweeney, Academic Vice President Joan Bailey, Dean Laura Ellis and my own Division Chair, Jerri Frantzve are a large part of that. And two secretaries—Rosemary Stroebel and Vera Mezzaucella, as well as my present research assistant, Eleanora Tornatore, help make the campus function smoothly.

My colleagues in the Association for Death Education and Counseling and the International Work Group for Dying, Death, and Bereavement also are an ongoing source of stimulation and support. So many over the years have become not only good colleagues, but very special friends.

My family, too, has been a strong source of support. I need to acknowledge those friends and family, especially Kathy, for the support and strength they offer. It is a privilege to watch my son, Michael, grow into young adulthood and to view with great joy his flowering relationship with Angela. It is a privilege, too, to watch my godson, Keith, grow into adolescence. And I know his mother, Linda, and I will have a special joy in watching him grow out of it.

Finally, we both want to acknowledge and thank all the authors in this book. They annually do a yeoman's job in responding to tight deadlines and tough editors. We want to thank Bernice Harper for the idea of this year's teleconference and book. As always, we need to thank Cokie Roberts for her yearly gift in making the teleconference sparkle.

Joyce D. Davidson and Kenneth J. Doka

Where We Grieve

In 1998, as we met to discuss the Hospice Foundation of America's teleconference for that year, and the accompanying edition *Living With Grief: Who We Are, How We Grieve*, the assembled panel began to consider the ways the factors such as culture, spirituality, gender, and age affect the grieving process. In the midst of this animated discussion, one panelist, Bernice Harper, reminded us not to forget *where* people grieve.

Her advice was sage. While the complexity of the issues at hand allowed us to address that concern only in passing, the idea remained.

Where we grieve is, in fact, critical. Our grief spills over, affecting all dimensions of our life. We grieve not only at home, in private moments or times of our own choosing, but in all the places we inhabit. We grieve at work, at school, at worship, and in our communities. The ways that others respond to, acknowledge, and support that grief can either complicate or facilitate the grieving process.

Two examples illustrate this. I recently dealt with a mother whose son, a young adult, had died. She worked in a school cafeteria. Sometimes as she saw the children her sadness would overwhelm her and she would shed tears. The principal called her in and told her that such behavior was inappropriate. Still a probationary employee, she was dismissed.

The insensitivity of the act rakes her still. Now she had to cope with two major losses: her child and her job. Moreover, she was removed from the critical support offered by her co-workers. Her own self-esteem suffered.

Her grief was disenfranchised. Disenfranchised grief refers to losses where the griever is denied the right to grief (Doka, 1989). Grief can be disenfranchised because the relationship is not acknowledged (for example, a friend or lover), the loss is not recognized (pet loss, divorce, job loss), or because grievers, such as persons with developmental disabilities or the very young or old, are seen as incapable of grief.

Corr (1998) has expanded the concept of disenfranchised grief.

Many aspects of the grieving experience, he asserts, can be disenfranchised. *Where* one grieves can be one of these. Probably everyone would acknowledge the right of a mother to grieve the death of a child. But here the message of her employer was that, while we recognize your grief, do not grieve here.

Perhaps we can understand the principal's misguided attempt to protect the children from an event about which they, in reality, know far more than we acknowledge (Doka, 1995). Ironically, he denied them the opportunity both to learn about grief and to learn how to support grieving individuals.

It does not have to be that way. In the summer of 1998 my family and I vacationed on a magical resort in the Bahamas called Atlantis. Its very name suggests an escape from reality, the ambiance that the resort projects. Yet one night, as we dined at one of the resort's most elegant restaurants, we noticed that many of the staff attached a black ribbon to their tuxedos and evening wear. We questioned our waiter. He told us that a very popular employee had died the week before, and the ribbons were a mark of mourning.

I was impressed. It would have been very easy for the restaurant simply to demand that the ribbons be removed as contrary to the tone of the establishment. They chose not to do so. Instead, management enfranchised the grief of their employees.

They did so, I found out, in a number of ways. They allowed employees to take a collection for the family. The restaurant contributed food for a traditional post-funeral meal. Moreover, they were flexible, drawing on staff from other restaurants in the resort so that employees could attend the funeral, even cook and serve the meal.

They had created an environment where people could grieve openly, in a supportive atmosphere. It was not only humane, it was good business. Even in the midst of loss, there was a sense of pride and rising morale in how they were able to respond. I am sure employees felt a renewed sense of commitment and respect to their employers, a sense that, I suspect, would be evident in many measurable, as well as intangible, ways for the restaurant.

So *where* people grieve, whether at work, at school, or at worship, can be a critical issue because those places afford or deny support, validation, and empathy. Subsequent sections will explore each of these dimensions.

This introductory section begins that process. Both the fore-word by Jack Gordon and the following chapter offer insights and information that establish a foundation. Gordon's chapter reaffirms why hospices and healthcare organizations should care. Gordon, the president of the Hospice Foundation of America, has long had an interest in the area of grief in the workplace. Bernice Harper's sug-gestion gave new urgency to Gordon's repeated comments that a teleconference should focus upon grief in the workplace. To Gordon, it is an issue for workplaces as well as hospices. As he reminds us, providing support and training in grief is central to hospice's mis-sion. Just as workplaces will find tangible benefits in offering support to their employees, so will hospices. Such a presence can increase sources of both referral and perhaps even revenue. Most importantly, it can enhance creative partnerships between hospices and other segments of the community.

My chapter attempts to provide a primer on grief. We hope that many people will find this book useful—from employee assistance and human resources personnel to those involved in hospice and in working with bereaved individuals. In such a wide audience, levels of understanding of the grief process may vary considerably. The primer offers a review of current understandings on the process of grief, in a question-and-answer format, that concludes with a brief introduction to the ways that grief may affect individuals at work, at school, and at worship.

Where people grieve is a critical issue. As we become increasingly aware of that importance we may be able to create humane environments at work, at school, and at worship, where grieving individuals may find the compassion and support so critical in their struggle.

Kenneth J. Doka

One

A Primer on Loss and Grief

Kenneth J. Doka

Introduction

One of the major problems with grief and bereavement is that so little information about the process of grief is widely disseminated. This seems strange for two reasons. First, there is much information that has been learned and studied throughout the last thirty years. And second, and even more basic, loss and transition are natural human processes, existent from the beginning of time. Certainly information about grief and loss should be widely known, an inherent part of folk wisdom.

Yet this does not seem to be the case. One of the most common questions asked by survivors of a death is whether or not their responses are, in fact, normal. And often the response of others seems to invalidate their grief. Others may expect survivors to quickly let go of their grief and get on with their lives. The understanding that grief is a long, uneven process that affects individuals on a variety of levels—physical, emotional, cognitive, spiritual and behavioral—does not seem to be widely known. In fact, a study of clergy indicated that even these frontline professionals underestimated both the nature and duration of grief (Doka and Jendreski, 1988). In a study of television depictions of grief, which both reflect and inform society, Wass (1988) found that grief was perceived as a short-term process.

In order, then, to address sensitive ways in which organizations such as workplaces, schools, and churches can address grief and grievers in their midst, it is essential that they understand the basics about grief—what it is, how it is processed, how individuals are affected. That information provides the basis of sensitive response.

What Is Grief?

Grief is a reaction to loss. While we often associate grief with death, any loss can cause grief reactions. For example, we grieve divorces, separations, or other losses of relationships. We may grieve the loss of a job or other work-related changes.

This recognition that loss causes grief can remind us of two critical things: First, during the course of a life-threatening illness, the individual experiencing that illness, as well as family and friends, may experience a variety of losses. In addition to the loss of health, patients, families, and friends may lose dreams and hopes for the future. The individual may experience the loss of work, physical capabilities, or appearance. All of these are likely to generate grief.

Second, any transition, however positive, may also entail loss. For example, a promotion may require changes in relationships with fellow employees, or a move to a new area. Similarly, developmental transitions, such as from childhood to adolescence or middle school to high school, can create a sense of loss. In all these situations, then, grief can be experienced.

Though losses can be due to many factors, this chapter will concentrate on losses caused by death, since that reflects the author's experience. But note that much of the discussion and suggestions can be applied to other losses.

Who Grieves?

That may seem like a foolish question. Obviously the person affected by the loss grieves. But it is critical to remember that many different people can be affected by a death or other loss. Family members are not the only people who grieve; friends and co-workers may grieve as well. Even people who seem to have a negative connection to the deceased may experience manifestations of grief. For example, co-workers or schoolmates who had an antagonistic relationship may still grieve, perhaps feeling emotions such as guilt, should one party to that relationship die. Negative attachments are still attachments. Even persons who seemingly have little or no relationship may experience reactions at a loss. For example, the death of a younger person or a work-related death might remind everyone of his or her own vulnerability.

How Is Grief Experienced?

Grief is experienced many ways—physically, emotionally, cognitively, spiritually, and behaviorally. Each person will experience grief in his or her own distinct way. There may be physical symptoms— pain, headaches, fatigue, lethargy, and others. Emotionally, people may experience a range of feelings that can include sadness, anger, guilt, jealousy, fear, anxiety, longing, and even relief. Cognitively, people may find it difficult to concentrate or focus. They may constantly think about the person who died, recurring memories, or aspects of their illness or death. It is not unusual to experience a sense of the deceased's presence or even to seem to hear, see, smell, or touch that person.

Grief, too, has spiritual effects as people seek to construct some meaning out of the loss. Some individuals may find comfort from their faith, while others experience a sense of spiritual alienation. Grief certainly affects the ways individuals behave. Some may avoid reminders of the loss, while others seek such reminders. Grieving individuals may seem irritable or withdrawn; others may constantly seek out activity as a diversion from pain. The key, though, is to remember that each individual grieves in his or her own way.

Do Men and Women Grieve the Same?

From the cradle, men and women are likely to have different experiences. It is not surprising that these different experiences may affect the ways they grieve. Martin and Doka (1999) suggest that many men may be *instrumental grievers*. This means that they are likely to experience grief more cognitively and physically than emotionally. Their affect is likely to be tempered. They may seek relief in activity or in thinking and talking about the loss. Many women are *intuitive grievers*. Their grief is likely to be experienced as waves of different feelings. And they are likely to be helped by sharing or ventilating those feelings with others. But again, it is important to emphasize the individuality of grief. Not all men are instrumental grievers, nor all women intuitive grievers. Grieving patterns are *influenced* by gender, not determined by them.

Do Children Grieve?

Certainly, but children may grieve in ways different from adults. For example, younger children may not understand death. They may be too young to realize fully what death actually means. Younger children, too, have a "short feeling span," meaning that they only can sustain strong emotions for short periods of time. So grieving children may have emotional outbursts that are followed by seemingly normal activity. But this does not mean children have quickly recovered from the loss. Children may manifest their grief in many of the same ways as adults, but they also may show their grief in different ways. Acting out, sleep disturbances such as night-mares, waking up or bedwetting, regressive behaviors, and changes in school performances—all can be signs of grief.

What Affects Grief?

The nature and intensity of a person's experience of grief can be affected by many factors: the circumstances of the loss, the type and nature of the attachment, the quality of the relationship, as well as many personal, social, and cultural factors.

First of all, each relationship is different. The loss of a spouse is different from the loss of a friend, child, parent, or sibling—not necessarily easier or harder, just different.

The relationship is not only different in each role, but also in quality. Each relationship is unique and distinctly mourned. Some relationships are more ambivalent than others. That is, they have mixed elements—things one liked about the person, and things one disliked. Often relationships that have very high ambivalence are harder to resolve. Some relationships are more dependent. Some, more intense.

The ways people die are different, and that, too, affects grieving. Often deaths that are very sudden, or follow long, painful illnesses, create problems for resolving grief. Grieving a suicide or homicide is different from grieving a natural death.

Sometimes the circumstances as well as the cause of the death can create special issues for survivors. In one case, Tom had great difficulty in resolving the loss of his parent, in part because the death took place on a day when he was skiing and was unreachable.

Not only are relationships and circumstances different—each person is, too. Each of us has his or her unique personality and individual ways of coping. Some people are better able to cope than others are. And everyone copes with a crisis in different ways. Some will bury themselves in work, seeking diversion; some will want to talk; others will avoid conversation.

A person's background affects grieving. Everyone belongs to varied ethnic and religious groups, each with its own beliefs and rituals about death. Sometimes these rituals, customs, and beliefs will facilitate grieving, other times they may complicate it. For example, perhaps our religious beliefs provide comfort that the person is in heaven or at peace.

Situations may be different as well. It is harder to resolve grief if one is simultaneously dealing with all kinds of other crises in one's life. It is harder to deal with the stress of grief if one's health is poor. It is harder to cope with loss if friends and families are unavailable or not supportive.

How Is Grief Processed?

Grief is rarely processed in predictable patterns—it is a process unique to every individual. It may be helpful to describe grief as a roller coaster, full of ups and downs, highs and lows. Like many roller coasters, the ride tends to be rougher in the beginning, the lows deeper and longer. Gradually, though, over time the highs and lows become less intense.

Often holidays, special days, and the anniversary of the death are the low times. Holidays and special days such as birthdays are heavily invested with memories. It is natural that the pain of loss would be especially keen then. The anniversary of the death, too, is often a low point. Here, even the season and weather remind one of the time of loss. And each date—the anniversary of hospitalization, the date of death, the date of the funeral—may have its own significance.

How Long Does Grief Take?

As long as it needs. Again, every loss and every individual is different. The popular misconception of grief is that people get over their losses in a relatively short period of time—perhaps a few months or a year at most. The reality is different. Generally, grief tends, in significant relationships, to be most intense for the first two or so years. After that the roller coaster tends to lessen. While persons still experience lows, perhaps even several years after a loss, they tend to be less intense, come less often, and not last as long. Hopefully, these lows will continue to become less intense with time. But there is no timetable for grief.

But People Do Recover from Grief?

Recovery perhaps is not the best word. It assumes that grief is an illness that one gets over in time. Rather, grief results from transitions that everyone faces. Once we experience such a significant transition, we are changed by it. One never goes back to the way things were. Life now is different as a result of the loss.

For most people, the pain of grief lessens over time, and they are able to return to levels of functioning similar to before the loss. Some may even experience a sense of growth, new insights, or skills sharpened as they deal with the loss. But they still live with the loss. They may have experiences even years after the loss where the absence of the person is felt keenly. For example, at her wedding, Kathleen sorely missed her grandfather, who had died six years before. She was well aware this was the only wedding of all his grandchildren that he did not live to see.

Other survivors may have more complicated reactions, still experiencing intense reaction to the loss years after. Here, the relationship or the circumstances surrounding the loss often created conditions that made it more difficult to deal with one's grief. Sudden, violent deaths, or losses in conflicted, ambivalent relationships are examples of types of situations or relationships that might complicate grieving.

How Does Grief Affect People at Work?

Grief can affect people in many ways. Some people actually use work as a diversion, spending more time and effort there as a way to seek respite from the loss. Others may be easily distracted. They may find it hard to concentrate or focus on work, and their efficiency may suffer. Some may find it difficult to maintain an emotional balance. They may struggle not to cry or seem overtly sad. Still others may be angry or irritable.

When work-related deaths occur, many co-workers may be affected. Not only may they experience grief over the person who died, they also may be influenced by the trauma or death, experiencing a greater degree of anxiety as they work.

How Does Grief Affect Children in School?

Children may be affected in many of the same ways. They may feel anxious and insecure. They may act out, showing flashes of anger. They may show regressive behaviors. They may seek attention or seem withdrawn. They may have physical complaints, constantly feeling unwell. Like adults, children may find it difficult to focus or concentrate, becoming easily distracted. Their performance in school may decline. Since many of the manifestations mimic learning disabilities, school counselors and psychologists are well advised to assess possible recent losses as they evaluate students.

Can Grief Affect People at Worship?

Certainly, grief has spiritual effects. Some individuals may feel angry. They may feel alienated from God or disappointed in the support they received from their worshipping communities. Others may struggle with their faith as they seek to understand their loss. Still others may experience a renewed appreciation of their faith and their faith community.

What Can People Do To Help?

While each chapter has specific suggestions, a few general comments might help. Four things may be helpful to persons who are grieving.

First, listen. Many grieving individuals simply need a safe place to explore their many reactions to a loss. One need not try to make people feel better. Nothing one can say can remove grief. Nor is it helpful to share one's own losses at this point. Simply ask the person how they are and listen as they share their grief and problems.

Second, if you can, share memories of the person who died. Sharing one's own stories and memories can assist persons who are grieving as they struggle to understand the life and the death of the loved one.

Third, offer tangible support. There are many ways one can show one cares, including participation in rituals and contributions to memorials. But there are other ways one can help as well. Asking people how they are dealing with the loss demonstrates support. It is more helpful to be specific in your help—offering, for example, to assist them with work, or helping with childcare or a meal—rather than simply saying, "Call me," or, "Can I help?" Bereaved persons may be reluctant to seek help or even be too confused and disoriented to assess what they need.

Finally, watch for danger signs. Self-destructive behaviors such as drinking to excess, suicidal expressions, problematic behaviors, or actions destructive to others are clear signs that the persons may need professional assistance in dealing with the loss. Sensitively assisting individuals in seeking such help shows one's own support and demonstrates caring.

Kenneth J. Doka, PhD, is a Lutheran minister and professor of gerontology at the College of New Rochelle. He serves as associate editor of Omega *and editor of* Journeys, *a newsletter to help in bereavement published by Hospice Foundation of America.*

Part I

Living with Grief:
At Work

Certainly one of the places where individuals grieve is at work. One question that arises is whether workplaces should care. After all, it could be argued, is it not appropriate to expect that workers will leave their problems at home? Can the effective worker not compartmentalize, concentrate on work when there, and on home difficulties or personal problems at more appropriate times? Workplaces are not, after all, therapeutic organizations, but organized to deliver services and create profits.

Yet as much as employees try to compartmentalize, to focus on their work, grief will intrude in numerous ways, affecting grieving employees emotionally, cognitively, and behaviorally.

Not only are organizations and supervisors sensitive for caring, but sensible as well. No one has yet put a price on the cost of workplace grief. Such an estimate would need to take into account days missed directly as a result of loss, days missed due to other aspects of grief (such as a compromised immune system, the stress of loss, or physical manifestations of grief), lessened productivity, and other costs such as litigation. This cost would be great, but can be lessened by sensitive supervisors and sensible policies. Moreover, companies that are perceived as caring are more likely to hold the loyalty of their employees and maintain a higher level of morale. This is particularly critical for professionals with skills in high demand. These people often cite the atmosphere of an organization as a prime consideration for employment.

But any organization will find it makes good sense to minimize high rates of turnover and other signs of low morale such as high absenteeism. The Families and Work Institute's *Business Work-Life Study* (1998), a comprehensive assessment of employees in both profit and not-for-profit business, found that more supportive workplaces led to greater levels of satisfaction, higher employee commitment to their companies' successes, and a stronger intention to remain with the organization. Supportive supervisors and assistance with life problems were found to be two critical attributes of supportive workplaces.

Lattanzi-Licht, Zucker, and Coleman broadly address ways in which work organizations can create more effective and supportive environments. Both Lattanzi-Licht and Zucker begin by acknowledging that grief has many facets in the work environment. Loss of a family member certainly may evoke grief reactions. Both authors consider other aspects of loss that may impact broadly on a workplace: Loss of a fellow employee by death or downsizing, or other changes in the workplace culture, even through the growth of an organization, can engender grief.

Lattanzi-Licht emphasizes the need for balance. The employer/employee contract does not mean that employers have sole responsibility for an employee's well being. But they do share that responsibility with all employees. Lattanzi-Licht stresses that hospices can provide a model for creating a healthy, supportive environment, one that uses both outreach referral and the presence of supportive team members.

Zucker also considers a formula for supportive environments that is echoed throughout this section. Any successful workplace will need to review policies and plans, provide training and education, and offer skilled interventions and debriefing when necessary.

Coleman's chapter focuses on the particular problems caused by the HIV/AIDS epidemic. Despite advances in treatment, HIV/AIDS is likely to be a workplace issue for years to come. In fact, these very advances in treatment make it possible for HIV-infected individuals to continue to work. Coleman states that HIV/AIDS is one of the most litigated of diseases, giving another reason for businesses to pay attention. Like Zucker, she calls for reviews of policies and plans, and emphasizes the value of broadly based educational programs. Coleman's chapter addresses a particular issue that workplaces need to review as they consider policy—that of domestic partners. American workers now live in a wide variety of situations. Many homosexual couples now live with lovers, as do many heterosexuals. The issue of domestic partners has implications not only for health benefits but also for issues such as caregiving and bereavement leave.

Both Lattanzi-Licht and Zucker remind us that workplaces can experience sudden trauma, such as violent death. Just reading the newspaper headlines reinforces the fear that no workplace is free of the threat of such trauma. Violent trauma not only leads to losses of fellow employees, it also shatters the assumption of safety, reminding individuals of their own personal vulnerability and how quickly life can change. Years ago I consulted with a foster care agency. Two employees were in a home, making a routine visit, when intruders forced entry and killed a family pet as a warning to this family's young adult son. While the social workers themselves were not assaulted, every worker in the agency became acutely aware of the fact that they often ventured into unsafe areas. These feelings of vulnerability took time to ebb. The agency provided support by allowing debriefings, as well as reviewing and modifying policies that allowed for a sense of increased security. These new policies involved escorts and gave meaning to the agency's claim that the safety of their workers remained paramount.

While in many work environments violence or sudden death is rare and unexpected, other fields such as the military or police face such losses more frequently. The fact that such losses do occur does not make them less traumatic. In these organizations the assumptions of safety that allow one to work are still violated. Nor are employees in the military or police any less likely to form strong bonds and relationships within the work environment than in other settings. In fact, the very nature of the work can strengthen ties. Both Kirby's and Carroll's chapters consider loss in these work settings. They describe successful programs and useful intervention strategies such as support groups and rituals that add richness to earlier examples.

A final chapter by Brenner further addresses an issue raised by Lattanzi-Licht. Many times those responsible for caring for others are themselves grieving. How do counselors, caregivers, health professionals, hospice workers, employee assistance counselors, and

personnel employees assist others when they themselves are grieving? Again, Lattanzi-Licht's notion of balance is critical. The key,
both authors suggest, lies in developing collaborative models of care
and in a sensitivity of the individual, a reflective self-awareness that
alerts the grieving caregiver to the ways the loss is affecting his or
her own abilities and capacities to care for another, as well as a sensitivity to his or her own needs.

Two

Grief in the Workplace: Supporting the Grieving Employee

Marcia E. Lattanzi-Licht

Gerry is walking through his first day back at work in a daze. It's only been a week since he lost his 18-year-old daughter, Beth. She'd had a routine appendectomy and then died from a blood clot six days later. It all feels like a nightmare. Gerry wanted to return to work because he needed something to distract him, to help him get back into a routine. The hardest part about this first day back was that no one mentioned Beth's death. Even those who had come to her funeral said nothing beyond a quick hello. They seemed to be avoiding Gerry. He felt resentment and anger that no one recognized how hard this was for him. Was he imagining it all? Did people expect him to go on as if nothing had happened?

As a society, our discomfort with grief becomes even more exaggerated in workplace settings. Gerry's experience is an all too familiar one for people returning to work following a major loss. Societal pressure toward either the extreme of quick healing or of treatment as a cure for grief influences our responses to people who are struggling to cope with grief in the workplace. It is difficult to find a balanced approach that acknowledges the needs of grieving employees and the performance demands of the employer.

The Experience of Grief in the Workplace

Grief is experienced in the work setting in several major ways. The first is in the death of an employee's immediate family member. The loved one may have been a member of the nuclear family, such as a spouse or child, or part of the family of origin, such as a parent or sibling, or part of the extended family, such as a niece, nephew, or grandparent. It is often difficult for a grieving employee, given the nature of work associations, to represent to co-workers the meaning of the relationship with the person who has died. And in a mobile society, many family members live at a great distance, making co-worker attendance at the funeral impossible. As a result, there is often a sense of disconnection between the intensity of the experience surrounding the death of a loved one and the inability to convey it to co-workers and friends in the employee's own world.

The second way grief is experienced in the workplace involves the death of a co-worker. Co-workers represent day-to-day relationships in which there can be a sense of camaraderie and shared understanding. Many of us form friendly acquaintance relationships with our co-workers during our employment tenure. Few of these relationships extend into ongoing friendships outside the workplace, particularly when employment ends. These co-worker relationships are typically time and context defined as in Viorst's (1986) description of special interest friends, who are involved with shared activity and concern without being intimate.

The death of a co-worker can generate feelings of vulnerability and an undercurrent of anxious concern in the workplace. Co-workers are people we identify with and relate to on an almost daily basis. The death of a co-worker can leave others feeling "survivor syndrome." We are left to wonder why that particular person became ill or was involved in an accident and died. It is difficult to reconcile why the person next to you was struck down and you are left standing. The death of a co-worker not only represents an unwelcome reminder of the reality of death in all of our lives, it also brings about change in the workplace. When the employee dies on the job, all of these responses are intensified and typically involve a post-traumatic stress response. A post-traumatic stress response involves generalized distress manifested in anxiety, irritability, increased arousal, and sleep disturbances.

The third area of workplace-related losses involves catastrophic losses. Examples include airline crashes where a number of crew members die, natural disasters such as earthquakes, floods, or hurricanes, or events such as a chemical fire or mine collapse where several employees perish. These events all involve multiple losses and require well-planned and comprehensive responses on the part of employers.

The Employee's Response

In addition to personal coping abilities, there are several additional key factors that influence how an employee will respond to the death of a loved one:

the nature and quality of the relationship,

the roles played by the person who died,

the circumstances of the death, and

the availability of support.

These considerations shape our responses and are determining influences upon our individual abilities to cope with a major loss. The quality and nature of the relationship, along with the roles the person played in a family, are the dynamic elements that make every individual unique and irreplaceable. When the grieving person discusses these aspects of their relationship with the loved one who died, they offer us some understanding of the importance of that relationship. We often know little of substance about the details of our co-workers' relationships.

Because it greatly affects day-to-day patterns, the death of a family member who is part of the nuclear family and living in the household has the most significant impact upon employees. Responsibilities and roles held by the family member who died must be absorbed and fulfilled by remaining members. In small families, surviving family members may feel burdened or overwhelmed by the new demands.

Many writers and clinicians acknowledge the complicating elements of a sudden, traumatic, or premature death. If the death involves traumatic circumstances, adaptation is more difficult. In addition to happening suddenly and without warning, trauma, by definition, implies an event that is outside the range of typical human experience. The death of a loved one in traumatic circumstances is emotionally overwhelming, with sensory overload and over-stimulation (Raphael, 1983). One of the legacies of trauma is an exaggerated sense of vulnerability and perceived danger to ourselves and our loved ones. In the case of a premature death, a surviving spouse may struggle with the burden of new roles. For the young widowed person, childcare and financial pressures can feel overwhelming. For some employees, multiple losses, or numerous losses within a short period of time, can make adaptation problematic.

Several human responses to loss are commonly manifested in workplace settings. These include exhaustion, withdrawal, difficulty concentrating, depression, or irritability. The inability to concentrate, the tendency to make mistakes, and decreased motivation or interest are all common grief-related symptoms. A major loss can undermine a bereaved person's coping abilities and can interfere with social and occupational functioning. Previously effective employees may become less able to perform their required activities. In the short run it helps for supervisors to check in with the grieving employee frequently to jointly discuss his or her ability to manage the workload. Supervisors and managers also need to be aware of behaviors or patterns that are potentially harmful, including substance abuse, lack of care or attention to personal hygiene, or excessive anger.

> *I can see it in my coworkers' faces—the pity and the fear. They all feel sorry for me since my husband Jim died from a heart attack two months ago. He was only 63. I know that the women are thinking that it could happen to them, to be suddenly alone and a widow. And some people just avoid me. Sometimes they try not to even look at me. Am I invisible? It would help if people recognized that even though this is a tough time for me, I need to feel that I can still be an important contributor at work, a valuable part of the team.*

Individual Responsibilities for Coping with Grief in the Workplace

The individual bears the largest burden in his or her attempts to regain functional abilities and integrate painful losses. The best time to develop coping skills that can be utilized effectively during bereavement is prior to times of loss.

One major coping response required of all grieving persons is the ability to compartmentalize. This setting aside of personal concerns and responses to tend to the responsibilities at hand is a major aspect of skilled coping for healthcare professionals. As a coping ability, compartmentalization also involves accountability for addressing the concerns and emotions that have been put aside. Our society asks grieving people to compartmentalize in many situations, particularly at work. Compartmentalization is an effective coping method when it is coupled with deliberate efforts to examine personal responses in private moments of reflection.

Other personal responsibilities related to coping with grief in the workplace include self-awareness and recognition of personal limitations. In addition, the grieving employee needs to develop support-seeking behaviors: Who will the employee go to when he or she has difficulty completing a task? Is there an understanding co-worker to meet for lunch occasionally?

One of the challenges facing all grieving persons is learning to tolerate distress. For healthcare professionals, this is an essential lesson. It is coupled with a personal spiritual search that involves developing a meaning context as a framework for working with people in difficult and painful times. This area of personal belief sustains us and has a powerful impact on our ability to integrate losses.

Another significant consideration for grieving persons involves the perception of social support (Rando, 1993). When an employee perceives a lack of support in the work setting, it can be considered a possible warning sign. In general, people who perceive a lack of support from others are more at risk for poor outcomes following a loss. While the perception of support involves the employee's personal orientation, experience, and possible distortions, it can be influenced by tangible acts of assistance. This element underscores the importance of workplace support and acknowledgment of the grieving employee.

A Crisis of Meaning

Many people who endure a profound loss experience a crisis of meaning. Things that seemed important or worth working toward are now thrown into question. Part of the personal searching that follows a major loss centers on a re-ordering of values and priorities. In that re-evaluation, one's work may, at least in the short run, become less significant. In *Signs of Life*, Tim Brookes, National Public Radio commentator and author, describes how the remedy for grief is often seen in the return to routine. Brookes speaks eloquently of his experience: "The five months after Mum's death had shown me how shallow, mechanical, and unsatisfying the routine world was, and during this vulnerable time the last thing I wanted to do was to go back there" (1997, p. 258). For some employees, the life-changing experience of the loss of a loved one can mean taking a more extended leave, or exploring other possible types of work.

Understanding the Employer/Employee Contract

By its very nature the employer/employee relationship implies a contract of joint responsibility. In exchange for performance of duties, the employer provides a wage, benefits, and a safe working environment. Beyond basic safety, employers today recognize that it is in the corporation's interest to address employee concerns that influence performance, productivity, or morale. A 1995 poll by the Managed Health Network, Inc. showed that over 90 percent of both employees and their bosses agreed that psychological and relationship problems had a negative impact on attendance, productivity, and turnover. The poll also showed that illness or death in the family was the second most common problem, cited by 58 percent of workers (National Hospice Organization, 1995).

The Family Medical Leave Act stands at the heart of the understanding that family members' health and well-being are of great personal concern to employees. In the same way a family illness can create inordinate energy and lifestyle demands, so can the death of an immediate family member.

Family leave time is the first rung on the ladder of corporate responsibility. Most corporate policies allow for three days of paid leave at the time of an immediate family member's death. There are few situations in which three days would be sufficient time to deal with the emotional and physical realities surrounding the death of an important loved one. For family members who live across the country, travel would consume a great deal of the allotted leave time. For employees who feel punished by the loss and who experience a sense of victimization, bereavement leave policies represent limited support. Employees typically use additional days from vacation time, or take time off without pay.

Family leave policies are intended to allow workers to retain their jobs in the face of significant family needs. Most corporations allow an employee access to family leave only after all other paid leave days have been used. In spite of problems with administering the Family Medical Leave Act, many human resources experts believe that the law basically represents good management practice (Barnett, 1997).

While attention must be given to the financial realities employers face, attention to the symbolic messages of family and bereavement leave policies, and the manner in which they are administered, is critical. For example, some employers allow co-workers to donate vacation or sick days when an employee is facing his or her own life-threatening illness, or that of a loved one. There is increased awareness of this mutual level of concern and commitment in a number of job settings (Ziegler, 1996). Realistic yet compassionate policies that integrate support for family concerns create goodwill and engender loyalty among employees. A number of companies are learning that adapting work to fit their employees' family needs results not only in loyalty but also in a competitive edge (Hammonds, 1996).

Beyond bereavement leave, a number of employers offer training for managers and supervisors that focuses on developing skills to support employees facing crisis and loss. Managers and supervisors influence the day-to-day work life of employees and set the norm and tone for how employees will be treated in times of loss. Front line supervisors and managers are the people most involved in supporting bereaved employees.

Marty is not doing well at all. He still seems distracted and is not as productive as he used to be, even though it's been three months since his wife died. I sent him to the Employee Assistance Program and I don't know what else a supervisor could do. I'm losing patience with him.

Supporting the Grieving Employee

Support for a grieving employee begins with acknowledging the loss experience. This can take the form of attendance at the funeral by co-workers, or tokens of remembrance including cards, flowers, or food. After the return to work, support for the bereaved employee involves individual understanding and interactions with co-workers and with the supervisor. Co-workers will offer varying degrees of support based upon their own personal loss experiences, their closeness with the grieving employee, and their own individual capabilities. Supervisors should meet with the bereaved employee upon the return to work and check in with him or her frequently in the weeks and months that follow. An employee who is bereaved may no longer be able to sustain previous levels of activity or performance. Frequent supervision and problem-solving efforts can help the employee maintain self-esteem and a sense of contribution. Brief meetings, approximately 15 to 20 minutes every one to two weeks, to set mutually agreed upon short-term goals and where any difficulties the employee is having can be discussed, are an effective supervision strategy. Allowing the employee to identify the areas of adequate functioning and those where additional help may be needed builds trust and support and enhances functional potential for the employee.

Finally, supervisors and managers should be aware of referral resources for employees who may need additional support. If the corporation does not offer an Employee Assistance Program, the employee can be directed to his or her family physician. Hospitals and hospice programs can be resources for support groups, referrals, and classes. Self-help groups and faith communities can also offer important support to grieving persons.

How the death of an employee is handled in the workplace determines to a large extent the adaptation process for co-workers. Following the death of an employee, a debriefing session utilizing mental health professionals from outside the corporation is suggested. Another possibility involves a personalized ritual or a staff-only memorial service for the co-worker. If the death is a work-related accident where employer culpability is possible, feelings of victimization and anger at the employer can be significant. Outside mental health resources can be an essential resource for employees in their efforts to deal with the negative responses associated with an on-the-job death. For example, after the deaths of two young firefighters in a training accident, the department arranged for trauma-debriefing sessions followed by mandatory educational sessions on coping with grief. Written materials and access to counseling were also available to all employees.

In the hospice setting, where death and grief are ever-present realities, staff and volunteers are often greatly affected by the death of a co-worker. While hospice professionals and volunteers have learned a great deal about supporting families dealing with loss, they are not always able to support themselves adequately in the face of a personal loss (Lattanzi-Licht, 1994, 1995a, 1995b). Individual coping with work-related losses progresses through a developmental process of learning to balance personal needs, vulnerabilities, and expectations (Harper, 1994).

Hospices have an additional buffer against the tolls of work-related losses in the interdisciplinary team. As a balancing force against the stresses and difficulties involved in care of the dying, the interdisciplinary team works effectively to support itself (Lattanzi, 1984). Healthcare professionals typically have a need to believe they can "make things better," giving them a sense of omnipotence and limited vulnerability (Schoenberg, et al., 1970). In that context, loss of a family member or co-worker can be more difficult for helping professionals, particularly for hospice workers. When a hospice co-worker dies, it is wise to seek outside resources for employee support.

Hospice workers display a range of observable responses in situations of personal loss. The illness or death of a hospice co-worker or of an immediate family member can bring about role re-adjustments and boundary concerns. Distancing and detachment are perhaps the most commonly observed emotional responses. There can also be a sense of exaggerated vulnerability and increased anxiety for hospice workers. Related understandings that can shed light on the impact of loss in the hospice workplace include burnout, compassion fatigue, post-traumatic stress response, disaster or battle zone phenomena, and chronic, compounded grief (Lattanzi-Licht, 1995b; Lattanzi-Licht, et al., 1998).

A Balanced Approach

An employer cannot assume responsibility for providing all the support for employees in times of crisis and loss. The development of self-directed work teams and flexible workplaces has encouraged high levels of shared responsibility. Employers no longer function in paternalistic patterns. Employers can, however, do much to create a healthy environment for their workers, including supportive responses in times of illness and bereavement.

In a world where we all feel time pressure, the responsibility to each other as co-workers adds another dimension to our workplace functioning. Under the pressure of day-to-day demands, we often pull back from the needs of our bereaved co-workers. We don't want to be reminded of our own vulnerability, and we don't want to be asked for more than we feel able to give. Perhaps the workplace is the new frontier for exploring collaborative ways in which we can support each other in times of grief. Rather than expecting employees' lives to fit into rigid schedules, the current trend is to rethink work processes in order to find successful solutions (Hammonds, 1996).

In an atmosphere of shared responsibility and concern, employees can feel a greater sense of control in their work situations. The investment of energy, creativity, and human potential can only lead to a more positive and productive work environment. The time-honored truth is that we do not exist in isolation from each other, we live in relationship to each other. The understanding that family crises are powerful human experiences that influence workers calls for a new and more integrated approach. The possibilities are as varied as the cultures of our thriving corporations.

Marcia Lattanzi-Licht, MA, RN, LPC, is a psychotherapist, educator, and author. An early voice for hospice care, Ms. Lattanzi-Licht was a co-founder of Boulder County Hospice (Colorado), where her work in the areas of education and bereavement care are widely recognized. She also specializes in team building and communication programs.

The Family and Medical Leave Act

The Family and Medical Leave Act (FMLA) became effective August 5, 1993. FMLA was designed to help employees balance their work and family responsibilities by allowing certain employees to take reasonable unpaid leave for certain family and medical reasons.

The Family and Medical Leave Act entitles eligible employees to take up to 12 weeks of unpaid, job-protected leave per year for specified family and medical reasons. It also requires that group health benefits be maintained during that leave, and requires that employees be restored to the same or an equivalent position.

A covered employer must grant an eligible employee up to a total of 12 workweeks of unpaid leave during any 12-month period for one or more of the following reasons:

- to care for an immediate family member (spouse, son, daughter, or parent) with a serious health condition
- to take medical leave when the employee is unable to work because of a serious health condition
- the birth and care of the newborn child of the employee
- placement with the employee of a child for adoption or foster care

Under some circumstances, employees may take FMLA leave intermittently—which means taking leave in blocks of time, or by reducing their normal weekly or daily work schedule. FMLA leave may be taken intermittently whenever medically necessary to care for a seriously ill family member, or because the employee is seriously ill and unable to work.

FMLA requires only unpaid leave. However, the law permits an employee to elect, or the employer to require the employee, to use accrued paid leave, such as vacation or sick leave, for some or all of the FMLA leave period.

Employees are eligible to take FMLA leave if they have worked for their employer for at least 12 months, and have worked for at least 1,250 hours over the previous 12 months, and work at a location where at least 50 employees are employed by the employer within 75 miles. If you are an eligible employee who has met FMLA's notice and certification requirements (and you have not exhausted your FMLA leave entitlement for the year), you may not be denied FMLA leave.

A number of states have also enacted family and medical leave laws, some of which provide greater amounts of leave and benefits than those provided by FMLA, or include coverage for employees who are not eligible for FMLA.

For more information, contact the nearest office of the Wage and Hour Division or call 800-959-FMLA. You can also find information at the Department Of Labor Wages and Hour Division FMLA Web page at **http://www.dol.gov/dol/esa/fmla.htm**.

Three

Grief in the Law Enforcement Workplace: The Police Experience

Michael Kirby

On December 14, 1975, William V. McDonough, first-time father-to-be and New York State trooper for two years, went to work at the Monroe barracks for a routine 3 to 11 shift. It was just another workday for the street-wise, good-natured young man who had recently emigrated from the Bronx with his young wife, the former Helen O'Donnell. He would die violently that day, shot to death by a drug-crazed individual who would then be shot to death himself by two of Bill's responding brother troopers. There were several young troopers assigned to the Monroe barracks at that time and, for many of us, our already dwindling alliance with the age of innocence ended that day.

A few days later a several-mile-long line of New York State Police vehicles crossed the Tappan Zee Bridge and convoyed into the Bronx, joining with a few thousand troopers and other police officers from throughout the Eastern seaboard to honor and pay homage to their fallen brother officer. The pomp and circumstance of the police funeral was on display in the ceremonial way the police profession says good-bye to one of its own. Those of us from the Monroe barracks stood tall in military formation in front of St. Margaret's Church, proudly wearing the gray class-A uniform and

Stetson, honoring our brother Bill. The feelings of pride and honor, in conjunction with intense feelings of sadness for Bill and his pregnant wife, Helen, were overwhelming and too difficult to process, so many of us just drank too much beer after the ceremony that day. There was no program in place back then to assist us or Bill's family with our grief. It would be another decade before the New York State troopers would establish an Employee Assistance Program (EAP). Nevertheless, we vowed not to forget him and his family.

We erected a monument in Bill's honor and placed it prominently in front of the Monroe barracks. His police academy photo was proudly displayed on the center wall in the squad room. We had anniversary rituals at the monument for a few more years. Eight years later, I became the Commander of the Monroe barracks. Helen and her daughter, Megan, who never saw her father, always drove up to the barracks from the Bronx during the Christmas season, delivering cookies for a mostly younger crop of troopers who never knew Bill. Out of respect, the troopers always reciprocated with a gift for Megan.

On December 14, 1995, twenty years after Bill's death, the number of police officers who gathered at St. Margaret's Church was down to about seven. The only gray I saw was in the hair of the attendees, as the uniforms had been replaced through the intervening years by the sign of a successful police career, the business suit. A few attendees were even dressed casually, the allowance and indulgence of the final promotion, retirement. The lines in the faces defined the police experience—something one cannot even begin to comprehend unless he or she has been there.

No one talks about Bill or how they feel, just as the feelings have generally gone unexpressed at previous memorial services. But we show up and honor Bill, Helen, and Megan, and we always retire to Helen's apartment after the Mass and talk about that oh-so-familiar topic, the job. For we are troopers, New York's elite, too tough, too hard, and too proud to express what we all commonly feel. Yet, in our own manly, fraternal, way we have healed. Little did I know at the time of Bill's funeral that 14 years later I would turn in my uniform to work as a counselor in our Employee Assistance Program. Time and time again I have been there for the tragedy of line-of-duty death and other sudden, violent deaths of local police officers and State troopers. Some of it is the same and some of it is different, yet we always learn and grow when the survivors permit us to enter their private domain and journey with them.

Co-worker and Survivor Grief

The loss of an employee through a sudden, violent act can have a profound impact on the workplace. The sudden, violent death of a loved one or family member can be a traumatic and life changing event (Hodgkinson, 1989; Gerberth, 1992; Parkes, 1993; Rando, 1993). According to Gerberth, the grieving process under these circumstances is more intense and commonly accompanied by acute feelings of rage and anger, as well as a sense of injustice and helplessness. When disaster strikes, most companies react by employing outside mental health professionals and their Employee Assistance Program, if they have such a program, to assist their employees who are experiencing traumatic grief. All employees, at one time or another, will face the loss of a loved one or co-worker. Grief can be a traumatic experience, diminishing our energy and affecting our motivation and ability to think clearly.

Stillman (1987) reports that surviving family members of police officers killed in the line of duty may be more at risk than other survivors after their loss. Relatives of slain officers often experience emotional distress over a long period of time and do not seek assistance or share their feelings because of embarrassment or the desire to avoid appearing weak. They may also refuse existing resources in their community because they believe that only members of the police culture can understand their problems.

Meanwhile, the entire situation may be exacerbated by the police department's lack of awareness of the devastating impact of the death on the survivors. Many police personnel mistakenly believe that family members are somehow more prepared for their losses than civilian survivors. Stillman's report indicates that the reactions of police survivors, including spouses, parents, siblings, friends, and co-workers, may be so profound as to meet the criteria for post-traumatic stress disorder. Studies of traumatized police officers indicate that the consequences often include administrative leave, less demanding assignments, or extended leave with workers compensation (Mann and Neece, 1990). Diagnostic data include adjustment disorder, personality disorder, PTSD, and alcohol abuse (Saathoff and Buckman, 1990). Alcoholism is a major problem for police departments across the county (Gilbert and Bolger, 1986; D'Angelo, 1994), resulting in deteriorating work performance, increased absenteeism, on-the-job accidents, and medical claims, marital difficulties, depression, and even suicide.

In a police department the bond between fellow officers is so strong that the loss of a brother or sister officer may be experienced as the loss of a family member. The loss of these close relationships may result in overwhelming feelings of grief complicated by the police personality traits of self-control and blocked emotions. The highly traditional masculine culture, which emphasizes the lack of emotional expression, the suppression of feelings, and a reliance on alcohol as a coping mechanism tends to inhibit expressions of mourning. Although it is sad, it is not surprising that 67 percent of the police departments responding to Stillman's survey lacked formal policies concerning the death of an officer.

It was the survivors themselves who decided to do something about the situation. In 1983 ten surviving families traveled to Washington, DC for the National Peace Officer's Memorial Day Service. They planned a seminar to coincide with the following year's service, and the result was an increase in attendance to 110 survivors in 1984. They then formed an organization to address the needs of surviving law enforcement families, and COPS (Concerns of Police Survivors) was born. COPS has grown into a national not-for-profit organization that offers emotional and moral support to surviving family members and others, including fellow officers, who have been impacted by line-of-duty police deaths. Every year in May the organization hosts workshops during National Police Week in Washington, DC. COPS also holds seminars for police departments throughout the US and responds to those impacted by line-of-duty deaths. The organization, comprising individuals who are survivors themselves, remains an exemplary resource to any police counseling service or Employee Assistance Program.

In 1985 COPS received a National Institute of Justice grant to research the psychological impact of survivors and to gather data on law enforcement agencies that had experienced line-of-duty deaths. The research (Stillman, 1987) disclosed the following information regarding line-of-duty death:

- *A survivor's level of stress is affected by the department's response to the tragedy.*
- *Spouses who were not notified of the death in person experienced additional trauma.*
- *Fifty-nine percent of the survivors met the criteria for post-traumatic stress disorder.*
- *Younger widows, especially if married for ten years or less, had a more severe reaction to the death than women married for a longer period of time.*
- *The same level of distress is experienced by surviving spouses of officers killed accidentally or feloniously. There is no difference in the sense of loss.*
- *Fifty-eight percent of the departments surveyed had psychological services units, yet only 31 percent of these departments offered these services to survivors.*
- *Sixty-seven percent of the departments surveyed lacked formal orders addressing line-of-duty death.*

The study found that when police officers die in action, survivors are not more prepared for the death just because they are part of the law enforcement family. Knowing that the job is dangerous does not prepare an individual for the experience of having a loved one die. According to the study, the following are common police survivors' reactions to their loss:

- *Having difficulty concentrating, making decisions and feeling confused*
- *Feeling hostile*
- *Feeling alone and different from others*
- *Being uncomfortable in social situations*
- *Anxiety about one's ability to survive*
- *Re-experiencing the trauma via intrusive images, dreams or thoughts*
- *Feeling emotionally numb*
- *Sleep disturbance*
- *Diminished interest in previously enjoyed activities*
- *An inability to return to prior employment.*

These symptoms are similar to the diagnostic criteria of post-traumatic stress disorder, the psychological disorder experienced by prisoners of war, combat veterans, hostages, and victims of physical assault, rape, and disasters.

COPS subsequently produced a handbook, *Support Services To Surviving Families of Line-of-Duty Death* (Sawyer, 1989), which was designed as a follow-up to the aforementioned research of Stillman. The handbook provides useful information regarding essential tasks that should be undertaken by police departments, such as:

- *Proper death notification,*
- *Assisting the family at the hospital and acknowledging their right to view the body of the deceased at the hospital,*
- *Supporting the family during the wake and funeral,*
- *Providing assistance regarding benefits to the surviving family,*
- *Continuing follow-up visits with the family,*
- *Supporting the surviving family during the ensuing criminal proceeding, and*
- *Assisting co-workers.*

Traumatic Grief Interventions in the New York State Police

The New York State Police (NYSP) was established in 1917 to combat crime in the rural counties of upstate New York. The original "gray riders," a horseback patrol, has grown into a force of over 4,000 sworn police personnel, the tenth largest police department in the United States. Trooper James A. Skiff was the first member of the New York State Police to die in the line of duty when, on May 25, 1920, as a sidecar passenger on a motorcycle, he was killed in a collision with a trolley car. Seventy-seven years later, on August 24, 1997, trooper Fabio Butita became the 108th member of the New York State Police to die in the line of duty when a drunk driver struck his vehicle.

There was no existing program to help the surviving family members and co-workers of the New York State Police until the Employee Assistance Program (EAP) was established in 1986. Although dreadfully understaffed and without a written mission statement until just a few years ago, EAP personnel have been responding to line-of-duty deaths, off-duty traumatic deaths, and other significant deaths since the inception of the program. The current leader of the New York State Police, Superintendent James W. McMahon, has taken a proactive position regarding assistance to his troopers and their families. To this end, the EAP has expanded in size and scope, and the members of the EAP unit have been extensively trained in various areas of counseling. We are particularly fortunate to have received comprehensive training in the areas of critical incident stress management (including debriefing individuals and groups who have been exposed to trauma), bereavement, and traumatic grief.

The EAP has an organizational membership in the Association of Death Education and Counseling, and members regularly attend the annual conference of this professional organization. The EAP is an internally based program, staffed entirely by police personnel who have been carefully selected for the position of regional coordinator. In addition, there are peer contacts in the field, officers who have received basic training in peer counseling and are available on a voluntary, as-needed basis. The director and one coordinator have graduate degrees in social work. Referrals to civilian therapists are also made regularly; however, for line-of-duty and other traumatic deaths, the EAP remains available to our people for weeks, months, and sometimes years, while they grieve and mourn.

The EAP is immediately notified when there is a line-of-duty death. The regional coordinator for that area of the state proceeds forthwith to the residence of the surviving family. The program director also goes to assist the family, while two other coordinators travel to the workplace of the deceased trooper to conduct debriefings and assist fellow troopers with their grief process. Mitchell and Bray (1990, p. 143) discuss the critical incident stress debriefing process as follows:

> *Critical Incident Stress Debriefings are structured group meetings that emphasize ventilation of emotions and other reactions to a critical event. In addition, they emphasize educational and informational elements that are of great assistance for emergency personnel in understanding and dealing with the stress generated by the event. Critical Incident*

Stress Debriefings are essentially discussions of the critical incident in confidential meetings. They are not considered psychotherapy, nor are they psychological treatment. Instead, debriefings are discussions designed to put a bad situation into perspective. The two major goals of debriefings are to reduce the impact of a critical event and to accelerate the normal recovery of normal people who are suffering through normal but painful reactions to abnormal events.

"Defusings" are considerably shorter and less formal versions of Critical Incident Stress Debriefings and are usually conducted within a few hours after the event. According to Everly and Mitchell (1997), they might take place at the crisis venue after disengagement from the crisis activity. Defusings are usually 20- to 45-minute group discussions about the event and are designed to reduce acute stress and tension levels.

A plan is put into place to meet other family members and relatives who will be arriving from out of the area. The troopers union or Police Benevolent Association assists with funding in this regard, paying for hotel rooms and transportation for the extended family members. Union delegates assume an important "peer contact" role during this time also, providing emotional support to fellow officers. In addition, an informal process is in place whereby troopers who are close to the family are relieved of their normal duties for a few days in order to assist EAP personnel with providing services to the family, such as transportation, child care, answering phones, shopping, and keeping the media at bay. These services are invaluable and facilitate the grief process for both the family members and the informal helpers themselves, who often express their gratitude to the EAP for having permitted them to "be there." A bond is created that facilitates both the family's and co-workers' healing as time goes on. The family never forgets the co-workers who were there for them, and this permits the co-workers to overcome defense mechanisms of avoidance that they may otherwise experience in the aftermath of the loss.

As family members and other relatives arrive at a central location—usually the home of the spouse or the parents of the deceased—funeral plans begin to unfold. At this stage the EAP assumes a crucial role in ensuring that the needs of the family are met. The ceremonial aspects of a police line-of-duty death can be quite ostentatious, but it should be that way only if it is congruous with the wishes of the family. Throughout the ceremonies the formula is simple: The needs of the family are placed above the needs of the police department. It is imperative that the ceremonies not become a "police event." The EAP Director assumes the role of liaison between the department and the family and also coordinates with the funeral director.

It is important to ensure that the family's religious, ethnic, racial, and cultural boundaries are not encroached upon. A therapeutic alliance with the family is created as they begin to see that their needs are not overlooked. It cannot be emphasized enough here how much sensitive members of the department, who are not counselors, can comfort the family by just being available in a responsive way. This is a crucial ingredient in the healing process of the family, as these officers live and work nearby and can be most helpful in the months to follow.

The real work for EAP personnel begins in the aftermath of the ceremonial aspects of the death. Stillman (1987) reports that in the months following an officer's death survivors often feel abandoned by the very department that was supposed to be close to their loved one but which now seems to have forgotten them. Simply stated, this never happens in the New York State Police. We educate our troopers in this regard and listen closely to survivors to ensure that the troopers in their area maintain contact. Memorial services and scholarships, funded through annual marathons and other competitions, are rituals that foster contact between survivors and troopers and facilitate mourning for all involved.

The EAP provides long-term follow-up care to the surviving family and co-workers, depending upon their wishes and needs. If a strong bond is created with an EAP coordinator, as is often the case, the coordinator will assume a counseling role and continue to join with the survivors on their journey. There is no time limit placed on this intervention. A surviving parent who lives out of state continues to maintain regular e-mail contact with one of our coordinators.

Some survivors seek outside professional assistance and still maintain a relationship with the EAP coordinator, who may assist with concrete services and assume the role of a peer contact. Other survivors feel comfortable maintaining contact with local troopers and access them as a resource. Some survivors elect to use previously established resources and maintain minor contact with the EAP and only casual contact with other members of the State Police.

What is most important here is that the value of self-determination is upheld and that the organization, whether it be the EAP or local members of the department, not invade the boundaries of the survivors. We have had several cases where the survivors elected to "go it alone" and subsequently availed themselves of the service many months later because of the positive experience with the department or EAP during the ceremonial aspects of the death. In one case, a surviving spouse was thinking about going back to school and accessed the EAP for advice. Over the course of her academic program, she came for regular counseling sessions to assist her with the stress of being a single parent and a student.

Other survivors access EAP personnel from time to time, often after long intervals, as new issues arise in their lives. In another case, a young widow without children continued to access the EAP from time to time over several years. During this period of time she was able to leave the workforce and obtain a college degree. She spent many hours talking to an EAP counselor in an informal setting and has subsequently remarried. It is personally rewarding when a survivor calls after a few years, desiring to just touch base. They are not our clients, they are our people.

Honoring Our Survivors

A person walking to the cafeteria at the New York State Police Academy cannot miss the memorial wall that honors our fallen troopers. A book on display relates the story of how each trooper lost his life. On the wall are 108 photographs of the men who gave their lives in the service of others. A picture of the most recently deceased trooper is displayed on a lectern in front of all the others. In my 25 years with the New York State Police I have seen the picture replaced exactly 25 times. I have stood there a number of times with a widow or surviving parent as they viewed the exhibit, observing their loved one's prominently displayed photograph for the first time. Words cannot describe the emotional impact this has on a recently bereaved survivor. They always express a profound sense of gratitude for the way their loved one has been honored. Still, we felt that we should do more.

When the idea of having a weekend to honor our survivors was presented to Superintendent McMahon in 1994, he wholeheartedly put the power of his office behind the concept. The implementation of the idea was tasked to the Trooper Foundation, a not-for-profit charity authorized by the New York State Police to accept and solicit contributions for the agency. The foundation supports the New York State Police in the areas of police training, special services to the public, public safety education, technical support, and special services to the police profession. Funding for the police survivors' tribute weekends comes from a charity golf tournament with the New York Jets football team.

The foundation, under the guidance of the executive director, Dr. William Trigg III, mailed 150 letters to the known children, parents, spouses, siblings, and other survivors. At this time a committee was formed to design the itinerary and logistics of the weekend. Three survivors were an integral part of the committee, which also included the EAP Director, Mr. Trigg, and a representative of Superintendent McMahon.

Sixty-three survivors attended the inaugural tribute weekend in 1995. The youngest person in attendance was an adolescent and the oldest was the daughter of a trooper who was killed more than 50 years ago. Attendees arrived at a local hotel on Friday evening and were transported to the police academy in State Police vans for a dinner and lecture. Afterwards there was an informal gathering in the hospitality room at the hotel.

Saturday's agenda included breakfast and lunch at the academy, along with morning workshops relating to issues surrounding grief. The survivors were offered tours of the academy, personal relaxation time and a boat ride in the afternoon. Additionally, two buses transported the survivors to the police memorial in downtown Albany, where they could observe the names of their loved ones on the police memorial wall, which honors all police officers throughout New York State who have died in the line of duty. At a banquet on Saturday night Superintendent McMahon delivered a speech on the recent history and direction of the State Police. The evening again ended in the hospitality room with the attendees relaxing, getting to know one another, and very importantly, bonding as a result of their common experience.

Sunday morning the survivors attended religious services and then participated in a memorial service in front of our own memorial wall at the academy. The memorial service was a powerful ritual as the survivors placed flowers in a large vase in the name of their loved ones. Clergy expressed words of comfort and survivors offered readings. After the memorial service the survivors gathered in the main auditorium for some final remarks, and the weekend concluded with lunch at the academy. The survivors unanimously voted to hold a second tribute weekend the following year.

The fourth annual tribute weekend was held in the fall of 1998. Seventy-four survivors were in attendance, an increase of 11 over the original weekend in 1995. The survivors decide, via a written survey, what changes should be made. And each year the EAP staff is present and available to survivors who like to talk or discuss their issues individually. Dr. Trigg is always present (he has become plain old Bill to the survivors), and he and his staff have worked tirelessly on behalf of the survivors. Superintendent McMahon and his wife, Joan, always appear throughout the weekend. Dr. Ken Doka has become an integral part of the weekend, serving in his capacity as a minister as well as an authority in grief and loss. Mary Jo Morrison, MSW, representing a consortium of funeral homes, has been a regular speaker and is always asked to return by the survivors. But in the end, it is the survivors who have made this weekend a success. Many of them never before had the opportunity to deal with their grief in this way. They have provided us with excellent feedback regarding their participation with others who share a common experience.

In the past two years there have been two more line-of-duty deaths in the State Police. It has been heartwarming to observe the comfort and support provided to the more recent survivors by those who have journeyed before them. This is what we see unfolding before us at survivors' weekend. We also see relationships forming among survivors that go beyond the weekend. There have been many tears, but is has become clear that they are the tears of healing. It has been a moving experience to join with the survivors and be a part of their weekend.

Other Grief Interventions by the New York State Police Employee Assistance Program

In the fall of 1996, Lieutenant Jeffrey P. McCormick was diagnosed with cancer of the pancreas. The day after his diagnosis he was admitted to one of the most prestigious cancer hospitals in New York and seen by a highly regarded physician in the field of pancreatic cancer. He was airlifted to the hospital by a State Police helicopter and was met there by two old friends who were his supervisors during his earlier days as a trooper. The two old friends, one a retired Sergeant and the other the Employee Assistance Program Director, would coordinate a variety of concrete and emotional supports for the McCormick family in the ensuing months.

Jeffrey had been promoted a few years earlier and had worked in three different locations of the state before permanently relocating. During this time many members of the department became familiar with the outgoing Lieutenant. His illness sent shockwaves around the department as everyone became aware of the prognosis associated with pancreatic cancer. There were fundraisers for his wife and three children aged eight to thirteen. There were many trips back and forth to the hospital, but there was always the helicopter and someone waiting at the heliport. There were always a number of State Police personnel in his room, with others standing by in the waiting room.

After the initial period of shock and denial, Jeffrey was able to talk about the likelihood of his death. He was candid about his wishes regarding his family and was assured that those wishes would be met. His children were not kept in the dark about the severity of his illness, and although everyone prayed for his recovery, they were prepared for his death. During the nine months of his illness, he and his family received a tremendous amount of emotional support from his friends, on and off the job, as well as the EAP. Several of his co-workers also received peer support from the EAP. His wake and funeral were so well attended that one would have thought it was a line-of-duty death. Two years later, I still have dinner with the family on a regular basis.

In the past two years we have experienced three off-duty deaths due to motor vehicle accidents. The EAP responds to these deaths in a similar fashion to a line-of-duty death. The pain is the same for the survivors. The survivors of line-of-duty death are aware of this and therefore have voted unanimously to invite these families to the tribute weekend.

From time to time we are also faced with the sad and untimely death of a child of one of our troopers. Most recently it was a SIDS death and less than a year ago it was an accidental death. Currently, one of our EAP coordinators is assisting a fellow trooper's family as they experience the traumatic stress of dealing with the cancer of their five-year-old. As so often happens in our line of work, the EAP coordinator and the mother of the child are friends, two female troopers who worked together a few years back. Again, they are not our clients, they are our people.

Conclusion

Grief and traumatic grief in the workplace are significant issues that must be addressed by management. Management courses do not teach about grief, so it may be difficult for some managers to find a balance between organizational productivity and caring for the emotional well-being of employees. A company with established policies concerning grief may actually experience enhanced productivity over time. Sunoo and Solomon (1996) report that 88 percent of the managers they surveyed indicated that they or a colleague recently faced, or anticipated facing, the loss of a loved one. Employee-centered organizations often have an Employee Assistance Program to assist their workers with myriad issues, including grief in the workplace. This is critical, as employees do not routinely check their grief at the workplace door.

Additionally, their grief may not be evident until later in the grieving process. Stein and Winokuer (1989) report that employers tend to respond to their grieving employees with an empathic response that focuses on the early days of bereavement. This response does not acknowledge that many bereaved people are initially in a state of shock and numbness and that grief may be manifested weeks, months, or even more than a year after a death. Their grief, then, may not be acknowledged or recognized at that time by managers. Instead, it becomes "disenfranchised," that is, not socially sanctioned or acknowledged (Doka, 1989), or even stifled (Eyetsemitan, 1998). This disenfranchisement may be the case when an employee dies, as others may not acknowledge the close bonds that have formed between partners and co-workers. Furthermore, the disenfranchisement can be exacerbated by a culture that looks at overt grief as a sign of weakness.

One effective approach has been to use a peer model of grief counseling, utilizing trained paraprofessionals to respond to the organizational needs of grieving employees. The concept of providing services to officers and civilians by trained peer counselors is not new. The Los Angeles Police Department Peer Counseling Program has been effectively working since 1981 (Klyner, 1986). Empirical research has also supported the effectiveness of paraprofessionals. Professionals have not demonstrated measurably superior outcomes compared with minimally trained individuals. The results of over 42 research studies comparing professionals to paraprofessionals on counseling effectiveness have shown that these trained paraprofessionals fared as well as the professionals in 29 studies and were rated superior in 12 studies (Durlak, 1979, cited in Klyner).

There are several other advantages, according to Klyner (1986), that peer counselors may have over professionals in providing counseling:

1. *They would not be tied to an office and could meet people in neutral or non-threatening locations, such as coffee shops, where the counselee might feel more relaxed than in an office.*

2. *Since the police population is very stable and "normal," most counseling could be expected to be short-term crisis counseling, in which it is usually desirable to spend more time with a client during the first sessions and to cluster initial sessions closer together. The flexibility to accomplish this is much easier for the peer counselor than for the professional.*

Many peer counselors have been through similar difficult experiences in a variety of areas (e.g., death of child or spouse, disciplinary issue, alcoholism, divorce). An individual seeking help often believes that someone who has been through what he is experiencing is more likely to be helpful.

Program staff are police officers who have received formal training in grief counseling, crisis training, the identification and recognition of behavioral, emotional, and physical signs of distress, active listening skills, assessment, and referral, and alcohol abuse. They are granted a significant degree of confidentiality, and, although there is a formal mechanism in place for contact, a peer counselor is most often contacted is through personal acquaintance.

We have raised the peer model in the New York State Police to a higher level, with training that far exceeds that of most peer counseling programs. Our peer counselors receive over 100 hours of training in the first year alone, including basic and advanced training in trauma counseling and basic training in grief counseling. Just as important as the training is the background and personalities of our peer counselors (regional coordinators). They bring their hearts and souls to work every day and are fully aware that the grief issues of the people they work with could become their issues at any time. Survivors have responded well to working with counselors from the inside who bring knowledge, compassion, and unconditional regard for those they work with into the workplace. That is the least we can do for our people.

Michael Kirby, MSW, LCSW, is a 25-year veteran of the New York State Police, Director of the New York State Police Employee Assistance Program, and team leader of the New York State Police CISM team. He is an adjunct lecturer at Dominican College in Orangeburg, New York, and a member of the Association for Death Education and Counseling.

Four

Grief at Work: New Challenges and New Opportunities

Robert Zucker

Our places of work represent the best and the worst of the human condition. No longer considered cold places of concrete where feelings do not belong, they nevertheless are still institutions where the bottom line is financial survival—often at the expense of the people who work there. As businesses turn toward a new century, many leaders have come to believe that to show compassionate concern for their employees not only makes good business sense, it is simply the right thing to do. For instance, over the last decade we have seen dramatic changes in the workplace due to significant demographic shifts: Job sharing, on-site childcare, and flexible scheduling have been implemented by management to meet the demands both of single-parent households and households with two working parents. Now, as baby boomers turn 50 and juggle the demands of parenting with concerns for their own aging and dying parents, businesses face new challenges. Illness, death, and dying have surfaced in the workplace as never before.

This chapter will address several dimensions of grief on the job. It will examine ways in which businesses can better understand how illness, death, trauma, and other losses all affect the workplace, and how businesses can benefit from understanding the grieving process. It will also address the risks of avoiding and denying loss issues at work and will introduce skills to support workers during times of change, loss, and crisis. Businesses must become better prepared to manage both expected and unexpected bereavement challenges.

Businesses Are Changed by Loss and Grief

- *An employee returns from work after the death of his child.*
- *A work group is recovering from the death of a supervisor.*
- *Staff members are in crisis over recent layoffs.*
- *Workers witness a colleague's sudden death in the workplace.*
- *A unit manager is diagnosed with AIDS.*

Workers experience loss and grief as a result of all of the above situations, and there is no blueprint or predictable pattern of behavior when workers grieve. Groups of workers may grieve together but will often feel differently at any given moment. Workers may experience periods of numbness and shock, as well as denial, fear, anxiety, anger, overwhelming sadness, and guilt. Feelings may come and go unexpectedly, and reactions may take days, weeks, months, or even years to evolve. As in families, groups of workers are affected by one another's reactions and feelings. Some may keep their feelings hidden, others may have a need to share with co-workers, some may not wish to listen to others' feelings at all.

Organizations also suffer when employees are grieving. There may be changes in job performance because grieving people frequently experience impaired concentration and memory loss, difficulty making decisions, and missed work days. Some staff may be unable to stay in particular work areas that trigger painful memories following a trauma. There may be damaged work relationships and impaired team effectiveness as a result of unresolved feelings and misunderstandings. And companies may experience loss of morale and motivation when managers are perceived as insensitive or slow to respond to the needs of grieving employees.

There are often financial losses, particularly when businesses are affected by critical incidents, situations in the workplace which produce strong emotional responses—responses so stressful that they overwhelm a worker's ability to cope. Types of critical incidents include serious occupational injuries, employee violence, work-related fires, natural disasters, or deaths of employees. As companies face these dramatic losses they suffer from lost work time, business interruptions with customers, the need for salary continuation for injured and traumatized personnel, medical expenses, higher insurance premiums, higher levels of absenteeism, and increased expenses from building repair and cleanup. Estimates of expenses resulting from such workplace incidents in the United States are $23.8 billion a year, and the cost to an organization from a single critical incident can reach $250,000 (Frolkey, 1996).

When organizations demonstrate flexibility and compassion they are able to cut some of their losses. The largest organization of employee-benefit professionals in the United States, The Employee Assistance Professional Association, has begun organizing bereavement seminars for corporate benefit managers across the country. These seminars provide advice and information on bereavement support to such major corporations as American Express, Mobil, the staff at the House of Representatives, and the FBI (West, 1998). Whether human service organizations, healthcare agencies, or Fortune 500 companies, institutions and businesses of all sizes are discovering that they need to know more about grief in order to become better prepared to respond to their grieving employees.

Where Do Businesses Begin?

When considering how to respond with compassion to bereaved employees, corporations can learn from the work of pastoral care providers like Rabbi Mychal Springer, Director of Pastoral Care and Education at Beth Israel Medical Center, New York City. At the Hyman-Newman Institute for Neurology and Neurosurgery, children come from around the world with brain and spinal cord tumors. It is not uncommon for staff members to become highly stressed and grief-stricken when their patients die. Springer sees her work as caring for staff as much as for patients and their families.

Healing Circles are held weekly where staff pray for their patients as well as for themselves. Following a patient's death, staff-only Rituals of Remembrance are attended by a cross-section of employees, from maintenance workers to surgeons. These events last anywhere from ten minutes to one hour, and are held on patient units so they will not disrupt the workday. After a brief opening prayer, staff share memories of the deceased patient and also discuss how patient deaths may have triggered memories of their own loved ones' deaths. To further support their employees, rituals of remembrance for staff who have died are held each year, where a gospel choir sings and staff are given opportunities to contribute to a book of remembrance.

Another example is *The Grieving, Caring, Growing Project*. Developed at Baystate Medical Center in Springfield, Massachusetts, this program has been duplicated by hospitals and hospices around the country. It grew out of concern for the cumulative grief of healthcare providers.

Each spring, staff members from across the institution, including nurses, physicians, secretaries, technicians, and social workers, are issued packets of seeds or cuttings from plants. They make a commitment to nurture these plants throughout the spring and summer. In the early fall staff members bring the mature potted plants to the hospital's annual memorial gathering as gifts for bereaved families in attendance. As a healing and commemorative ritual, *The Grieving, Caring, Growing Project* provides an opportunity for staff to express their own feelings of grief when patients die, and an opportunity for staff to communicate their caring to the families of the patients they have served.

Administrators and managers in all types of businesses can attend to the spiritual concerns of their employees. Managers or supervisors may designate private places for co-workers to mourn and talk together. They can become role models for their staff by expressing their own grief openly and honestly. They can also model appropriate expressions of care, reaching out to family members of the deceased by sending cards, attending funerals, and visiting. They can familiarize themselves with different ethnic, cultural, and religious bereavement practices represented in their places of work. They can also encourage informal office rituals such as joining together to clean out a deceased co-worker's desk, organize a fundraiser in his or her memory, or leave a particular work station or piece of equipment unused for a period of time. They can remind their staff that grief is a slow healing process that often changes the bereaved for a lifetime. Finally, managers can suggest holding a non-religious memorial service. These events are most effective when the closest associates of the deceased are given key roles in planning the event (Tyler, 1996).

An engineer at a Northeast-based high tech company employing 50,000 people collapsed and died on-site. Employees watched the failed attempts to revive the woman. Since the employee's husband wanted a private service and none of her co-workers were allowed to attend, Malaena Nahmias, employee assistance counselor and designer of corporate memorial services, saw this as an opportunity to help employees design a personalized on-site memorial service. A grassroots committee was formed, made up of Nahmias, a human resource representative, the deceased woman's secretary, and a core group of three co-workers and friends. This committee grappled with such issues as finding a quiet, appropriate space. They were able to convert a conference room into a safe space for employees to share feelings. E-mail invitations were sent to staff. Invitations were mailed to former employees who had been close to the deceased, who were asked to RSVP so that security would anticipate their arrival. The corporate cafeteria provided food for a reception, and it was agreed that any cost incurred could be charged to the cost-center of the deceased employee. Lights were dimmed and simple flower arrangements placed on conference tables covered with white tablecloths. Nahmias began by explaining the order of the meeting. Friends and colleagues were invited to read poetry, and messages were read from those unable to attend. Since the deceased had been a composer, some of her songs were performed by fellow employees. A few colleagues had been designated as speakers, but many others chose to speak spontaneously. Food, stories, laughter, tears, and hugs were shared during an informal reception that followed. One appreciative employee later remarked, "I've been in this conference room hundreds of times, but this morning when I walked in I felt that I was entering a sanctuary."

Grief takes time to unfold. Compassionate management practices cover many areas: sharing information with staff in a timely manner, being willing to relax deadlines, temporarily reformulating job responsibilities, hiring extra help as required, expressing appreciation for any extra work that may be required of some co-workers while others are debilitated, and allowing trusted employees to work at home (Ramsey, 1995).

Cancer and AIDS: Examples of Life-Threatening Illness in the Workplace

The American Cancer Society tells us that when an employee is stricken with cancer, managers need to remember that this illness does not necessarily end an employee's career. Many who undergo cancer treatment are able to continue to work effectively. Nonetheless, workers with cancer may need more flexibility from their employers and extended time away from work. Managers should keep lines of communication open, work with the employee to determine appropriate workloads and schedules, and check in periodically as treatment progresses. The American Cancer Society also suggests that managers take cues from the employee, offering support, respecting requests for confidentiality, and keeping employees abreast of company policies affecting medical conditions, including the Americans with Disabilities Act (The American Cancer Society, 1998).

HIV/AIDS in the workplace must be addressed head on. Nearly 500,000 Americans have contracted AIDS since the late 1970s, 97 percent of whom are of working age (Centers for Disease Control and Prevention, 1995). It is most important for management to develop a thorough understanding of how the Americans With Disabilities Act applies to people with HIV/AIDS, as well as an understanding of what the virus is and the many workplace ramifications of the multiple diseases associated with the virus. James D. Slack, Associate Professor in the Department of Public Policy and Administration at California State University, Bakersfield, and consultant throughout California on the policy and workplace impact of HIV/AIDS, suggests three activities that managers can establish and maintain in the workplace.

1. Establish a plan of action for dealing with HIV in the particular workplace and include this plan in the personnel handbook. The plan should include a statement supporting the workplace rights and civil rights of employees living with HIV/AIDS, specific procedures for helping employees challenged with HIV, general examples of reasonable accommodations to assist infected employees, and a plan to educate employees and supervisors about HIV/AIDS.

2. Education and training should focus on improving employee and management understanding of HIV/AIDS and its impact on productivity, morale, and health in the work force. For instance, Slack suggests offering a one-day management seminar that addresses the workplace ramifications of AIDS. Topics should include basic AIDS information, information on how the Americans with Disabilities Act applies to persons with AIDS, suggestions for sensitively dealing with employees who are infected with HIV/AIDS, suggestions for modifying the workplace, confidentiality issues, managing relationships between infected and non-infected employees, information on community-based assistance programs, and information on how managers can design specific AIDS planning that is unique to their particular work areas.

3. Managers are advised to develop workplace strategies that are job-specific and respond to individuals living with HIV disease at each stage from asymptomatic HIV to full-blown AIDS. People infected by HIV can be asymptomatic for anywhere from two to ten years, and during that time managers can help strengthen their immune system by reducing stress and anxiety. To reduce stress, Slack suggests that employers offer HIV support groups in the workplace. They can also offer support for dealing with shock and depression by allowing for greater flexibility in use of sick days, transferring workers out of work environments that might further challenge their immune system, and discouraging employees with HIV from working overtime.

When the illness progresses to persistent generalized lymphadenopathy (PGL), various lymph nodes become enlarged throughout the body, marking the decline of CD4 T-cells that fight off diseases and viruses. PGL may last for years and is followed by full-blown AIDS. A host of opportunistic infections can then occur throughout the body, and malignancies such as Kaposi's sarcoma may become visible. Depending on immune and environmental conditions, full-blown AIDS may last two to four years before death. Employers can have an impact on environmental conditions. Workers with PGL or full-blown AIDS need increasing amounts of time away from work and will often use up their sick time. Managers can suggest that fellow employees assist their co-worker by pooling their unused sick time. Workers with AIDS will sometimes benefit from the option to work at home or to switch from full-time to part-time hours without losing full health benefits. Managers can also provide opportunities for frequent rest periods, privacy, and time for reflection (Slack, 1995).

There Are Many Reasons to Grieve

There are many faces of grief in the workplace in addition to death and illness. Grief may be caused by fear of downsizing, "work re-design," and other changes that result in transfers and layoffs. Even a promotion may produce grief reactions as an employee assumes new roles and responsibilities and loses old roles and relationships. Following major transitions at work, staff may experience feelings of failure, decreased trust among workers or between workers and administrators, and increased feelings of self-doubt. Disruptions following layoffs may result in "survivor guilt" among those remaining, increased feelings of insecurity, and profound disruption in on-the-job social networks. Unfortunately, organizational denial and fear can seriously impede a company's ability to support workers during these times of great upheaval. Bill DeFoore, PhD, executive coach and president of the Institute for Personal and Professional Development, shared the story of one manager who assumed the role of "corporate chaplain" by creating opportunities for expression of both humor and pathos among his employees.

For economic and supply reasons, a West Coast paper products plant that employed 600 people had to relocate 150 of its employees. The plant manager knew this would disrupt many lives and the culture of the plant itself. This was a very close-knit group of employees, strongly attached to their jobs, their particular departments, and their fellow employees. Many had been working at the plant for over 20 years. Several families had been there for generations. The plant manager anticipated serious backlash among his workers, including disruptive disputes and productivity declines, unless the feelings associated with this major transition could be addressed head on. His solution was to design a funeral for the plant. Plant carpenters built a 10' by 4' coffin that was placed on rollers. The plant was shut down for half a day and employees were invited to participate in a funeral ritual to acknowledge the impending reassignments. All employees were given a 10-penny nail tied with a black ribbon and were invited to hammer the nail into the coffin as the processional passed. A few employees chose to dress up as the Blues Brothers and lie inside the coffin as it slowly rolled through the plant. Others simply cried quietly as the coffin passed. Some laughed and chose to join the processional, while others, hands trembling, drove their nails into the coffin. A group of employees disassembled the coffin when the ceremony was over and the community returned to work.

Crisis Management Teams and Plans of Action

The good work of creative managers alone will not prevent the high cost of grief in the workplace. Systematic plans of action are needed to further protect employees and companies. Managers need to be empowered to handle the many-faceted ramifications of a crisis in the workplace with sensitivity and creativity.

The first step for a company might be to choose a crisis management team. Members should include representatives from legal, security, human resources, senior management, medical/EAP/mental health, as well as a union/employee representative. This team would be responsible for addressing legal, security, safety, and emotional needs of workers, as well as organizational issues. Teams would establish guidelines to identify what constitutes a critical incident in a particular setting, to determine the organization's particular areas of vulnerability, and to develop policies and procedures to respond to critical incidents. Crisis management teams need to become well trained in all areas of crisis management. They in turn become key players in training managers and supervisors throughout the company (Frolkey, 1996).

As soon as a critical incident is identified, the crisis team should be convened. Since teams are multidisciplinary, each team member plays an important role in determining an appropriate and timely response. Although teams need to be flexible, checklists addressing an array of potential problems can empower managers to prevent the chaos that often follows a crisis. Items on crisis team checklists should include:

1. Escape plans following an internal or external disaster
2. Determining which employees are most affected (individual teams, a single site, or the entire work force)
3. Determining whether the worksite requires maintenance or repair as a result of an incident
4. Identifying "special needs" employees (physically injured, victims of crime, friends or close colleagues of injured or deceased personnel, witnesses to a violent crime, etc.) who may require attention from medical or mental-health providers and/or trauma debriefers
5. Procedures for reporting a death or any type of incident to employees (For example, avoid e-mail and memos. When information is shared more personally, it is greatly appreciated by bereaved employees and strengthens their morale.)
6. A plan to take care of the body of the deceased when a death occurs in the workplace
7. A plan to inform employees of various in-house supports such as employee assistance program services and outside bereavement resources such as area hospices, bereavement centers, and self-help groups

Protocols should also name a specific crisis team member to handle all media inquiries, as well as another team member to be responsible for both identifying and contacting any outside crisis/bereavement consultants (Henderson, 1997).

To address the possible sudden death of a top executive, Tari Schreiber, a partner with Contingency Planning Research in New York State, advises crisis management teams to imagine the impact on a company if key figures in the company were no longer there. They are then advised to develop a "succession of management plan" for key individuals. In the event of a top executive's death, a four-component crisis management plan would include:

1. Providing information to employees in order to avoid rumor, and making counseling available to employees
2. Determining the impact of the death on the customer base and informing and reassuring customers
3. Preparing a press release
4. Assuring stockholders (Kuhar, 1995)

Debriefings are facilitated by specially trained debriefers and should be scheduled within 72 hours of a traumatic event. In order to provide time for feelings to surface and for employees to have the benefit of contact with families and friends outside of work, debriefings are most effective when held the day after the traumatic event. Onsite interventions for employees should be educationally focused, informing employees of expected physical, emotional, behavioral, and mental reactions to trauma (for example, short-term memory loss, difficulty concentrating, high anxiety, intrusive thoughts, irritability, difficulty sleeping, and depression). Participants should be encouraged to talk about what they may have witnessed and how they have been feeling. All employees should be provided with information on available supports offered by a company, such as onsite, time-limited and confidential grief support groups. Debriefing meetings should be voluntary and held at the worksite in a location that provides accessibility, privacy, and confidentiality (Mitchell and Everly, 1995).

No matter how well conceived, crisis protocols are only effective when managers are familiar with their contents, when manuals are not merely collecting dust on a manager's bookshelf. Protocols work best when managers and human resource personnel are trained in crisis management and have an understanding of the grieving process. Training for managers and human resource staff must include concrete and practical use of all protocols and procedures, as well as information on how to sensitively interact with traumatized and bereaved employees (Reigel, 1998).

Teaching Groups of Workers About Grief and Healing

A secretary in the president's office at a small Southern college suffered from a chronic illness that caused her to be out of work frequently. Some of her co-workers, faculty members, and administrators were very sympathetic to her situation and grew close to her as they pitched in to lessen her workload. Others believed that she was exaggerating her illness and taking unnecessary amounts of sick leave. When her absences caused them extra work and frustrating delays, they expressed resentment and questioned her sincerity. News of her sudden death shook the office deeply. Their grief was complicated by strong conflict among staff members due to feelings of guilt, as well as resentment and anger towards one another. Relationships among co-workers deteriorated for months. One upper-level administrator who was perceived as having been insensitive to the secretary quietly took early retirement.

How can businesses support their employees as they grapple with such painful struggles? Sheelah Sodhi, a training and development coordinator at the Department of Juvenile Justice for the Commonwealth of Virginia, believes that personnel can develop the skills to manage grief with all its various complications. She has developed *Coping with Loss in the Workplace*, a comprehensive loss curriculum. The training is available to all levels of staff in the Juvenile Justice Department, from parole officers to supervisors and managers. Sodhi is also called on to provide modified training to teams and departments in the aftermath of critical incidents. Her efforts are an example of how organizations can support their employees through a difficult healing process instead of running from painful conflicts.

Using didactic and experiential methods, Sodhi's one-day workshop examines the many-faceted dimensions of loss and grief -- from death to more subtle change-related losses. The training provides a safe environment in which to explore primary and secondary losses, factors that may complicate grief, techniques for managing grief in the workplace, and conflict management skills related to loss and grief. The workshop includes opportunities to practice skills in simulated scenarios representing a variety of critical events, tragedies, or more subtle transitional challenges that can occur at work.

One particularly interesting component to Sodhi's curriculum involves inviting participants to make drawings about losses that have had an impact on their work environment. She has found that such opportunities for creative expression help many workers express and communicate complicated feelings.

Following are two examples of drawings by probation officers who attended Sodhi's workshops. The drawing entitled *Mixed Emotions* by Andrew Dickerson pictures a worker leaving a site where he has worked for 21 years, as he anticipates being transferred to a new worksite. And Tim Jones' untitled drawing powerfully depicts boats at sea as metaphors for various responses

"Mixed Emotions" by Andrew Dickerson

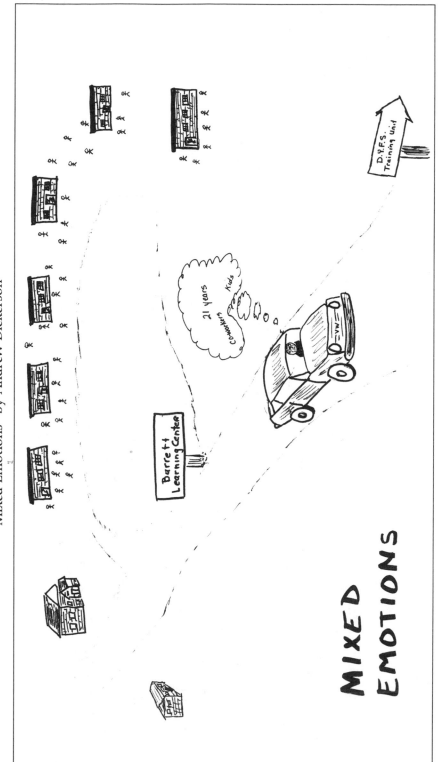

Untitled by Tim Jones

to loss in the workplace. Grievers are represented by four boats, each boat managing rough waters with different degrees of resilience and vulnerability.

Conclusion

There are many reasons why businesses need to take grief seriously. People will always face loss, and they will always bring their feelings with them to work. When workers find sanctuary in their places of employment, their lives will be enriched and businesses will be better able not only to weather these tragedies but to thrive.

Robert Zucker, MA, is a bereavement therapist, founder of Caring Communities Respond, and co-director of the Sturbridge Group, providing bereavement consultation and training. He is editor of the Grief and Healing Newsletter, *and an associate faculty member at Antioch New England Graduate School.*

Programs That Work

Starbucks Coffee Company

On July 6, 1997, three Starbucks employees were shot to death after the close of business in what was likely a failed robbery attempt. Starbucks likes to think of its workers as family and partners. They responded to the deaths as a family often does.

First, they held a memorial service to celebrate the lives of the three employees. To make sure that all workers had the opportunity to attend, Starbucks closed all of its 70 stores in the metropolitan area at 5pm. More than one thousand people attended, including Starbucks Chief Executive Howard Schultz.

The store was reopened in February 1998. But it is now a living memorial to the slain employees. A memorial wall, created in their honor, was installed in the store. And all net profits from that store go to organizations dedicated to the prevention of violence and providing assistance to victims of violent crime.

Finally, like any family member, Starbucks wishes to assure that justice will be served. They recently raised the reward for information that will lead to arrest and conviction in this case.

Starbucks response emphasizes two key aspects of an effective corporate response. One is a true sensitivity to the grief and trauma of employees—a sensitivity reflected at the highest level. Second, Starbucks understood the real need to provide an opportunity to come together to mourn—just like any family.

Special thanks to Kevin Carothers and the Starbucks Coffee Company for allowing us to share their story.

Five

Death in the Military Workplace

Bonnie Carroll

When a death occurs, many lives are changed forever. The ripple effect extends to an average of ten people, and that circle includes not just immediate family but friends and co-workers whose lives are now marked by this event. Sometimes that list also includes those who meet the deceased only in death: the recovery worker in a plane crash, the ambulance crew at a car accident, the innocent bystander who witnesses a homicide, or the passerby who happens upon a heart attack victim and administers CPR to no avail.

This chapter will look at one workplace, the armed forces, and examine how this culture deals with the circumstances that accompany a death of one of its own. While the number of us who currently serve in the military is decreasing, vast numbers of people have been exposed to the "workplace" through television shows such as *MASH* or movies such as *Saving Private Ryan* and *Courage Under Fire*. These shows share a common thread in their examination of how fellow service members cope with death. As General Douglas MacArthur said during his famous "Duty, Honor, Country" address at West Point, "The soldier above all other people prays for peace, for he must suffer and bear the deepest wounds and scars of war." General Colin Powell (1992) echoed those sentiments when he wrote, "In war, we take it as a given. In peace, when no resolute foe is intent upon our destruction, death comes as a painful reminder of the price of peace."

Many complicating factors come into play when a death occurs in the armed forces. The surviving family often must move out of base housing. While regulations now allow "dependents" to remain in that housing for up to 180 days after the death, and may even extend that time if special circumstances exist, the fact remains that as soon as the service member dies, the clock starts ticking for the family's inevitable move.

In the civilian population, grief counselors caution the bereaved not to make any quick decisions and not to move for at least a year. This is not an option in the military. The first task of grieving is simply to accept that the death has occurred (Worden, 1991). This can take days, weeks, months, or even years. It is only after the impact of the loss is fully felt that one can then grieve the death. During this devastating period, the bereaved may experience a wide range of emotions: sadness, anger, depression, anxiety, panic, confusion, and tremendous loneliness. For many, this most traumatic period comes between four and six months after the death. If we overlay this on the military timetable, we see families packing and moving during their most trying time.

After the surviving families have begun to work through their grief, another task of grieving in Worden's model is to adjust to the physical environment in which the deceased is no longer present. Worden notes that this is done without forgetting the past and the person who has died. This is the time during which a grief-stricken spouse might begin to consider a change in venue, yet it is often the time when those who made quick decisions during difficult times are waking up to find themselves in situations that are not what they had hoped for. One young widow moved herself and her three children within 30 days of her husband's death in an Air Force plane crash. She went "back home" to her parents, who had recently sold their family home and now lived in an assisted-living facility. She found herself in the role of their caregiver at a time when she herself needed care. Her friends were involved in their own marriages and lives, and despite their best efforts they could not understand her grief. She was left out of the very social milieu that she had hoped would be her salvation.

Moving presents yet another complicating situation when the relocation is from a military installation to a private community. Those who reside on a base or fort drive to their homes through gates manned with armed security officers who ensure that only those with proper identification gain entry, assuring the resident that they belong and that once inside they will be safe. When a death occurs and a military family moves away, they often find that the security in their new civilian neighborhood pales in comparison. In a civilian neighborhood, security alarms and bars on windows may be the norm, while it is not unusual for houses on a military base to be unlocked and for people to feel protected by the security forces standing guard day and night. At a time when one is already feeling vulnerable, this may bring a whole new wave of insecurity.

Another aspect of a loss in the armed forces that complicates the grieving process and is a byproduct of the work environment is the media coverage that accompanies military casualties. When a multi-million dollar aircraft goes down, the media are on the scene to cover every aspect of the loss. We hear about the deaths almost immediately, see live footage, and sometimes even watch bodies returning from foreign lands or solemn funerals taking place with centuries-old ceremonial honors. This has an enormous impact on the family's ability to cope and heal after the loss. They find themselves temporarily living in a fishbowl, hounded by media for comment or photographs. Then, just as quickly as their story was the lead on the national news, they are left alone to cope and heal in a vacuum.

What is also lost in the rush for media coverage following a major military disaster is the family's individual right to honor their loved one. When a family member dies in the civilian sector, there is normally a chance to quietly and thoughtfully write the obituary that will capture a life and offer a tribute, and select a photograph for use by the newspaper. Yet in the military workplace scenario, the same Public Affairs office that is coordinating CNN's coverage of the disaster scene is also controlling the flow of information released about the servicemembers killed. The information may even be released without coordination from the next of kin, preempting the family's traditional right to this final honor.

Even the way a death in the military is spoken about—honoring *those who have made the ultimate sacrifice*, or saying a soldier *gave his life in service to his country*—sets it apart from other loss experiences and complicates the unique experience of those who grieve that loss. We even have national days of remembrance and mourning—Veteran's Day and Memorial Day—for all who have served and died, regardless of the circumstances.

How do these complicating factors in this one particular workplace affect the grieving process of those left behind, and how can we help the bereaved most effectively? In the civilian community, people choose first where they are going to live, and then establish from that base their work, family, church, civic activities, and friends. In the military, it is just the opposite. People choose their job first and then accept as their home the place where they are sent to serve. The community and the job are one and the same, for in the military those with whom you serve become your neighbors and friends as well as your co-workers—in essence, your support system and social network.

The impact of a workplace death ripples throughout the entire military installation, affecting everyone, from the family who loses a loved one to the fellow service members who lose a friend and colleague, the neighbors in base housing to the children attending the military school. The chaplain on the death notification team, the commander working to heal his unit, as well as the various support personnel, are faced with the reality that, much as in law enforcement and other perilous professions, the business of the armed forces is fraught with danger, even in peace time.

In times of tragedy, the military community expands to encompass all those in the chain of command, up to the Commander in Chief. The memorial service is often attended by the entire base population, shutting down the installation as it touches every family in the base community. Watching the televised memorial service for the airmen killed in the bombing of Khobar Towers in Saudi Arabia, we saw dignitaries that included the President of the United States and the Chief of Staff of the Air Force paying their respects alongside the family, friends, and co-workers of those who died.

When someone dies in the line of duty, those around them are forced to re-evaluate their own mortality and take stock of their life choices and actions. If this happens to pilots who lose a fellow aviator, for example, they risk losing their own nerve to fly, which can be paralyzing. Many military air crashes are ruled publicly to be "pilot error." A Vietnam combat veteran once told me that the belief among other pilots that a crash occurred only because the pilot made a mistake—a mistake that they themselves certainly would never make—enables them to continue flying. If the ruling was "mechanical failure," or if they were sent by the command into a scenario that was beyond their control, they might lose their own confidence in the plane or the leaders and be unable to fly again.

When an Airborne Warning and Control Systems (AWACS) plane went down at Elmendorf Air Force Base in Alaska in 1995, killing 24 crew members, the Wing Commander made a point of flying onboard the first AWACS to go up after the crash. This show of confidence in the plane and his personal commitment to the continuation of the mission were critical to the psychological survival of the co-workers in this military workplace.

Service members who worked with the deceased in a support role may also feel guilt: a mechanic who worked on a plane that crashed, a parachute packer after a skydiving accident, or a commander overseeing a preventable training accident. After an Army aviation crash killed eight people, the instructor pilot who had trained the crew, and even saw the plane off that day, felt a great deal of responsibility for the crash, even though he could have done nothing to prevent it. His personal assumption of guilt led to alcoholism, hospitalization, a failed marriage, and finally the loss of his aviation credentials and career. No one connected "co-worker guilt" with the deterioration of his life until it was too late.

How can we as caregivers see these effects and help those in the workplace who suffer a loss? The military has ways to handle the aftermath of death from which the civilian sector can learn. There are very specific regulations to uniformly honor those who die and to minister to those left behind. There are casualty regulations on everything from how to tell a family that a loved one has died to how to perform the burial ceremonies. This organized approach has been developed in an attempt to aid in the healing process of those who are left behind, including co-workers in the military workplace. It sends the resounding message that "We take care of our own," and that the organization will stand by its soldiers, sailors, airmen, and Marines and will see that their service is honored and their families are not abandoned.

The military also has a long-term support system for the emotional support of its families and service members. The Tragedy Assistance Program for Survivors (TAPS) is a private, non-profit veteran service organization that provides services to those affected by a death in the armed forces. TAPS' services are simple but critically important: peer support, grief counseling referral, crisis intervention, and caseworker assistance. The organization acknowledges the psychological needs of those affected by the death of a family member, friend, or co-worker. Those needs include the validation of grief, assistance in coping with the need to go on and perform the mission at hand, survivor guilt or loss of nerve, and the need to feel that one is not alone in his or her feelings. TAPS was born out of the recognition that death in the military workplace is a unique experience. It is patterned after other workplace-related groups, such as Concerns of Police Survivors (COPS), for law enforcement deaths.

TAPS was formed in 1992 by a group of survivors who lost loved ones in the crash of an Army C-12 aircraft on a routine mission. The plane went down in bad weather and treacherous terrain. It was not unlike many other military losses, the result of a dangerous occupation.

For me, however, it was very different. One of the soldiers on board was my husband, and I was at the time a Captain and a member of the Critical Incident Stress Debriefing (CISD) Team for the unit that responded to crashes such as this. When I got the news that the plane was missing, and later learned that it had gone down with no survivors, I allowed my professional side to take over. I found myself in a support role, organizing activities and working to assist other families. I later learned that this was more an example of shock and denial in action than superhuman leadership skills. I felt that if I kept moving forward and acting positively things would somehow turn out all right and we would find this had been some terrible mistake.

As time passed, the media coverage faded, and the mission continued, I came to the realization that the crash had not been a dream but a very real nightmare that I would live out for the rest of my life. Just as so many therapists predict, the worst times came when I passed into the second task of grief, mourning the loss, after accepting that the death had indeed occurred and I would never again see my husband. As I mourned his death, I felt overwhelmingly alone. Yet how could I be? Surely others had suffered such a loss. I had worked with the community CISD team and the local homicide survivors' support group, as well as the hospice in our area. I went to those resources for validation and comfort. I even went to widows' groups to find someone to whom I could relate.

But I found that I didn't feel the anger of a homicide victim, couldn't understand a loss from long-term illness, was far more intimately involved than my fellow response team members, and was younger than most in the local widows' group. Just when I felt that I was surely going mad I ran into one of the other young women made a widow that fateful day. As we talked we both had the stunning realization that we had been living parallel lives, feeling many of the same emotions, wondering about many of the same things, and even having similar dreams. We both longed for the association with our husbands' military unit, a part of our own lives now gone forever. We discovered a bond that joined us closer than sisters, which had finally given us not only comfort and validation but also healing.

It was out of this realization that TAPS came to be. The informal network grew, and we researched existing support for those impacted by a death in the armed forces. We found that there are a number of widows' groups, such as Gold Star Wives and Society of Military Widows, which do wonderful work with those who have lost a husband in the line of duty. These groups came out of World War II and Korea, and their members work diligently to lobby for veterans' survivor benefits and provide a long-standing social network. We talked to those groups and to the Departments of Defense and Veterans Affairs, and created an organization that would fill a void for those who did not fit into the existing programs, whose needs were immediate and emotional.

TAPS is a peer support network that is both made up of, and provides comfort to, those impacted by a death of any cause in the armed forces (including but not limited to widows). TAPS provides four services that meet immediate needs: peer support for everyone impacted by the death, grief counseling referral when military families relocate, crisis intervention for coping with casualties, and caseworker assistance that complements the work of military casualty officers. All services are available 24 hours a day through a toll free information line.

TAPS serves as the organization that connects all those impacted by a loss in any branch of the armed forces, in the common bond that their co-worker and loved one died while serving their country. They are united in that common experience, share the bond of service and, regardless of the actual cause of the death, are brought together by a special sense of patriotism, mission, and duty. TAPS becomes their link back to the armed forces, and provides those who want that connection the chance to participate in seminars, the kids' camp, on-line chats, official ceremonies, and military activities that are part of the patriotic traditions so important to their lives with their loved ones. Commanders can also use this network to have easy access to information about how to help their soldiers and family members cope with a traumatic event. TAPS has given the military workplace a central clearinghouse for finding support for families and resources for units when a death occurs. Support systems outside the military fail to take into account the unique elements of this loss experience. Nowhere else in society would a mother whose son died in a terrorist bombing in a foreign land be connected with the perfect person to comfort: another mother who had lost a son a world away in an major military air disaster. Both felt a tremendous sense of pride in their sons' service to America, both were reeling from the shock of the sudden loss, and both were dealing with traumatic death. They understood each other, and in that understanding, came healing.

Groups such as TAPS are effective because they take into consideration the specific circumstances of the death and the workplace in which the death occurred in order to facilitate healing. A person's life is defined in large part by his or her education and work, as well as the co-workers who share in that camaraderie and bond through their daily experiences. When a death occurs, the way in which those who are left behind respond is likewise going to be determined by this shared culture and acknowledgment of the complicating factors of the loss. As one military widow explained, "You can't discuss burnt dog tags and bent wedding rings over the backyard fence with your neighbor, but you can with someone who tragically possesses those same personal effects." That in itself can validate and heal.

For the co-workers, there is comfort in witnessing the recognition that a life was lived and was valued, that the person was honored for the service they rendered his or her country, and that they themselves would receive like recognition and honor. They are also reassured that their loved ones will be wrapped in the warm blanket of support offered by those who have walked through the valley of the shadow of death and are now there to provide encouragement and hope.

TAPS is one example of giving back to those in a specific workplace a part of themselves, a connection with the military service that was so dear to their loved ones. These programs work because they offer validation and hope, camaraderie, and comfort. Words spoken by someone who has raised children alone and answered questions about "daddy's death" ring truer than even those of the most educated counselor's. These programs are here for caregivers as well, as a resource and a referral, and they bring another dimension to the healing process of grief.

Bonnie Carroll, founder and president of the Tragedy Assistance Program for Survivors, Inc., is a Captain in the Air Force Reserve currently serving as Chief, USAF Casualty Services, and is the widow of Brigadier General Tom Carroll, US Army.

Six

AIDS in the Workplace

Veronica Ryan Coleman

What Business Managers Can Do: Policy and Program

A health threat of great magnitude, affecting businesses large and small in the United States, as well as in other parts of the world, has developed since the detection and spread of AIDS. An estimated one million Americans are currently infected with HIV, the virus that causes AIDS. Given that fact, it is likely that many large companies have an employee with HIV infection. HIV/AIDS has caused more individual lawsuits than any other disease in American history. Under the Americans with Disabilities Act (ADA) of 1990, employers may be held liable for discriminating against an applicant or an employee because of his or her HIV/AIDS status.

Beyond concern with litigation, however, businesses have other reasons to respond wisely and compassionately to the HIV/AIDS epidemic. The stigma and fear that HIV/AIDS generates can complicate the grief of those infected with the virus and experiencing their own losses, as well as all those family, friends, and co-workers affected by the illness or death of another. And the issues raised by HIV/AIDS, such as the need for education, policy, and grief support, certainly provide a model for the handling of other chronic illnesses within the workplace.

About one in 300 Americans is infected with the HIV virus. AIDS is the second leading cause of death among 25-to-40 year olds in this country. The majority of people now infected and likely to be infected are in this age group (Centers for Disease Control, 1997). In the US this age group represents 50 percent of the current workforce and is the largest age group at risk. Considering that HIV/AIDS is one of the most costly and litigated diseases in American history, the economic impact is staggering.

However, in a supportive workplace workers with HIV/AIDS can continue to be productive. Medical treatments allow people with AIDS to live and work longer. Survival time can vary due to individual response to disease and the presence of new drugs; many infected persons can be symptom-free for years. In any event, even though the prognosis is serious, infected persons can manage the infection as a long-term, chronic condition. The numbers of people with HIV, combined with extended life expectancy from more effective treatments, mean we can expect more employees on the job with HIV in the future.

However, there remain widespread discrimination and physical, emotional, and financial hardship due to lack of understanding and misinformation about HIV transmission. Unnecessary fear of infection can complicate co-workers' feelings of impending loss as well. Policies and education programs for the workplace can help prevent such discrimination.

Business and labor have vital roles to play in dealing with these issues. All businesses, from small independent businesses to multinational corporations, will benefit from developing a cost-effective, sensible, and sensitive workplace HIV and AIDS program. These programs help employers clarify their compliance with federal, state, and local laws, and confirm their hiring, promotion, transfer, and dismissal practices. Also critical are benefit programs for employees and family members, including domestic partners.

Labor unions have long been in the forefront of the struggle to provide basic healthcare, social insurance, and safe, healthy working conditions. These are issues of paramount importance with regard to AIDS caregiving, grief, and loss in the workplace.

Medical Facts

Basic knowledge about how HIV is transmitted is critical when considering how to set up an AIDS policy and education program. HIV is transmitted through sexual intercourse (vaginal, anal, or oral) with a man or woman infected with the virus, or by sharing needles or syringes with an infected person. It can also be transmitted from an HIV-infected woman to her child during pregnancy or childbirth or, in rare cases, through breastfeeding. Other modes of transmission include receiving HIV-infected blood or blood products, or through blood-to-blood contact (World Health Organization, 1992).

The HIV virus cannot be transmitted through casual contact such as a handshake, a sneeze, or a hug. It is not transmitted by sharing dishes, tools, telephones, computer keyboards, bathroom facilities, or drinking fountains. HIV cannot be transmitted via air, food, water, insects, or animals. Company policy should make these facts clear to all employees.

Legal Issues

The Rehabilitation Act of 1973 prohibits any company that either receives Federal aid or does business with the Federal government from discriminating against persons with disabilities. The Americans with Disabilities Act of 1990 prohibits employment discrimination by *any* business with 15 or more employees. Under these laws a covered employer may not refuse to hire a qualified applicant because that applicant is perceived to have a disability, including HIV/AIDS. The employer is also required to make reasonable accommodations (unless such accommodations create undue hardship for business). Examples might be job modifications, flexible scheduling, and leaves of absence that would allow an employee with HIV/AIDS to continue to perform essential job functions. Employers must ensure that applicants and employees are not subjected to discriminatory hiring practices, job assignments, eligibility for benefits, or termination. Additionally, many states and local communities have enacted other legislation that may go beyond the provisions of Federal law.

HIV/AIDS Workplace Policy

Businesses should prepare themselves to deal with AIDS by developing a comprehensive written policy that defines their response to

HIV as well as other chronic conditions and illnesses. They should prepare employees by clearly communicating company policy and providing workers with information about employment practices and health benefits. This policy establishes a company's leadership in confronting major public health concerns. It also establishes a company as a responsible employer, provides for consistency, and sets standards of behavior for all employees. A written policy should let workers know where to go for information and assistance, and indicates to supervisors how to address HIV/AIDS in their work groups. It may also help to prevent a crisis situation, such as a work stoppage or co-worker fear when an employee discloses that he or she has AIDS. Written policy defining a company's response to HIV and AIDS should address the following issues, which have specific application to individuals with HIV and AIDS.

- Compliance with federal, state and local laws, including the Americans with Disabilities Act, the Federal Rehabilitation Act, and the Occupational Safety and Health Act
- Hiring, promotion, transfer, and dismissal policies with regard to employees and potential employees with HIV and AIDS
- Maintaining confidentiality of employee medical records and information
- Identifying expected behavior within the company
- Examining social benefits programs available to employees and family members with HIV/AIDS (Of special note are issues such as funeral leave for domestic partners, family leave to care for a dying domestic partner, and establishing a grief and bereavement program that recognizes domestic partners as well.)
- Clarifying, and perhaps adjusting, medical benefit coverage
- Defining management strategies that address potential worksite discrimination of employees with HIV/AIDS
- Developing employee education that promotes understanding and prevention

Successful HIV/AIDS policies already exist and can be adapted to suit specific work environments. A sample policy can be obtained from the Centers for Disease Control (CDC) Business Responds to AIDS Resource Service. A basic seminar on HIV/AIDS can be useful; consultants are available from agencies such as local departments of public health and the Business Responds to AIDS Resource Center to assist companies in developing an HIV/AIDS policy. The costs of developing programs and policies should be identified and allocated in the company budget. Naturally, such a policy can serve as a model for approaches to other chronic illnesses and conditions.

Education Programs

There is currently no cure for AIDS and no vaccine that will prevent HIV infection. Prevention education is therefore the best available way to slow the spread of this disease. An HIV/AIDS training and education program should be organized for managers, supervisors, and union leaders as well as for employees. Such a program must involve a planned, ongoing strategy that is responsible, effective, and cost effective.

In order for individuals to be receptive to disease-prevention education they must understand that they could, in fact, become infected. They must know that their degree of risk depends on their own behaviors. They also need to know that something can be done about infection and that help is available (Rosenstock, 1996).

Setting Up an HIV/AIDS Program

Once a company has decided to establish an HIV/AIDS program, a steering committee of managers, supervisors, and union leaders should be set up. Building a strong foundation for a company's program requires leadership and teamwork from a supportive management; it is crucial to have key high-level managers on this committee in order to give power and weight to committee decisions and policy enforcement.

A permanent committee should include representatives from each of the company's departments and operating units. The committee should include a labor representative.

A managers' education program should be set up. This can be accomplished through HIV/AIDS seminars or onsite workshops by health professionals with expertise in this area.

Employee education should focus on means of transmission and prevention, as well as on detection methods and resources for confidential testing. Employee anxiety and misinformation, which can lead to discrimination and work disruption, can be reduced by an accurate understanding of HIV transmission and prevention.

Family education is also important in addressing workers' concerns about HIV/AIDS. Depending on company size, lectures, and educational films can be made available as a community service.

Effective grief and bereavement counseling services are important in assisting employees facing all types of death and loss. However, it is of particular importance as an integral part of a workplace HIV/AIDS program. Even though, with treatment, an individual may live with HIV/AIDS for years, impending mortality has a profound effect on the infected individual and on those who love and care for him or her. Onsite grief and bereavement counseling programs can be provided during lunch breaks, or before or after work hours. Employee Assistance Programs often provide such services or refer workers to outside agencies.

Planning an Education Program

Identify a leader. It is important to select a person who is both willing and able to develop the program and to make it work. A company may hire an outside health professional on a consulting basis to head up the program. This consultant would work with a team or a key leader inside the organization.

Establish goals and objectives. An overall goal might be to establish responsible leadership in this area and to provide for the well-being of employees. A basic objective for management education should be to ensure that all managers have a thorough knowledge of company policy. Other objectives for all levels of employees would be to provide accurate information about what constitute high risk behaviors, methods of prevention, and where to obtain confidential testing and counseling, as well as grief and bereavement counseling.

Do a needs assessment of employees. Find out what they want to know and what they already know. With the help of a health professional find out what they *need* to know.

Identify needed resources and those already in place. What funding is available? Are appropriate facilities and equipment available or will they need to be rented? What can be obtained free or at low cost from outside agencies? Identify and order materials well in advance.

Create a timetable. Allow for planning and implementation, as well as follow-up.

Plan learning activities. A variety of approaches can be used that fit in with your business culture and environment. Posters can be displayed in key locations. Brief educational messages can go out as payroll inserts. Bulletins, memos, brochures, workshops, and discussion groups can be utilized as appropriate.

Include effective evaluation tools. Make sure that the evaluation process matches your timetable and your goals and objectives.

Implementation

Successful implementation of an HIV/AIDS education program is more effective when it utilizes approaches that workers are familiar with. The program should be introduced by a senior company official. Some businesses have sent out a memo from the president explaining the company's position on HIV/AIDS and inviting all employees to a meeting. When the first communication comes from the top, credibility for the program is quickly established.

A guest speaker who is an HIV/AIDS health professional might be invited. It is important that outside consultants be appropriate to the company's culture, and to tailor their approach to the audience. Have audio-visual equipment in place, encourage an open atmosphere, and leave adequate time for questions. Remember, this is only the beginning; people can't learn everything at once. Describe future programs and goals. Make it clear that the company will continue to deal with HIV/AIDS accurately and openly. Again, these principles can guide programs for other types of illnesses should that become necessary.

Conclusion

The HIV/AIDS epidemic will not disappear, nor can employers hide from it. No workforce is immune to the possibility of HIV/AIDS infection among it employees. Employers who ignore current legislation regarding HIV/AIDS not only increase their potential liability, but critically, limit their ability to educate and support their employees. That failure, too, has its cost in days lost to caregiving or grief, as well as in morale, turnover, and productivity. Companies that confront the issues directly and responsibly join thousands of other businesses making an effort to ease potential or existing burdens and contribute to a caring workplace environment.

Veronica Ryan Coleman has a PhD in Community Health Education from New York University. She is an RN whose area of expertise is in providing technical services for the delivery of health promotion and disease prevention services to communities, especially worksites.

Seven

When Caregivers Grieve

Paul R. Brenner

Carol works in an emergency room at a large urban hospital. In addition to her nursing duties, she is expected to deal with grieving families and friends who routinely come to the ER and are informed of the sudden death or serious injury of a loved one. While challenging, Carol has always found this part of the job both critical for families and meaningful for her. But ever since she returned from her sister's funeral, her work is increasingly stressful and seems unfulfilling. At shift's end, she is emotionally and physically exhausted.

Carol's ability to do her work while processing her personal loss will be impacted, among other things, by the culture of the hospital in which she works. It can either complicate or facilitate her grief process. The dominant culture of healthcare in the US is grounded in a model that emphasizes objectivity over subjectivity, rationality over emotion, winning over collaboration, and the science of care over the art of care. This model complicates the caregiver's ability to provide care when the caregiver is personally dealing with loss.

Institutional Assumptions About Caregivers

Professional caregivers are expected to be servants of the institution/agency of which they are a part. The institution expects professionals to act "professionally," which means to behave competently, autonomously, and efficiently, not troubled by personal problems or in reaction to patients or family members, and, in particular, not creating problems for the institution.

When Caregivers Grieve Within this Context

Institutions may grant a short bereavement leave, but upon return to work the caregiver is expected to function at full professional capacity. The assumption is that the grief is taken care of in a matter of days and the institution is not responsible for what happens in the personal lives of their professionals after the leave is over. If the caregiver's behavior is less than "professional" due to grieving, the conclusion is that something is wrong with the caregiver, not that something is wrong with the institution's assumption about the nature of loss and grief.

Implications of this Model

It is not that the approach of this culture and model of healthcare service-delivery is deliberately less than humane or consciously destructive. It is simply that such matters are outside the scope and comprehension of this model and culture.

It is within this model of professionalism that most caregivers are trained. Medical training, for example—in its required sleep deprivations, long work hours, and technical bias—seems almost deliberate in its attempt to downplay the humanity of physicians and turn them into technical machines. Therefore, it is not surprising to find a significant level of personal dysfunction in the lives of many healthcare professionals, as indicated by substance abuse, addiction, poor personal health, and family relationships in disarray.

Further, because death is the ultimate enemy and represents defeat within this model, there is little structure to support the grieving of loss by family members or staff members. Grieving is not something that receives clinical attention or is considered important enough to address within its structure of care.

Building Other Models

The creation of other models is dependent upon the ability to break through the restrictions of the existing model and its culture of caregiving. Ultimately, a new culture must be created regarding how professional caregivers are trained and supported in their institutions, as well as in how clinical practice is structured in the delivery of service.

While the existing dominant model is based on the "old" science, the new culture will emerge through the worldview articulated by quantum physicists. Perhaps the single greatest difference between these worldviews is that the dominant inherited model sees the world as a collection of static entities that relate by unchangeable laws within a vacuum called space.

The quantum world, on the other hand, is one in which the earth and the cosmos are perceived as one vast, complex, interconnected living system. The quantum worldview does not make claims to objectivity, moral/ethical neutrality, or the revelation of absolute truth, but deals with probabilities, uncertainty, the relationship between contradictions, and the subjectivity of scientific observation and study. This science does not focus on objects and entities as such, but on connections, relationships, and complex interdependent systems. In this perspective the whole is much greater than the sum of its parts, and by understanding the whole, one better understands the many systems contained within.

Implications for Healthcare

Moving from an objective, deterministic way of understanding truth and reality implies significant changes in how one approaches healthcare within the quantum framework.

The most immediate change is that the focus of care moves from a disease-centered, body-focused approach to a whole-person approach—that is, a whole person within the context of one's significant relationships and systems of family, religion, culture, ethnicity, sexuality, and psychological coping.

Within the quantum model, death and life, disease and health are not absolutes unto themselves or categorically in opposition to each other, but are interrelated, interacting, interdependent systems. Therefore, healthcare must focus not only on disease in the body with cure the only goal; it must also focus on the person as a whole and on the person's suffering as a result of disease and disease treatment, clarifying choice and self-determination throughout the course of treatment. Healthcare must also achieve changing quality-of-life needs, and support those individuals who are part of the patient's support and care.

In this new model the person who is sick is not regarded as a victim and therefore the object of care, but is an active participant to the fullest degree possible. Curing the disease is only one of many operative goals, including total care of physical, emotional, spiritual, and existential needs. From this perspective healing is always possible, even when a cure may not be.

Dying and death are acknowledged not as a medical failure but as a fundamental part of the human experience, from which one has the possibility of learning much about life and living. For some healthcare professionals, care at the end of life is fulfilling, challenging, and significant. Such care requires creativity, emotional maturity, spiritual integrity, and intuition, as well as technical competency and careful attention to details.

Caregiving of the Dying

It is not surprising that the model of the interdisciplinary team, which includes all relevant professional caregivers, as well as lay volunteer caregivers, originated with the work of hospice care. Effective and efficient care cannot be provided to patients and families by an endless array of disconnected and unrelated healthcare providers and professionals. The assumption of the interdisciplinary model is that no one profession can address the multiplicity of physical, emotional, spiritual, existential, relational, and practical dimensions involved. At the same time, all professionals are needed for what each one has to bring to the whole. However, the whole of the team is much greater than (and even other than) the individual professions involved.

Patients and their families do not need distance, objectivity, and separation; they need caregivers who are not threatened by intimacy—the intensely personal dimensions of the work and the vulnerabilities involved.

In this model the team as a whole is responsible not only for the delivery of care but also for ensuring the ongoing well-being of its own members in their giving of care. The team looks after its members because it recognizes that any of them may be affected by unfinished business that arises on occasion in their therapeutic relationship with patients and families.

Models of Care for Caregivers

The hospice model has pioneered the care of its own caregivers. The fundamental assumption is made that support is a necessity for all professionals involved in care. This support is part of the interdisciplinary model that operates, through the supervisory structures that exist within disciplines, by providing support through outside facilitators, and by intensive ongoing education, training, and skills building. The developing palliative care movement also pays attention to the need to provide systematic support to its staff.

When Caregivers Grieve Within this Model

When caregivers experience significant loss in their lives, the hospice/palliative program has a framework in place to respond to and provide care for its grieving caregivers. The institution or program acknowledges that grief is a natural response to loss, and does not have unrealistic expectations about quick recovery. It acknowledges that this is a complex process of its own, and the return of the caregiver to the workplace can both assist and inhibit the process. A significant part of the commitment of the institution or program to its staff is that it accepts responsibility to work with the grieving caregiver, especially in work-related issues. Significant support will be given by the members of the team to its grieving caregiver. This support will be ongoing and constant through the interactions of team members.

However, the institution or program will have provided training, direction and support to its supervisors who are in a one-to-one relationship with the grieving staff member. Supervisors will assess the work activity, assist in setting realistic expectations, and make referrals for additional assistance as needed and appropriate.

When Grieving Is Hidden

While grieving loss is generally acknowledged within healthcare institutions and programs, sometimes the loss is hidden or disenfranchised. This is particularly true of nontraditional significant relationships, such as gay and lesbian couples. If the institution or program does not recognize such relationships, it may provide no safe way for a gay or lesbian staff member to participate in informal staff conversation about family life or to display the picture of a partner at the work area.

Even more so, with the impact of AIDS on gay men and breast cancer on lesbian women, gay or lesbian professionals not only may need to closet the true nature of their relationships, but if they experience progressive disease and death with their life partners, they must conceal this as well.

Often these gay men and lesbian women do not have their losses acknowledged nor do they receive support from their institution or program when they are grieving. This isolation in the work place at such a vulnerable time can be devastating—and nearly impossible to hide. The further stress of feeling constrained to conceal one's grief and the true nature of one's most intimate relationship is additionally destructive. This all too frequent experience of gay men and lesbian implies an ongoing need to address this institutionally. Grieving is hard enough, but disenfranchised grieving is an intolerable burden to bear.

Practice Model for Caregivers

Under the existing model we noted that the message given to caregivers is to keep their personal life out of their professional activity. The fundamental assumption is that there is no connection or relationship between them, and that professionals are expected to perform as experts, always in control, objective, and emotionally detached in patient contact.

Within new models careful attention is paid to the interdependence of the personal and the professional. A "practice model" is the attempt to integrate personal human and spiritual development and awareness with professional development and expertise. An example of such a practice model is the work being done in the Zen Hospice Project in San Francisco, or at The Project on Being With Dying, Upaya, in Santa Fe, New Mexico. The central idea is that one's spiritual practice of meditation, inner cleansing, and focused awareness in the here and now are critical to the work of being with persons who are dying and those who are grieving the loss. The one can inform and assist the other.

We are challenged as part of the new model of healthcare to also develop a new model of what it is to be a professional. This task involves our working through our own assumptions, beliefs, values, and practices that have defined us, and to reframe and expand our self-understanding and practice.

We must develop a balanced model—one that does not require a divorce between the personal and professional, and one that does not flood the professional with such unfinished business that it inhibits competent care. From this perspective neither the existing dominant model nor its perceived opposite is satisfactory or desirable. This new model must transcend the either/or alternatives that drive practice to extremes on either hand, and must recognize that clinical competence combines technical mastery, psychological/spiritual development, and the ability to engage one's own humanity in the therapeutic relationship appropriately and effectively.

In Henri Nouwen's book, *The Wounded Healer*, he proposes the concept that being effective in a healing way with another is formed and transformed by the integration of an understanding, acceptance, and acknowledgment of one's own woundedness. Woundedness is frequently the place of connection with patients and with family members and even, we suggest, with professionals who grieve. This model offers an alternative to the current healthcare model, which knows how to *do for*, but cannot *be with* the person in his or her suffering. Both competencies are needed by those we serve, as well as by those of us who do the serving. To bring our woundedness to consciousness and integration is to enhance our professionalism, not diminish it—to deepen care, not decrease it.

While healthcare institutions and programs need to ensure that there are appropriate supervisory and supportive systems in place, the ultimate task is to assist the grieving caregiver in incorporating the experiences and teachings of this wounding into the increasing humanization of his or her clinical practice.

Paul R. Brenner, MDiv, is the Executive Director of Jacob Perlow Hospice, Department of Pain Medicine and Palliative Care, Beth Israel Medical Center, New York, and is Chair of the Board, New York State Hospice Association. He has served hospices in the Washington, DC area and Jacksonville and Palm Beach County, Florida, and has been active in the National Hospice Organization.

Practical Suggestions

When Illness Strikes

As an Employee

The diagnosis of a life-threatening illness is not only a medical crisis, it is a personal one as well. It turns your whole world upside down. Everything—career, family, future plans—now seems in flux. It affects you psychologically, socially, and spiritually. It challenges all of your assumptions and threatens your hopes. Often shocked by the diagnosis, you must grapple with whatever symptoms exist as well as deal with such practical issues as arranging for treatment.

- Recognize the ways that illness affects you and try to schedule accordingly
- Communication is key
- Find and cultivate effective sources of support
- Learn about health benefits and options
- Avoid rash decisions

As a Supervisor

When one of your employees is struggling with a life-threatening illness, you need to understand and acknowledge that he or she is in the midst of a deep crisis. Your support will not only be critical, it will set a tone for your workplace.

- Be supportive
- Respect confidentiality
- Help problem-solve
- Know your company's policies and programs
- Take care of yourself
- Maintain contact
- Assess effects on co-workers

As a Co-worker

When a co-worker becomes ill, you can play a big role in assisting that person. Because you may feel ill at ease with the situation, or do not know what to say, you may avoid that person. Instead, try to follow these few basic principles.

- Offer your support in tangible ways
- Follow their lead—ask them how they are doing, but do not force the discussion
- Continue to treat them as normally as possible; do not let the disease dominate your relationship

When Death Strikes: Encountering Grief

Not only does illness affect the workplace, but death does as well. Employees must return to work after the funeral of someone they loved. Co-workers may die—perhaps even in work-related deaths. Grief, like illness, will affect the work environment.

Coping with Your Own Grief at Work

- Accept your grief
- Be flexible
- Be gentle with others who may not understand
- Seek support
- Take care of yourself

Supporting Grieving Employees and Co-Workers

- Review policies before a crisis
- Get training
- Offer sympathy and support
- Participate in the memorial, if appropriate
- Offer tangible help
- Be understanding

When a Co-worker Dies

In addition to the above suggestions, a few other ideas may help supervisors and co-workers respond in a sensitive and compassionate way.

- Share information
- Plan memorials together
- Sensitively deal with personal effects
- Acknowledge the loss
- Consider professional intervention

Getting Help

While it is difficult to deal with situations involving illness and loss, you do not have to face these situations alone. Your local hospice or mental health agency, as well as any employee assistance program, can be of help. Professional organizations such as Hospice Foundation of America are available to assist in finding local resources.

These tips are summarized from a brochure entitled *Living With Grief: At Work*, a publication of the Hospice Foundation of America. Contact HFA for more detailed information and suggestions.

Part II

Living with Grief:
At School

Another place where people grieve is at school. Many of the same situations that employees experience at work are experienced in schools as well: Issues of life-threatening illness, losses due to death or divorce, even traumatic and sudden losses can occur within the school environment.

Matthews' chapter delineates these losses. She reminds us of the many faces of loss as well as the effects that loss has on children. Particularly important for Matthews is that grief can manifest itself in many ways. These include behavioral responses such as substance abuse, delinquency, acting out, and sexual activity. Cognitively, the manifestations of grief can mimic learning disabilities: an inability to concentrate, a short attention span, and a preoccupation with the loss that causes less attentiveness to environmental stimuli.

Matthews offers sound advice for interventions—what schools can and cannot offer. She highlights what they can do well, aspects, in fact, of their mission—education and modeling. Matthews emphasizes critical principles for developing interventions. One is that they have to be developmentally appropriate; the needs of an adolescent in middle school are far different from those of a child in the primary grades. And, Matthews reminds us that interventions are most successful when they are developed collaboratively with students.

Among the faces of loss are those presented by the HIV/AIDS epidemic. Levine and Khalili estimate that from 82,000 to 125,000 children will have lost their mothers to AIDS by the end of the year

2001. Others are themselves infected. Still others experience the loss of siblings or other family members. While losses related to AIDS are similar in many ways to losses caused by other diseases, there are some critical differences that provide a specific challenge to schools. The first is that AIDS still remains a highly stigmatized disease, creating fear and isolating those infected and affected by the disease. A second challenge lies in a paradox: HIV infection is spreading rapidly among adolescents and young adults, yet infection is preventable. Clearly this points to a need for schools to examine their educational programs. Levine and Khalili recognize the limits of the school, but remind schools that they need not tackle issues alone. Three models, or collaborations, involving not-for-profit agencies, community organizations, and hospice, offer excellent examples to spur local creativity.

In the development of programs, it is critical to both train staff and assess needs. For example, assess what support groups may be needed. In some schools there may be a critical mass of students with special loss issues: family losses due to incarceration or death by violence or suicide. In other schools students may deal with different issues.

Wrenn's chapter considers an oft forgotten population, late adolescents at college. As Wrenn reminds us, they may have excellent support systems within their family or community, but these are largely irrelevant if they are away at school. Wrenn's particular strength is his ability to give practical suggestions to colleges, ranging from death notification to work with survivors.

Wrenn emphasizes a point echoed in the other chapters: Interventions in schools and colleges have to acknowledge that those people asked to help, such as counselors or teachers, may be grieving as well. Staff members are likely to be affected, especially when the loss involved is that of a staff member or student. Schools, after all, are workplaces too.

Eight

The Grieving Child in the School Environment

Jennie D. Matthews

It was December when Mike entered the high school counselor's office hoping to adjust his schedule for the next semester. Schedule changes could only be made for "good reason," so the counselor inquiry took place. The primary reason for the request was Mike's concern about his ability to do well in college prep classes, given what could take place with his mother over the next few months. His father had died six years before after a brief bout with cancer. His mother had been diagnosed with cancer the previous July and treatment had not been as effective as hoped. Mike knew his mother had a short time to live. The decisions to be made included: Should Mike take courses that would allow him to graduate from high school a year early so that his mother could see him graduate? Should he be allowed to take a less difficult course of study so the stress involved in doing well in or just passing challenging courses would not add to the stress of helping care for his dying mother? How much emotional and academic monitoring should the counselor do? How much should the teacher be told? Should the counselor help Mike's friends understand what was happening and learn ways to support their friend? Should performance expectations be lowered? When the mother died, what was the school's responsibility to the child? How long should the counselor and teachers be concerned about the student?

The parents of a third-grader diagnosed with leukemia ask the school counselor for help. Their child is to receive a bone marrow transplant if a donor can be found. The sick child's brother and sister are also students at the school. Who does the counselor need to tell? What does the child's teacher do to help students understand why the desk is frequently empty? What should the teacher do to help the child make academic progress yet not feel pressured? Is home instruction a better idea for this student? Is it the counselor's or the teacher's responsibility to help the children understand? What is the teacher to do if the child dies? What does the school need to offer the siblings? What should the school do if religious questions are asked?

The grieving student is any child or adolescent who has experienced circumstances that alter what is known, what is safe, what defines life as they know it. When children deal with death, with divorce, with frequent moves, with a difficult medical diagnosis, with illness, or with giving up something meaningful, loss is experienced. Parents and teachers cannot protect students from the inevitable losses that occur in the natural progression of life. The loss of one's place in the family because of the birth of a sibling, the loss of an older sibling due to the natural process of leaving home, the loss of self-confidence when one fails a course or a much sought after goal, and the loss of one's youth when choosing to grow up too soon—all are losses experienced by most students (Hayes, 1988).

Grief is the process of reacting to all of the losses that occur in one's life experience. The grieving student has lost something significant and will react in unique ways. Teachers and school counselors must understand the emotions involved in the grief process and must respond in ways that provide physical and emotional safety for the child.

There are many questions to ask and decisions to be made by school counselors, administrators, teachers, and other school personnel when loss comes to school. There are many facts to know and many decisions to be made about handling any loss responsibly and compassionately. Communication between school personnel within the school environment is critical to effectively respond to the student in grief. It is also crucial that someone from the school communicate with the family.

One of the most important things parents of school age children need to learn is how to communicate with their child's teacher, counselor, or principal when something happens outside the school environment that impacts the child during the school day. These could include chronic or terminal illness of the child or a family member, family discord, lack of economic security, incarceration, substance abuse by a parent, and other family situations.

Some parents will not contact teachers because they assume their child will communicate the news, and the school will have planned an appropriate response to the child. Some parents may not communicate the news because they consider the event a private family matter that does not involve the school. It is important for the adults in a child's life, especially parents and teachers, to react to a death or other significant loss and to answer questions honestly. If the trusted adults fail to answer a child's questions, confusion, anger, and guilt can result (Stevenson, 1995).

The losses experienced by children and adolescents have many faces, and a loss of any magnitude can affect the actual and/or perceived emotional and physical safety of all children. Teachers, administrators, and counselors must know as much as possible about how loss and grief impact academic performance. Educators must be trained to recognize the emotions and behaviors of children and adolescents that are grief reactions to school-wide crisis events and to their daily, individual loss experiences.

The goal of education is multifaceted: to nurture academic success; to encourage preparation for the workplace; to promote artistic, athletic, and individual potential; and to attempt to motivate students to achieve their intellectual capacity. A central mission for educators is to teach the life skills necessary for the development of responsible, healthy, moral, and compassionate adults who will become the citizens, leaders, and parents of the next generation. To reach these goals, teachers, school counselors, and other school personnel must have as part of their training an understanding of the impact of loss and grief on children and adolescents. Educators must also plan effective intervention strategies to address the needs of grieving students in the school environment.

When tragedy or crisis comes to school, the opportunity exists for school personnel to equip children with coping strategies that enable them to respond to the inevitable changes, disappointments, and losses that occur naturally in life. These events offer opportunities to teach children how to reach out to others for support and how to offer support to others in need. This method teaches a sense of community within the school and, in turn, in the larger society. Schools have an ethical responsibility to provide leadership by responding to children throughout their educational experience in ways that teach and model the life skills of adapting, responding, and supporting. Schools can be places of preparation and transformation when loss sparks vulnerability in children (Whiting and Matthews, 1997).

The Faces of Loss in our Students

To best help the children we serve, educators must realize that loss has many faces. Loss happens to people of all ages, in all socioeconomic groups, in different geographic locations, and from different cultures. The following stories demonstrate the range of grief experiences among children and youth. The opportunities in loss can be seen only when we have a well-defined picture of what loss can be in the lives of our students.

Loss Is. . .

Sarah, a 12-year-old whose parents are divorcing. She feels confused, lost, scared, and angry. Her grades begin to fall. How can the school help this child balance the demands of school when she worries about things at home?

Michael, a 17-year-old who breaks up with his girlfriend after finding out she is pregnant. He feels sad, guilty, and different from his peers. He withdraws in class, even skips school. His parents call the principal after finding a note mentioning suicide. Should the principal handle this situation alone or seek assistance from the counselor and teachers?

Mrs. Rodriguez, the assistant principal who finds the principal slumped over his desk during school hours. She panics and is unsure what to do. The principal's children are students at the school. Who takes over when school personnel are unable to carry out their duties? Who informs his family of the immediate crisis? How is this event communicated to the school?

Ashley, a five-year-old whose kindergarten teacher is having chemotherapy and losing her hair. She feels upset and doesn't understand why no one is talking about this. The substitute teacher doesn't know how to answer the children's questions. Who at the school should handle this student and the class?

Kyle, a 15-year-old whose sister was killed in a car accident on the way to school several months ago. He is upset, angry, and dis-respectful to his teachers. The teachers want to reprimand him but are unsure if this is the right action to take. Is it the school's respon-sibility to acknowledge the loss and assist the grieving student?

Jermaine, age eight, whose Labrador retriever was run over during the weekend. He has had the dog since he was five and has never lost anything until now. He is very quiet. The teacher thinks he should get over it and has told him so. What should the teacher know to appropriately react to a student experiencing a loss?

Christina, a 16-year-old whose older brother has been charged with a serious crime. A family member of the victim is in her English and gym classes. The teacher and coach are concerned about problems that could arise when the case goes to trial. How do they prepare to offer support to both students and to other students impacted by the community event?

Latisha, a 12-year-old whose mother died suddenly. She feels angry and thinks it is her fault because she had been fighting with her mom. She has to help take care of younger siblings. Her grades drop below passing. Her teacher needs help talking with Latisha, her father, and the class. Does the school counselor help with this or should an agency from the community be involved?

Mr. Smith, the math teacher whose wife has just been diagnosed with a serious illness. They have three children in the school district. You teach next door and wonder what you and the school can do to help the teacher and his family. Does the school district have a sick-leave bank so that employees can share sick days with families battling a serious illness? How is personal information about faculty members shared within the school family?

Loss Is Also. . .

> *the fear of a hurricane, tornado, or earthquake;*
> *an unsolved crime in the community;*
> *a school bus accident;*
> *a flood, severe storm, or fire;*
> *a bomb threat;*
> *mobilization of national forces;*
> *placement of foster children with new parents or in a new school;*
> *children who are victims of abuse;*
> *diagnoses of diabetes, asthma, AIDS;*
> *not making the basketball team or cheerleading squad;*
> *physical disabilities—hearing, visual, or orthopedic;*
> *learning disabilities—ADD or ADHD;*
> *divorce or remarriage;*
> *changes in relationships.*
> *(Whiting and Matthews, 1997)*

The Nature of Loss in the School Environment

Many experiences of loss, particularly in children and adolescents, remain unrecognized and unacknowledged. Loss happens in many ways within the school community. Children and youth may lose a sense of safety, a sense of mastery, a sense of belonging, and a sense of security. When loss happens to children, adults need to offer support, set an example, and provide guidance in helping them move successfully through the loss experience. Children and adolescents are not equipped to do this alone. Therefore, adults must seize the opportunity to model positive, appropriate responses to difficult and painful occurrences. Children and adolescents need educators to have a working knowledge about the nature of loss. Educators often bring to the school and to the classroom what was modeled in their own life experiences. Some teachers, counselors, principals, and other school personnel learned appropriate responses and skills, but many learned inappropriate, even damaging responses. It is important that grief and loss training be incorporated into teacher education programs (Whiting and Matthews, 1997).

Only in recent years has our society acknowledged the needs of children and adolescents in grief. When adequate support systems are available and school staff are prepared for the needs of grieving children, a multitude of problems can be avoided or handled directly (Allen, 1990). When an event of school-wide proportion happens, the counselor and administrators must drop everything and be prepared to respond in a knowledgeable, compassionate way. It is often assumed that school counselors are well trained in the many aspects of crisis management and grief counseling. In reality, though some are so trained, most have had little or no training.

The nature of loss and how students are impacted within the school environment includes many characteristics:

Losses Must Be Mourned in their Own Way

Educators need to understand that all losses must be mourned. School personnel need to know how to react to different crisis situations. An illness and a car accident would require different responses. The school killings in Mississippi, Kentucky, Arkansas, Pennsylvania, or Oregon would demand a different protocol, one that would call for intense student and faculty intervention, and for involvement from professionals in the community.

Losses Must Not Be Compared

Parents and educators need to know that losses must not be compared. Each loss is different in intensity and in personal importance. Sudden death shatters a child's sense of security. Changes that happen so quickly have a painful impact and often destroy the safe, secure world that existed before the loss. Primary, elementary, and middle schools are concerned about protecting the self-esteem of children, yet the loss of a parent or other significant adult shatters self-esteem. Children who have experienced a significant loss seem to have a vulnerability and an "oldness" about them that manifests itself in classroom and other social settings. Adolescents who have lost a parent are often impatient with friends who complain about their parents. It is hard to be identified as a "motherless teenage girl" or a "fatherless teenage boy."

Loss Creates Fear

Loss sparks fears in children and adolescents: Who will take care of me? Am I still a big sister? Teenagers are encouraged to be strong for parents and siblings. Their fear for their own safety surfaces, and they wonder about their sources of strength (Sims, 1990). Some children will refuse to go to school. After the loss of a parent or significant adult, the fear that the remaining parent may get sick and die while the student is in school is real and must be carefully handled. Hospice workers, school counselors, school social workers, and other school personnel have worked with families to effectively help children and adolescents through this part of the grief process.

To soothe the fears of younger siblings, teenagers will often assume some of the roles of the sick or deceased parent. Bedtime stories, meal preparation, carpooling, babysitting, and grocery shopping are tasks for which older children assume responsibility. The pressure that adolescents feel to contribute to the home can cause them to drop out of school activities that had been important to them (Cragg and Berman, 1990). Schools can make an effort to work with families to minimize the isolation that extra responsibility can create.

The classmates of a terminally ill child need honest information about the impact of the disease on the sick student. They need to be reassured that the illness is not contagious. When the sick child is absent from school and if the parents agree, the teacher and/or school counselor should talk about the child's illness and how it is different from other illnesses (Peterson and Straub, 1992). Discussing symptoms, physical changes, and characteristics of the illness can reduce the fear of students when interacting with the sick child. Classmates should be kept up-to-date on the child's progress. Banners, posters, cards, letters, poetry, a video, and audio messages can give hope to a sick child and a discouraged family.

Loss Is Universal

Every loss has a ripple effect. It moves from those most affected outward to others. Children and school personnel become a type of family that must be aware of the direction the ripples take. Depending on the nature of the event, one member of a school family may be most impacted, or an entire school community can be equally impacted. Schools must organize a crisis response team and devise a plan ahead of an event to provide an emotional safety net for the affected students (Whiting and Matthews, 1997).

More often than many people realize, the responsibility of informing a child of a family crisis or death is carried out by school personnel. Many administrators, counselors, and teachers have taken students home, sat with them at the hospital until parents arrived from work, visited at home and at the funeral home, and attended funerals and memorial services to show their support for the student and his or her family.

Loss Alters Direction

Loss alters direction in both slight and dramatic ways: academically, socially, personally, and economically. During his senior year in high school, Taylor planned to attend a large university an hour away from home. Acceptance to the school, scholarships, and roommate assignments were all in order. Throughout his senior year Taylor, an only child, maintained an active extracurricular schedule while juggling cleaning, cooking, and caring for his dying mother and older father. Emotional support came mostly from his marching band "family," and from teachers and counselors.

Taylor's mother died two days after the graduation ceremony. Trips to a friend's home became more frequent over the summer. Taylor continued to take care of the home—cooking, cleaning, shopping, and taking care of his father. Then came time to go off to school and leave Dad home alone. New issues surfaced. The school counselor received a call from the friend's parents, concerned about Taylor's ability to deal with leaving his father, the need to maintain the home, and the thought of canceling plans to attend the university.

When is the school no longer responsible for the needs of its students? The grieving adolescent needs the help of friends, family, and school personnel in order to adjust to the changes that loss forces upon him or her. Returning to school may create tremendous social pressure to demonstrate a resolution of grief and to do so in an unrealistic time frame (Allen, 1990). The child, dealing with the range of emotions brought on by loss, can often be distracted. The ability to give new concepts full attention is an unrealistic expectation of the grieving child regardless of age. Teachers may need to teach and reteach specific concepts and classroom rules to help the grieving student progress.

When the only parent in the home dies, many children are forced to leave familiar homes, churches, neighborhoods, friends, or schools—support systems that are critical for the healthy development of a child. Shayla and her three sisters moved from New Jersey to Georgia after the death of their mother. The move caused the additional losses of friends, teachers, familiar neighborhoods, and church groups. Children experiencing multiple losses such as these need extra support from all areas of their new life. Abused and neglected children placed in foster care suffer the same grief responses when moved and need extra support.

The terminally ill child may work hard to reach an important milestone before his or her death. Students, teachers, counselors, and other school personnel can perform vital roles. Involving students in creative, compassionate activities that help support the child enhances the sort of learning that educators seek to impart (Peterson and Straub, 1992).

Loss Erodes Trust

When loss erodes trust, children can begin to question their parents' ability to protect them from harm. Loss disrupts life in ways that can be difficult to define and understand. When a spouse or other family member dies, the surviving parent or parents are so impacted by their own grief that the children may be left to deal with their grief alone. Bereaved families do not always know what to do with adolescents who are grieving, and adolescents will rely on peer support for comfort and for direction in how to respond to each other (Cragg and Berman, 1990). When a parent is dying, it is important to keep the children of all ages informed in language they can understand and in portions they can accept. Teachers and school counselors may need to assist in the monitoring and support of a child whose family has been tragically affected.

Loss Causes Stress

Loss is stressful and can cause negative behaviors. Loss forever changes one's perception of self. With the support of intuitive, knowledgeable adults, the changes caused by loss can result in positive growth. With no support, the grieving child or youth can turn to inappropriate groups or behaviors.

Loss Is Isolating

In the process of grief, the loss of something or someone significant will cause us to pull back from those who care about us. Students of all ages experience feelings of being alone and different.

A dying child is often isolated from peers to protect him or her from illnesses that could further weaken his or her condition. School personnel should be willing to work cooperatively and compassionately with the family to reduce the isolation the dying child will naturally feel. Videotaping a science or math lesson with students greeting the sick child can give the homebound child a sense of belonging to the class and to the teacher. It reassures the child and the family that he or she is not forgotten.

Loss Takes Time

Adjusting to the loss of someone or something significant takes time. Each person, child or adult, has a unique personal timetable. Loss magnifies individual differences in our minds. Loss provokes us to try to make sense out of why it is happening and what it all means in the big picture of life. Teachers and counselors must help students realize that loss has no specific timetable nor set stages. Children and their parents may need the help of school personnel to understand and accommodate the difference in the grieving child's energy level. Teachers may need to make use of outside resources.

Reactions to loss go far beyond the actual event. Grief responses may begin long before a death or loss occurs, and can last for years. Educators need to know that *loss is the noun* that describes an immediate response to an event, and *grieve is the verb* that describes both immediate and long-term reactions (Riethmayer, 1997).

Physical, Emotional, and Behavioral Aspects of Loss in Students

Grief demands flexibility by all those impacted. Physical symptoms of grief include appetite and sleep changes, frequent sore throats, earaches, nausea, upset stomachs, anxiety attacks, headaches, and colds. Physical illnesses are common in the newly bereaved child, adolescent, or adult, and it is important for school staff monitoring attendance to know this. Exceptions may need to be made regarding school attendance.

The emotions of those experiencing a loss can include confusion, denial, fear, sadness, anger, and guilt. Thoughts that come to mind include: Why? What does it mean? What do we do? What will happen to me? Was it my fault? How can we fix this? In children and adolescents, educators and parents may see more open defiance or withdrawal. The ability to concentrate and maintain academic performance could become a problem for the grieving student (Whiting and Matthews, 1997). Children and adolescents could lose interest in extracurricular activities at school, at church, and in the community. If an activity is tied to the loss, the student may lose interest completely. Parents, teachers, coaches, and counselors should communicate if a child loses interest in an activity that has always been significant. Bereaved parents are often so consumed with their own grief that they are unaware of some of the difficulties of the surviving siblings.

Bereaved children and adolescents can be at higher risk for substance abuse and sexual activity. Parents are often impacted in the same ways as the child, and will not be as able to support the child in his or her grief. It is imperative to provide structure within the classroom and create opportunities to help make sense of what has happened (Whiting and Matthews, 1997). Teachers should be aware that behavioral changes are a common grief response and should communicate directly to the parent, or to the parent through the school counselor.

When a loss occurs, the child or adolescent is forced to redefine his or her role in the family, in the classroom, and in groups to which he or she belongs. Responsibilities held by the child can become greater. When a parent dies, one or more of the children may be forced to leave the home, school, church, and community to live with extended family members. Losses are multiplied and grieving can become more complicated. Siblings may become only children—no longer big sisters or little brothers (Sims, 1990). Roles like 'caretaker,' 'housekeeper,' and 'only child' become part of the adjustment. Some losses impact the economic status of the child and the family. A loss of income may force the family to move from a large home to a smaller one. Loss can also impact the hopes and dreams a child may have for himself or herself or for the family.

Loss Affects Development: Children

Each person confronted with a crisis responds differently. People have unique personalities, coping styles, support systems, circumstances, and diversity issues. One factor in how a person reacts is age. Children under the age of six years do not understand loss as final. They may view it as reversible ("Mom will be back by school time" or "Dad is asleep and will wake up"). It is important to be cautious about explanations that feed these misperceptions.

Children between three and six years of age focus on fantasy and magical thinking. Their imaginations can run wild as they try to understand what has happened and why. It is important to offer honest explanations. Children require the presence of adults to maintain security and trust in the world. The loss of predictable schedules, routines, eating and sleeping patterns threatens the child's trust. Attention should be given to maintaining the "usual" for children in loss situations.

Children learn how to grieve by modeling the behavior of the adults around them. Adults teach children how to cope—how to express hurt, sadness, and anger. They feel these emotions and need some means of expressing them. Children may need assistance putting words and behaviors to feelings they experience. Children need to be given choices about attending the visitation and the funeral when they lose a family member or a friend. Teachers and school counselors may be asked to help the parent make decisions about how much the child should participate. Teachers also need to communicate with parents if signs of distress begin to show.

Grade school children see the world literally and need concrete and detailed explanations of loss situations. Expect specific questions and give short, clear, honest answers.

Children have short attention spans and move rapidly from one feeling and activity to another. For this reason, grief is often misunderstood because "sad" emotions are quickly turned into joy and playfulness. Children grieve with the same emotions as adults, but these emotions come and go differently than they do with adults. Often grief feelings manifest themselves in masked ways. Parents, teachers, counselors, principals and other school staff must understand how grief looks in children. Children believe they cause and affect everything that happens. The child's world is "I" centered. Children, therefore, frequently blame themselves for the loss. They must constantly be reassured that the loss is not their fault.

As children grow in their abilities to think and feel, new questions arise about the loss. We must recognize this and be available to go back over the loss in new ways, sometimes over a period of years. As a child matures physically and emotionally, holidays, anniversaries, and other losses can be occasions to help children discuss the lost loved one from new developmental perspectives. When a fourth-grade student loses a parent, the other family members often provide extra support and attention. As everyone grows older and changes roles in life, new grief responses can surface and may require support and understanding. If the fourth-grade child experiences another loss on the way to becoming an eleventh-grade adolescent, the previous loss could and probably will be mourned all over again (Hayes, 1995; Whiting and Matthews, 1997).

Loss Affects Development: Adolescents

Adolescence is a time of identity formation. Loss must be affirmed as it uniquely impacts the individual adolescent. There can be a heightened sense of aloneness. Sharing similar hurts, while giving attention to the particulars of the loss, can be helpful. Intense anger may be triggered if a loss interrupts life as it begins to be felt in an independent way. There may be a sense of being cheated just as life begins. The future may feel especially threatened.

Adolescents believe that nothing can happen to them. When loss does occur in their lives, intense shock results from the collapse of this belief (Hayes, 1995). Schools have the difficult task of interpreting behavior and responding appropriately. We can assist teenagers in constructing new assumptions when predictability is lost (Whiting and Matthews, 1997).

Adolescents prioritize physical presentation and peer relationships. Alteration of either is extremely frightening and needs specific attention. A chronic medical condition, a broken romantic relationship, a learning disability or physical disability, and the appearance of being visibly upset are examples of vulnerabilities that are keenly felt in adolescence.

Adolescence is a time of self-consciousness. The adolescent may suffer embarrassment and guilt over a loss. Adolescents will censor feelings viewed as socially unacceptable. They fear being different from peers. Educators need to offer acceptance of a wide variety of feelings. Encourage the peer group to show their reassurance and acceptance. Confidentiality can be important to adolescents who fear rejection from peers because of a loss incident.

When a member of the student body is diagnosed with a terminal illness, schools can do small things to teach life skills that impact the sick child and the child's family. These same efforts can impact the lives of those students and friends participating in the illness and eventual death of the child. Teachers must be very aware of cruel comments and behaviors of classmates of sick children. They need to isolate negative behaviors and teach appropriate, compassionate responses. An example of an appropriate school-wide gesture would be to allow, even encourage, children to wear a cap to school in order to support and make less noticeable the child whose hair is lost due to cancer treatment. A group of male students in one high school arrived at a Christmas party for their ROTC unit with shaved heads to show their support of their instructor, who had shaved his head when his wife lost her hair during chemotherapy.

Adolescents may not readily reach out for adult guidance in times of loss. They often cling to those in their own peer group who have good listening skills. This is a time of rebellion and distrust of authority (Allen, 1990). Although often frightening and frustrating to adults, it is developmentally appropriate for adolescents to pull away in search of independence. Educators must take the initiative and reach out to them. Schools need to have counselors trained in grief to help students, teachers, and administrators properly respond to each other during difficult times.

When death happens to a classmate or teacher, many teenagers are unaware of how to express their condolences to the family and to their friends. Schools can help teach proper funeral home and family visitation etiquette. When announcements about funeral arrangements are given, simple funeral home behavior can be reviewed. Teachers can also assist with teaching culturally appropriate practices. Many teenagers think that they honor the loss of their friend by staying for an entire two-hour visitation. They often will pass adults in line to speak to the family or crowd together around the casket. It is helpful to the family and to the students if a few school personnel are present at family visitations and funerals. Teenagers often attend these services without parental support and may need the support of a familiar adult. School personnel should also be aware of which students are having the greatest difficulty with the loss and may need to be monitored for inappropriate grief responses later.

Adolescents may express feelings in dangerous or unhealthy ways. Teach healthy coping skills as options to unwise displays of aggression, to acting out, to excessive withdrawal, to recklessness, to apathy, to the use of chemicals, to sexual experimentation—all common adolescent choices for handling grief.

When a friend, parent, or relative dies, the adolescent can be overwhelmed by the loss of a part of his or her support system. Peer support groups facilitated by a trained school counselor, school psychologist, or mental health worker can be an excellent preventive program for the bereaved child or adolescent. Participation in a support group can help students process thoughts about the deceased loved one. When sharing their feelings about their loved ones, they not only learn the importance and pain of expressing feelings, but they realize they are not alone. Talking about their loved ones helps them and the others in the support group. Many students report that participation in a peer support group renews their energy to study and their desire to go on with life. They become less embarrassed when expressing emotion and learn that adults can be supportive of them. Through group interaction, students learn that grief reactions are different and have different timetables (Allen, 1990).

Conclusion

The losses experienced by children and adolescents within the school environment increase the school's responsibility to be prepared to deal with the immediate and long-range needs of the students impacted. Schools must have flexible plans and trained personnel to guide decisions when crisis comes into the school environment. Crisis response plans and teams must become a part of every school safety plan.

For a child to be able to resolve grief, someone needs to recognize the loss. Often educators take the view that what happens at home is separate from school. When children bring the "extra baggage" of loss to school, learning will be affected. Educators have a responsibility to help the student make sense of the situation. All school personnel, including the bus driver, the cafeteria worker, the media specialist, the custodian, the counselor, the teacher, the principal, and the school volunteer, can play a part in meeting the needs of the grieving student.

Listening to the child to help him or her discover fears and other feelings associated with the loss is the most helpful thing educators can do. Helping the grieving child make sense of what has happened by being expressing feelings can help the child move through the process of grief (Hayes, 1988). Educators can assist children and adolescents as they make the adjustment to new situations created by the loss, allowing a class to make decisions about the empty chair in the classroom. Sharing rituals that honor the memory of a classmate or relative can be very helpful. Valuable life skills can be modeled for children and for adults who have learned inappropriate responses. Student responses can be shaped or reshaped, and more positive responses can be learned.

Teachers and counselors can work together to use a variety of activities including writing, art, and creative projects to facilitate healthy student grieving. Teachers can use journal writing, letters, and essays to help students get in touch with their emotions. These activities also help teachers know and understand the depth of the impact of loss on students. Art teachers can use creative methods to help students remember a classmate and honor the life that has been lost. Memory books, cards, and collages can be created in memory of a classmate or teacher and then can be given to the family. The act of creating memories is healing for the students involved with the project, as well as for the family. Cards, letters, and school newsletters prepared for the chronically ill or dying child encourage the sick child and his or her family. Classmates learn that their touch in difficult times not only makes a difference to the sick child but also impacts them (Goldman, 1994; Peterson and Straub, 1992). When teachers take the time to model culturally appropriate behavior, students learn lifelong skills in compassion.

Each person confronted with a crisis responds differently and will move through the grieving process at a different rate. Educators must also realize that as they offer support to the grieving student, their own issues regarding loss must not be added to the burden of the grieving student (Barrett, 1995). Teachers need to know the developmental characteristics for the children they serve, with special attention and support given to children with disabilities. Developmentally delayed children should be responded to at their appropriate level. Some special education students and their parents are frequently confronted with educational losses that must be mourned. Parent communication and student encouragement are essential to the grieving student with emotional disabilities.

School personnel should be knowledgeable of community resources which could provide valuable assistance during a school-wide crisis event. Local professionals trained in loss and grief issues can assist a teacher in order to help students better understand and support a dying classmate. Bereaved parents and siblings may need assistance from the school in locating professional counselors or support groups. Counselors with expertise in grief and loss can train school personnel to recognize grief responses that require professional intervention, such as a child who expresses little or no emotion after the death of a parent, a child who clings to adults, a child exhibiting self-destructive behaviors, or a child who begins to fail academically (Goldman, 1994).

With a high percentage of today's children coming from divorced homes, with children committing murders at school, with the preponderance of television violence, and with the mobility of families, loss and grief have become a regular part of student life. How teachers, counselors, administrators, and other school personnel respond to loss and crisis is as important as teaching students basic reading, writing, and mathematics. As teachers balance the academic progress of each student, monitor behavior, and guide students toward realistic career goals, they must be prepared to recognize and properly respond to the grief reactions of their students. As school counselors balance college applications, scholarship recommendations, academic progress, parent/teacher meetings, special education planning, testing, and career counseling, they must take a leadership role in being ready to deal with the many losses children experience. School administrators must provide leadership by organizing crisis response teams and plans so that the school is ready to respond appropriately when crisis occurs. All school personnel must seize the opportunities presented through crisis events and other losses to impart to students valuable life skills in responding to loss compassionately, sympathetically, and empathetically.

Jennie D. Matthews is a counselor at Rock Hill High School in Rock Hill, South Carolina. Her professional experience includes crisis intervention, guidance counseling, grief counseling and consultation, and teaching at the high school and university levels.

Handling Mother's Day and Father's Day

A traditional school activity for children in the primary grades is to create a gift or card for Mother's Day or Father's Day. For children who have experienced the loss of a parent—through death, divorce, or other forms of separation such as foster care placement—such an activity can both be painful and accentuate a sense that the child is different.

Rather than avoid the holiday, there are effective ways to reframe the exercise. One that I suggest is to begin a discussion about what mothers or fathers do. Create a list on the blackboard. This is "fathering" or "mothering." We can point out that many people may actually do "mothering" or "fathering" in our lives. Now the project can be introduced as one to honor that person, whoever he or she may be.

Kenneth J. Doka

Nine

Schools as a Resource for HIV-Affected Children and Youth

Carol Levine and Azadeh Khalili

Schools exist to educate children and youth by giving them the skills, experience, and perspective necessary for a productive and responsible future. In today's world, it is not possible, if it ever has been, to separate education from the culture that sustains it and that it sustains. Schools not only reflect but also inculcate, societal values and mores. They mirror societal discomforts, one of the most pervasive of which is talking about death. When death is stigmatized, as with suicide, drug abuse, violence, and AIDS, that discomfort is magnified. When those stigmatized deaths occur in families with children or adolescents, the barriers to explicit discussion become even more formidable. Adults are doubly concerned; they want to protect children from upsetting information, and they fear that children will pass on this information to others. Death becomes even more taboo.

Most adults, including educators and many healthcare professionals, avoid thinking or talking about death. Only a small percentage of adults, even those with serious illnesses, have prepared an advance directive or have named a proxy for healthcare decision-making to carry out their wishes should they become incapacitated.

When a tragedy such as a student murder of other students, an

earthquake, or an airline disaster strikes a community, crisis intervention teams are brought in and the community rallies to comfort
the bereaved and traumatized. This immediate response does not
prevent the possibility of delayed reactions or long-term consequences, but it does at least provide a protective environment where
initial grief can be shared openly.

In communities affected by HIV/AIDS, the crisis is not a single
event but an endless repetition. Death comes to one family, then
another, then a third, and frequently returns to take another
member at another time. Families and communities suffer multiple
losses. Deaths related to AIDS are often preceded by a long period of
erratic illness; patients' and families' hopes alternate with recurrent
opportunistic infections or, more recently, the side effects of new
and powerful therapies. But there are no crisis intervention teams
for the bereaved here; there is no widespread community catharsis
for grief. The majority of affected children and youth mourn
silently and alone. Not surprisingly, their feelings may cause
immediate behavioral problems, or may be suppressed until some
later time in their development when these hidden emotions can
reappear in diverse and destructive ways.

Like the society they reflect, most schools in the United States
still struggle with incorporating AIDS into their daily lives. Nearly
two decades after AIDS was first identified, it remains a stigmatized
disease, largely because of its links to sex, drugs, and death. Despite
governmental-, school-, and community-based attempts to present
factual information, many adults and young people still have erro-
neous ideas about HIV transmission, treatments, and supposed
"cures." Some schools have limited HIV-related instruction. A 1994
Centers for Disease Control and Prevention (CDC) study found that
78 percent of health teachers taught about abstinence, while just 56
percent spent time on the effectiveness of condoms in preventing
HIV infection. Only 37 percent taught students how to use condoms
properly (Donovan, 1998).

Furthermore, because of rapidly changing information and
widespread distrust of government in many communities, there is
often an underlying skepticism about public health messages.

Educators confront their own and community values in curriculum decisions about how to teach AIDS and HIV prevention,
how to deal with HIV-infected children in the classroom, and how

to balance children's right to medical confidentiality with concern about their health and the need to protect all children from infectious diseases. Relatively few schools have even begun to address questions concerning the impact of parental, sibling, or family HIV-related illness and death on uninfected children. Yet this may be the most far-reaching consequence of the epidemic. Fortunately several models have been developed to meet the urgent need. Since there is considerable information about HIV education, infection control, confidentiality policies, and other questions involving HIV-infected children and youth, the remainder of this chapter will deal primarily with loss and bereavement. First, however, it is important to describe the context of a changing epidemic.

The Changing Face of AIDS

By the end of 1997, over 640,000 cases of AIDS in the United States had been reported to the Centers for Disease Control and Prevention. About 60 percent have died. The actual number of people who do not have AIDS but who are infected with HIV is unknown, but the CDC estimates that there are between 600,000 and 900,000. Women and youth are the fastest growing segments of the HIV-infected population. In the early years of the epidemic women made up about 9 percent of people with AIDS; this proportion has now risen to 20 percent and in some areas is even higher. One in four new cases of HIV occurs in a person under the age of 25; increasingly the numbers of young women are equal to those of young men. A recent study of youth applying for the federal Job Corps found that HIV infection rates were 50 percent higher among young women aged 16 to 21 than among young men the same age (Valleroy, 1998). While men who have sex with men accounted for the majority of cases in the early years, heterosexual transmission is now rising. Intravenous drug users continue to be at high risk. The majority of new cases are reported among African American and Latino communities. HIV/AIDS has become endemic in poor communities of color, already devastated urban centers, and, increasingly, poor rural communities.

While the epidemic continues to take its inexorable toll, two positive developments have changed the future outlook. Both affect children and youth. First, perinatal HIV transmission (from HIV-infected mother to fetus) has been sharply reduced because many HIV-infected pregnant women are now identified earlier and because zidovudine (AZT) is widely administered in the late stages of pregnancy, at delivery, and to the newborn. In controlled clinical trials of AZT in pregnancy the infection rate was reduced from 25 percent to 8 percent. HIV-infected women have been advised not to breastfeed, thus preventing transmission by this route. The reduced rate has been maintained outside clinical trials, and some centers are now reporting few if any births of HIV-infected babies. This development will decrease the likelihood of a new surge of HIV-infected children in schools.

The second positive development has been in treatment advances for both HIV-infected adults and children. Earlier identification of HIV infection, new combination therapies, and more accurate ways to measure viral load (a good indicator of infection status) have resulted in longer survival and, in many cases, greatly improved quality of life. Some HIV-infected children are now living to adolescence, presenting some novel issues for schools but also re-creating some of the tensions that occurred early on when adolescent boys with hemophilia or youngsters who had been infected through transfusion were typical cases in this age group. Ryan White, who experienced significant discrimination in his school and community and for whom the most extensive federal support program is named, was a hemophiliac.

There are significant differences, however. The vast majority of the youngsters now reaching adolescence were infected perinatally and many have experienced some consequences of the illness, including developmental delays, since birth. (There are some cases, however, of HIV infection in children contracted through sexual abuse.) In the early 1980s hemophiliacs were the first wave of school-age children infected through contaminated blood products that were used to control their hemophilia. The parents of hemophiliacs were not themselves HIV-infected. Still, questions of confidentiality, discrimination, emerging sexuality, and chronic illness affect both groups.

Treatment advances for adults have been more successful among white gay men than among women and men from communities of color. The death rate for all people with AIDS has declined, but less significantly for the latter groups. The specter of AIDS as a rapidly fatal disease is being replaced by the sobering reality that AIDS at best is a chronic illness that requires adherence to a complex and rigid medication schedule. For children living in a family with an adult with AIDS, the difficulties are perhaps different but no less daunting.

There are no precise data on how many children and youth up to the age of 18 are affected by HIV/AIDS. An estimated 82,000 to 125,000 in this age group will have lost their mothers to AIDS by the end of the year 2000 (Michaels and Levine, 1992). More recent estimates for the United States are not available, but a recalculation by the same authors in 1996 of the New York City estimates found that the earlier estimates were far too low (Michaels and Levine, 1996). In the intervening four years, the number of women who died from AIDS had increased significantly. By the end of the year 2001, it is now estimated, 30,000 to 50,000 New York City children and youth up to age 21 will have lost their mothers. New therapies have unquestionably decreased mortality, but for how long is still unknown. These estimates included only youngsters whose mothers will have died; they did not include those whose fathers will have died, or, especially important, those with an ill parent or sibling. In the school population of urban centers hard hit by AIDS there are undoubtedly thousands of children and youth affected by the disease. These youngsters can also be found in small cities and rural areas, though not in such concentrations.

Psychosocial Impact of HIV/AIDS on Affected Children

While there is much to be learned about how death, especially the death of a parent, affects children, there is consensus that children mourn differently from adults and that developmental stage, not just chronological age, impacts a child's understanding of death and expressions of loss (Dane and Levine, 1994). Furthermore, when children reach new developmental stages, especially puberty, deaths that occurred earlier may resurface in the young person's thinking and actions. If the death was preceded by a long illness, children may feel uncertainty, fear, and guilt. They may feel that by being "bad," or failing to stay home when their mother was ill they brought about the death. They may interpret every good or bad day as a reflection of their own "magical" powers. Adolescents may be conflicted over their natural desires for independence and exploration and their responsibilities at home to care for younger siblings or even the parent (Hudis, 1994).

Many of these reactions are common to any situation involving serious illness or disability. What makes AIDS different and more complex is the secrecy and stigma attached to the disease, even within the family. Overwhelming social and economic problems may take priority even over illness. The background of multiple losses also affects a family's and a community's ability to mobilize both emotional and material support for the survivors.

The psychosocial impact of HIV/AIDS on children is often felt first and most dramatically at school. Students, particularly older children and adolescents, may be absent frequently or for long periods. There are many reasons, including the child's perceived need to stay at home to protect or help the ill parent, and the adolescent's inability to focus on school when family life is so chaotic. For children who are attending school, academic and behavior problems are typically the first sign of trouble at home. Not all youngsters act out; some hide their feelings and continue to behave as if there were no problems.

The following case, adapted from Siegel and Gorney (1995, pp. 50-51), shows how one child's difficulties were addressed in school:

> Michael, age 10, was informed of his mother's AIDS diagnosis about one year prior to her death. His father told him that his mother had contracted AIDS through her occasional intravenous drug use. Michael's. . . outward behavior remained unchanged. While his parents were open in their communication. . . they emphasized the importance of not discussing his mother's illness with anyone outside the family. This need for secrecy both confused Michael and led to feelings of shame and humiliation.

> Michael. . . began to [develop] headaches and stomachaches, which resulted in his frequently staying home from school. Remaining at home allowed Michael to be with his mother for extended periods. It soon became apparent that these physical concerns were related to a deeper worry [about] his own bodily safety. A secondary benefit of staying home from school was related to his recurring thought of his mother's illness and his worries about what his life would be like without her. Michael

had a magical belief that if he were with his mother all the time, he would have the power to keep her alive.

After his mother's death, Michael was visibly sad. Behavior changes both at home and at school became apparent. He changed from calm and compliant to angry and defiant. His schoolwork began to suffer.

Michael began to see the school guidance counselor. . . . [H]e was able to tell the counselor about his profound feelings of loneliness. He described a feeling inside him that his mother was still alive. He explained that he often felt his mother's presence and that this feeling had a calming effect. . . .

Over time the counselor was able to help Michael see how his defiant behavior was related to how much he missed his mother but also how angry he was at her for engaging in behavior that led to her death. The counselor was also able to help Michael understand that his wish to be reunited with her was normal. He encouraged Michael, with his father's and grandmother's help, to make a scrapbook containing pictures and other mementos of his relationship with his mother. . . .

Among adolescents, a typical response to death is depression, which may manifest itself in withdrawal, eating disorders, sleep disturbances, moodiness, and inability to concentrate. Other signs of depression may be excessive risk-taking, provocative behavior, or initiation of drug or alcohol use. On the other hand, some adolescents try to compensate for the loss of a parent by assuming adult parental responsibilities at home that eventually overwhelm them. Whatever the reaction, there is a good chance that school attendance and performance will be affected.

It is important, therefore, that school personnel recognize these indicators as more than normal or even "difficult" adolescent behavior. There may be many other causes of trouble at school, but where HIV/AIDS is prevalent in a community, there is a strong likelihood that the disease is at least part of the problem at home. Not every teacher or staff member need become a grief counselor. But all personnel who work closely with children and youth should be alert to signs of trouble that may be related to bereavement and should be familiar with the school-based resources that can serve as the first line of referral. For some youngsters, school-based services are most accessible and appropriate; for others, community-based services are a better choice. Many need support on a short-term or as-needed basis only. Some youth, however, particularly those in families in which drug use and domestic violence are prevalent, have serious mental health problems that probably predate the parent's illness and death; these require a more structured form of professional intervention.

School-Based Interventions

School-based interventions for bereaved students can be organized in various ways. Several factors influence the structure and program: the age and developmental stage of the students; those included in the program, whether HIV/AIDS affected only or mixed; the focus of the program, whether on support groups or on other activities; the type of community; and whether the program is open-ended or has a fixed duration. Following are brief descriptions of three models: a school-based model; a collaboration between a community-based organization and schools; and a hospice-initiated program.

The New York City HIV/AIDS Technical Assistance Project

In New York City the HIV/AIDS Technical Assistance Project (the TA Project) is a not-for-profit organization providing HIV/AIDS training and prevention programs for the public high school system. Supported by private foundation funds, it is located in the central Board of Education offices and enjoys broad support within the system.

Beginning in 1994, teachers and students told TA Project staff about their tremendous need for HIV bereavement-related services. In response, the TA Project sponsored a one-day, citywide conference on HIV-related loss and bereavement for high school staff and students. At every conference since that time, at least one workshop has addressed grief and loss. The conference is a full day and is attended by teachers, guidance counselors, administrators, district health coordinators, special education personnel, substance abuse specialists, and support staff from grades K-12.

To date, TA Project staff have provided training for approximately 90 teachers and guidance counselors who have volunteered
to address this problem in their schools. One-day training sessions
discuss how to recognize and identify HIV-related loss in students;
how to address the stigma and discrimination that can affect families in this situation; and how to advise the participants on helping
young people deal with grief, inside and outside classrooms. A number of New York City public high schools now conduct regular
bereavement support groups for HIV-affected students. In these
schools, guidance counselors, who are also psychologists, conduct
the support groups, bringing students together to share their experiences and identify their needs.

At the John F. Kennedy High School in the Bronx, for example,
a group called REAL (Reality Enters All Lives) has been meeting twice
a month since 1992. About a dozen students attend at a time; most
have lost one parent to AIDS, some have lost both parents. JFK High
School is the city's largest public high school, with about 5,000 students. According to a story in the *New York Times*, school officials
estimate that about 300 students have lost a family member to
AIDS (Richardson, 1998).

The bereavement group is coordinated by Paula Foster, the
school psychologist, and Bill Elmore, an English teacher. Mr. Elmore
reports that most of the participants come to the group through
teacher referral. He believes that there is such a stigma surrounding
HIV and AIDS that even among those who come forward, most prefer individual counseling with a psychologist to speaking before
peers on this emotional subject. The group's mood varies; sometimes the students criticize each other for holding back their
feelings; at other times they laugh and make plans for parties. One
student became so depressed after learning her father was infected
with HIV that she had to be hospitalized. She relies heavily on the
group: "They were there to listen. I had their comfort. I felt they
opened up their hearts to me. I feel if you don't talk to somebody,
one day you are going to explode."

The TA Project also carries out a number of other activities. The
BASE (Be Active in Self-Education) Grants Program funds student-
created peer education programs. In 1997 the project funded 117
programs in 90 public high schools. Thirteen BASE Grant projects
focused on HIV-related bereavement, including support groups and

various commemorative art projects. One project, called "The Tree of Remembrance," constructed a "tree" made of cardboard and foam and placed it in the school's lobby. Each leaf signifies a $1 donation used to buy a gift for a person hospitalized with AIDS. After the first year's tree was destroyed during a school cleanup, the students built a bigger, better tree and made a video, which provided them with an outlet for their grief over losing someone they care for.

Another BASE Grant project at the High School of Art and Design gave students an opportunity to create paintings while talking about the loss of parents, family, and friends to AIDS. These paintings were displayed at St. Vincent's Hospital in New York City. At the Bronx School for Career Development a group created a multimedia AIDS quilt, which used a computer program to show pictures about AIDS arranged in a quilt pattern. The viewer clicks on a picture to view it in a larger size and hear students talking about the loss of a mother, father, aunt, or uncle to AIDS. A follow-up project is taking the original quilt to other homerooms in the school and talking about the problem of AIDS and how many people it affects in the community.

Another project created a radio show called *AIDS—A Radio Quilt*, inspired by the Names Project. Tape recordings of students from Offsite Educational Services schools and GED sites served as the tapestry of the quilt as they remembered their loved ones. Project members edited interviews, added music, and presented the piece as a program on local radio stations.

These projects serve several purposes: They offer students a creative outlet for their grief and concern, they educate other students and staff about AIDS and its impact, and they enhance teamwork and skill building as the students master technical aspects of the projects.

The TA Project hopes to create a system-wide HIV-related bereavement support and services network for New York City public high school students. Staff are working to create a project that will train public high school teachers to identify students who would benefit from the assistance of a capable guide through their grief process. Teachers will be provided with basic skills in this area, and a network of resources, including qualified professionals who are familiar with adolescents and bereavement, will be established.

Henry Street Settlement's Community Consultation Center

Another model is found on New York City's Lower East Side in the collaboration between the Henry Street Settlement House, a large, community-based social service agency, and local elementary and junior high schools (Rusnar and Fiester, 1998). Beginning as early as 1988, Settlement House staff and local schools began to form positive relationships based around the needs of children in families affected by HIV/AIDS. Staff at both the Settlement House and the schools recognized that the most effective way to reach children in these families would be through the schools, which provide safe, neutral spaces where students facing similar issues can support each other and concentrate on school work more effectively. The team, headed by Lela Charney, CSW, with the cooperation of the administration, developed the school bereavement programs.

Because grieving students often experience school difficulties, the Community Consultation Center expanded its team to include a certified teacher, who visits both public and private schools to assist in the education of families involved in the program. The Center supports both the schools and families by providing the best education for the student, while responding to the special needs of a child or adolescent experiencing the death or serious illness of a parent.

Bereavement groups at Gustave Straubenmuller Junior High School, for example, are facilitated by Henry Street Settlement staff. They include mostly students affected by HIV/AIDS but also students who have lost family members to other diseases. Multi-age groups meet weekly for 45 minutes over a period of eight weeks. Sessions are scheduled at times least likely to disrupt regular school activities. Henry Street Settlement House staff stress that interorganizational communication, connections, collaborations, and commitment are essential components of the program's success.

The Hospice of Glen Ridge, Inc.

A third model was developed by the Hospice of Glen Ridge, NJ, now The Center for Hospice Care. Increasingly aware of the impact of AIDS and other deaths on children, the Hospice of Glen Ridge began training school personnel to run in-school group therapy sessions for affected children. Estelle D'Costa directed the Grief and Loss Project for the hospice. In this program, children and youth grouped by age attend weekly sessions during school hours over a ten-week period. Leaders guide them through a series of activities aimed at helping them understand and accept the death of a loved one. Surviving parents or other involved adults are invited to attend separate sessions to help them deal with their own grief.

In the first phase of the program, children are encouraged to get to know each other through activities that are unrelated to death, such as simply drawing pictures of things they like. In the second phase, they learn to express their feelings about the death and to create images that reflect these feelings. Finally, they are encouraged to address the reality of the loss and to begin to cope in positive, nondestructive ways.

In addition to running its own programs, the hospice has trained school guidance counselors and social workers to run bereavement groups in both urban and suburban areas (Van Tassel, 1995). In one school in Newark a hospice volunteer who is also a school employee has organized after-school bereavement groups (D'Costa, 1998).

Practical Suggestions for Working with Bereaved Children and Youth

For Teachers

Lockhart McElvy, a social worker at the Family Center in New York City, has constructed a list of actions teachers can take when helping students deal with the loss of a close friend or family member (HIV/AIDS Team Update, 1998, p. 3):

1. *Find a balance for young people, i.e., homework vs. not making them accountable. Though they are grieving, it is important that they continue to strive for academic excellence.*
2. *Communicate with the surviving parent or new caregiver.*
3. *Maintain limits on behavior.*
4. *Provide opportunities for expression, e.g., drawing, writing, and similar activities.*
5. *Provide opportunities for group interaction.*
6. *Be flexible with programs.*

7. *Adolescents often drop out during bereavement. Adjust programs to keep them around.*
8. *Stop any instance of teasing. Teasing students about deceased parents will make a child of any age fight or withdraw.*
9. *Rather than place students in a special ed program to minimize stress, remember that students who are grieving will return to their baseline grades and performance over time.*
10. *Don't underestimate your impact. A little extra attention can go a long way.*
11. *Try to keep students in [the same] school, if possible. Changing schools is a real loss for young people. It is overwhelming to lose a parent and to move or change schools.*

For Group Leaders

At a national conference on HIV/AIDS and the Family, sponsored by the Annie E. Casey Foundation in December 1997, members of a panel describing the Henry Street Settlement program offered these suggestions for establishing school-based mental health groups:

Screen group participants to ensure that children are referred for appropriate reasons. The screening process should include discussions with the individual who made the referral, with the child, and with the parent or guardian.

Create groups of mixed genders, ages, and stages of grief. One panelist found that mixed groups are most successful because they allow those who have been dealing with losses for longer periods to support those reacting to a more recent event. These issues may also be resolved in other ways, but should definitely be considered in the formation of groups.

Design culturally sensitive sessions. Group leaders should be sensitive to and respectful of the particular expressions of grief that are characteristic of diverse cultural and religious groups, and avoid stereotyping students on the basis of their familial origin.

Allow group members to guide activities. Staff should be alert to changes in children's moods and allow them freedom in choosing how fully they wish to speak and participate. Trust is essential before children will feel free to express their emotions.

Use a variety of developmentally appropriate therapy methods and materials. Young children benefit from concrete activities, such as drawing pictures or writing letters, while older children with a better abstract understanding of death and dying may enjoy poetry, role-playing, and skits.

Use a psycho-educational approach to encourage participants to discuss their feelings openly. Students can appreciate that their feelings are not "weird" but are normal reactions to stress and loss.

Acknowledge and discuss the role of the family in the grieving process. Other problems in the family, such as drug use, separations, violence, and poverty may have damaged family relationships. The family's grief has an impact on the child, and the family can help the child only if it is helped to understand the interrelationships of all these events. Where possible, home visits are an important means of communication, and in some cases may be the only way to establish contact with a family.

Involve staff from several service fields in the design and implementation of the school-based program. Many school staff are overwhelmed with the intensity and complexity of the needs of bereaved children, but they should not feel that they alone are responsible for addressing these needs. Successful programs integrate the expertise of teachers, counselors, social workers, and psychologists. (Rusnar and Fiester, 1998)

These suggestions are intended to stimulate discussion rather than present hard-and-fast rules. The most important step is the first one, serving as a "critical part of the early warning system" by recognizing the tremendous needs of children and youth in HIV-affected families and by bringing school, family, and community together to assist them through this traumatic experience (Geballe and Gruendel, 1998).

Carol Levine is director of the Families and Health Care Project, United Hospital Fund, New York City. She also directs The Orphan Project, administered by the Fund for the City of New York.

Azadeh Khalili is director of the HIV/AIDS Technical Assistance Project, New York City.

Programs That Work

Calvary Hospital

Show us your sun, but gradually. Lead us from star to star,
step by step. Be gentle when you teach us to live again.

This quotation by Nelly Sachs is on a condolence card sent to the family of every patient who dies at Calvary Hospital. It captures the concept of process fundamental in adjusting to life-changing events and characterizes the tenor of Calvary's many bereavement services.

Step by step, patients and their families are accompanied by our experts of care and comfort through the end of the terrible disease that brought us together at Calvary, a hospital for adults with terminal cancer. But our paths do not part with death. The continuum of care extends through the process of bereavement in a variety of ways.

While Calvary offers grief assistance and support to adults, it is also vigorously engaged in "helping little hearts mend." Certainly, children feel the death of a family member or friend either directly through their own loss or indirectly through the sadness in those around them. Calvary Hospital has included children in its special formula of care and comfort by offering the following programs.

Precious Moments

This after-school program runs for eight consecutive weeks in two locations. The program is conducted on Mondays and Tuesdays, with the intention that intervention early in the week can help to set a positive tone at home and in school. This has been proven to be the case; evaluations at the end of the program consistently indicate that there were notable differences in the children's behavior. All children are accompanied to the bereavement program by a parent or guardian, who must be willing to participate in the adult group conducted concurrently.

Camp Courageous

This summer day camp, offered to children who have participated in the after-school bereavement program, continues the mending process and restores to children what sorrow has often taken from them: childhood fun. Since grief often produces chaos, venturing into nature and then making connections with patterns in one's own life tends to promote harmony. The camp is located at Arrow Lake Park in Tuxedo, New York. Round-trip transportation is provided from Calvary Hospital. This opportunity for bereaved children is made possible by Calvary Fund donors and ABC, Inc..

Teaching Others about Children and Grief

The needs of grieving children have been so poignantly represented by the participants in our program that we feel compelled to represent them to the community at large, so that all of us will become more deliberate in the attempt to help little hearts mend. Thus, two videos on children and grief are being readied for production, thanks to a very generous grant from the Al Smith Foundation. One video will be for direct use with the grieving child, the other will be an instructional video to help adults understand the needs of grieving children and how they might better meet those needs.

Mentors Through Mourning

This is an education program in childhood bereavement offered to elementary school administrators, teachers, guidance counselors, and social workers. Sadly, many educators do not recognize or understand the needs of grieving children. With Calvary's expertise in bereavement, mentoring educators will ensure that faculty will be available to share critical coping skills with children. Our goal is that every school in the New York metropolitan area will have at least one representative trained by Calvary to be a mentor through mourning for the grieving children who will surely pass through their doors.

Catherine R. Seeley
Director, Bereavement Services
Calvary Hospital

Ten

The Grieving College Student

Robert L. Wrenn

Lisa Robinson has been driving 100 miles from campus each weekend of her senior fall semester to visit her mother, who is dying in hospice. The week before finals she receives a late night phone call from her father telling her that her mother has died. He tells her not to postpone her exams; they will wait until exams are over to have a memorial service for her mother. Lisa had hoped her mother would be alive to enjoy her graduation ceremony. She knows her mother would have wanted her to finish her senior year but she wonders if she will be able to concentrate for the upcoming final exams. She would like to go home and be with her family.

David Jenkins, a member of a national fraternity, was found in bed at the fraternity house, dead from an overdose. The house wants to plan a service for David but is not sure how to go about it or whom to invite. Several of the residents of David's floor are wondering why they were so unaware of his apparent problem, and the student who found David's body can't seem to get a good night's sleep or concentrate on his studies. The university is going to look into what else may be going on at the fraternity house that would be cause for alarm. Some of David's friends plan to go out and "get smashed" to celebrate David's life and death in their own way.

Sarah Smith came back to campus from spring break last year extremely upset. Her boyfriend Rick had suddenly disappeared while surfing. They could not find the body, and most people who were there think he must have drowned in the surf; he was a known risk taker. One year later Sarah feels she is coming back to life and has decided to dedicate her life to social work so she can help people who are having problems such as she has experienced.

Students arrive for their 10:00 humanities class only to find a psychologist from the student counseling service talking with the humanities department head at the front of the classroom. When the bell rings the psychologist says to the class, "The reason I am here today is to share some bad news with you. I am sorry to have to tell you that your instructor died last night. We are here today to answer any questions you may have and to talk about how the class will operate for the rest of the semester."

These are just a few of the kinds of situations students face on college campuses each year.

Institutional Preparedness

The colleges and universities that these students attend are often not expected or prepared to deal with these issues. Many of them have no written plan or procedure for handling the death of a student or a death in a student's life. A survey of 53 universities and colleges in the US found that 33 had no written plan, 24 offered no training to personnel for dealing with bereavement issues within the student body, and 22 could not say who would be responsible to notify the family in the event of a student's death (Wrenn, 1991a). We can expect approximately 4.7 deaths per 10,000 college students each year, and the causes of death for students age 18 to 21 are roughly 60 percent accidental, 25 percent illness, 12 percent suicide, and 3 percent homicide. These figures vary depending on the size and the mission of the institution (Wrenn, 1991b). You probably won't hear these figures discussed at new student or parent orientation, and you won't find many people who believe that students will be dealing with death while attending school—but they will. And they will do so at a time when they are vulnerable and uninformed about what they should be feeling and doing with the normal grief they will experience.

Students do worry about death and loss and it seems to be fairly universal. At the National Taiwan University in Taipei, a student survey of mental health issues indicated that the potential illness or death of a family member or friend was one of the top three concerns of the student body (Wu, 1989). In the United States we would expect that a significant portion of college students are dealing with a past, current, or anticipated death among family or friends. This chapter will look at some of the special issues students have to deal with in their grief and will detail some interventions that can be useful both to the student and to the institution.

Student Grief Issues

While there are a few excellent published resources that focus on the college campus (e.g., Zinner, 1985; Rickgarn, 1996; Marrone, 1997), there is very little written material generally available.

One of the primary issues students face when experiencing a loss through death is that there is often no specific place on campus readily recognized as a place to go for support or information. For the student who is trying to become independent from his or her family, or whose family is miles away, the only built-in support group may be a residence hall floor or an academic or social interest group of equally inexperienced peers. For some, there seems to be no support on campus at all. Those of us who teach courses in death and dying realize that our classrooms are filled with students who chose such a class as a safe place to explore their own feelings and questions about unresolved grief issues. Many students regard the counseling or mental health center, if one is available, as a place to go only if one is having serious problems, rather than a place where they can talk things over with an impartial and empathic professional who listens and relates to their grief, regardless of the severity of the situation. The campus ministry may be a place where some students will go based upon their own experience of religious support in the past. Students are hesitant to burden their friends with this "uncool stuff" for fear of making a fool of themselves or of suddenly losing it in front of their peers. Some will turn to their parents, but this may provide limited support.

One of the difficult issues in grief is adjusting to an environment that is changed by the death (Worden, 1991). This issue is complicated when the student has returned to school and senses that everyone else is going about business. But the bereaved student is preoccupied with the recent death and may feel "weird" being on campus because no one really understands and doesn't really seem to care about his or her special situation.

A third issue for grieving students is how to respond to people who ignore their grief, or who tell them that they need to get on with life, that it's not good for them to continue to grieve. A student in a residence hall had put his sister's picture above his study desk. Two months after her death, he regretfully took it down because some of the guys on his floor kept asking him if he was still dealing with her death and encouraging him to move on with his life. According to them, he should have gotten over it already.

A fourth issue is the feeling of "going crazy" because of experiencing the presence of the deceased in waking life as well as in dreams. One may see the person walking away or driving a car. A student may find himself or herself calling the deceased person on the phone, and not see this as normal grieving, even though it most likely is.

Finally, there is the practical matter of convincing teachers to allow late work, a make-up exam, or an incomplete for a class.

What Do Students Most Appreciate Learning about the Grief Process?

There are a few things that students most want to hear when they are grieving. They especially want to know that they are dealing with things normally and well and that they did what they could, knowing what they knew at the time of the death. The following diagram by Captain Jack Harris of the Tucson Police Department has been helpful in visually demonstrating to students that they shouldn't beat up on themselves with statements such as, "If only I had done x, y, or z, so and so would still be alive," when in fact they didn't have that information until after the death:

[-------------DEATH-------------]

The little markers before the word DEATH represent information that they had prior to the death. Then a death occurs. Then more information is gathered as noted by the markers that follow. For example, a mother whose daughter died in a car accident an hour after leaving the house said that if she had only held her daughter for five seconds more at the door she would still be alive. This mother was using information she had gathered *after* the death to explain what she should have done *before* the death. If you or I knew that in one hour we would die at a certain intersection, we would not drive that way, if we drove at all the rest of the day.

Next on the list of what grieving students want most to hear is that they don't have to fix their friends' or family's grief. Most students do not grieve the death of someone close to them in a vacuum—others are also grieving. To feel that they must put aside their own grief to accomplish the impossible task of resolving someone else's grief is of no help to either party. In fact it will postpone their own grief and compound the issue for themselves and others at a later date. The recognition that we all have our own unique pain and our individual way of dealing with it, and that no one can "fix" the pain experienced by another, is a new concept to some students. They have been taught that the way to help someone else is to reassure them that everything will be OK in time, and then cross their fingers and hope that it will be. Experienced grief counselors realize that the best procedure is to be available to grievers, to assist them in the process of coming to terms with their grief, in their own way, and to give them sufficient time to grieve while supporting individual needs in the grief process.

Students are also interested in learning how to deliver bad news to others. This information can be used in severing relationships, as well as in informing someone of a death, and students truly appreciate demystifying the process. In class we often role play around this topic and practice going over the following basic steps which, of course, must be adapted to a particular situation:

Guidelines for Giving Death Notifications

- *Decide who is the best person to deliver the notification.*
- *Help this person to have all the facts available about the death before approaching the survivor.*
- *Notify people in person, if at all possible.*
- *Make sure you are telling the right person.*
- *Find a comfortable place, preferably sitting down.*

- *Tell the person by first indicating how you feel in having to deliver the message, and then give them the bad news, using the word 'dead' or 'died.' Don't beat around the bush. Say something like, "I am very sorry to tell you that your son, Eric, died this morning."*
- *Then say no more. Wait for a response. Let the person be in charge of what happens next.*
- *Answer any questions you can. (This is why having all the facts is so important.)*
- *Ask if they would like to have someone with them. Do they want to make the call or do they want you to?*
- *Stay with them until help arrives.*
- *Write down how they can reach you if they want to.*
- *Follow up by phone later that day or the next day to see how they are doing.*
- *Understand that each situation is different and you can't do much harm if you are honest and stick to what you know and feel.*
- *Afterwards, talk with someone you trust if you are feeling upset.*

The importance of knowing about this process is brought home by the following example: Two students who had taken my course came to me incensed over a situation that happened to a classmate in another class. A department head stepped in the classroom and asked the professor if so and so was in class today. The student, hearing her name, said she was there, and the department head asked the student to come with her. The class then heard screaming in the hallway and when the door was opened the students saw the girl writhing on the floor. The department head had just told her that her mother had died. These two students asked me if faculty and department heads were unaware of the "how to give bad news" information I had given them, and would I please inform this person how to do it better next time. I called the department head, who was eager to know a better way to handle the situation. The event had frightened her almost as much as it did the student.

How, then, can a college or university facilitate the grief that students normally experience and how can the institution become better informed about initiating procedures so that death, even for the college student, is not so alien to campus life?

Helpful Interventions

- *Determine the point person or office to coordinate all student death issues.*
- *Assign someone to be the institution's spokesperson to the media.*
- *Compose a checklist that instructs the responsible person or office (1) whom to notify, (2) how to close the academic and billing records, (3) how to process a posthumous degree, and (4) how to inform the campus offices most likely to be affected, such as residence life, dean of students, and student body leaders.*

Informing Faculty and Staff

The point person for student death can make sure that each department on campus has a copy of the following ten-step plan. This plan can be modified, but the basic elements can help to educate those on campus not accustomed to thinking about the issues involved.

Humane and Helpful Procedures in the Event of a Campus Death

- *Students, faculty, staff and officials from the college/university attend the funeral or memorial service.*
- *Letters of recognition, appreciation or achievement are given to the dying student or to the family posthumously.*
- *One person is assigned to coordinate or handle information given to the press and to investigators.*
- *The presence and support of the president, vice-president, dean, department head, and faculty familiar with the student, convey to the family and friends that the student was important to the college.*
- *Police have good channels of communication with campus personnel.*

- *Professionals are available to work with roommates, friends, and family of the deceased.*
- *A place and time are provided for students and others associated with the deceased to ask questions and express sorrow, concern or anger.*
- *Follow-up procedures are carried out with students or faculty members most affected.*
- *Some public recognition of the death is issued, such as letters to those most concerned.*
- *Those closest to the deceased are encouraged to be involved in services and other events.* (Wrenn, 1994)

It is also useful to use some of the counseling principles Worden (1991) has suggested for individual counseling, adapting them to an institutional perspective. Examples of this model follow.

Help survivors actualize the loss. One small department on my campus suffered the death of a graduate student who was much beloved by both students and faculty. They called on me, the campus point person for student death, to meet with faculty and decide what should be done. Because the student was Asian, the faculty invited the on-campus and off-campus Asian community to join the students and faculty at a memorial service in the building where the graduate student had taught. After I outlined why we were there, people were invited to record a message that would be sent to the family. Two hours and two tapes later, the meeting adjourned. This is one example of how a public ritual can encourage people to participate in the mourning process and to become more in touch with the death.

Another example of how survivors are helped to actualize the loss occurred when a sorority sister was killed in an accident. I was asked to meet with the students to see what was needed. When I arrived, I saw that the sorority members were already taking care of each other. People were weeping and holding onto each other, a candlelight service had been planned, the parents had been invited, and all I could say was, "It looks like you are dealing with this tragedy in the best way possible—by supporting each other and honoring your friend and her family." In this case the natural support group for the survivors was already taking care of the issues at hand and outside intervention was not needed. Sometimes it's important to recognize that things that aren't broken don't need to be fixed!

A final example is an instance in which I met with the class of a teacher who had killed himself the night before. The class time that day was devoted to allowing students to ask questions, to vent, to sit and stare off into space, or to otherwise begin to come to terms with the death. It was also an opportunity to teach this particular class how to frame the experience for later reflection and to advise them of resources on campus that might be of help.

Help survivors be in touch with and express their feelings. The institution can offer campus-wide talks, workshops, videos, and discussions on topics that focus on how people come to terms with losses in their own lives. One example on my campus was a mock funeral sponsored by the Greek system, which had been given a grant by the parents of a student killed in a drunk driving accident. The grant was intended to allow fraternities to put on events that would educate students on the consequences of drinking and driving. Following the mock funeral there was a lively series of letters to the editor in the campus newspaper, where all could express their feelings and thoughts on the subject. Remember that learning can occur vicariously as well. When issues are brought into the public arena there are those in the community who begin to think about how they would want to deal with the issue if it happened to them. Training residence hall staff, offering peer or professional support groups through the counseling center, meeting with campus leaders, or organizing a crisis hotline are but a few of the ways that students, faculty, and staff can begin to get in touch with feelings that are often ignored on campus.

Becoming a death-education ombudsperson could become a full time job—which I have guarded against. Academic departments are likely to ask for help in talking with the faculty and staff when a fellow worker dies, or when a grieving staff member is having a particularly difficult time on the job or with an employer who is insensitive to the needs of the bereaved. Often a campus will have people within its human resources, counseling or health organizations who can be called upon so that the burden is shared by others who are trained in grief and loss issues. On one occasion, the football coach asked several of us to meet with the team when one of the players died. There seems to be no end to the number of ways one can intervene in assisting students in their grief. One of the most satisfying situations in an otherwise stressful event occurs when there is a built-in support system, which was the case with the football team, or in a residence hall, Greek house, or departmental unit. In these cases, everyone is hearing the same words and can see right away how they can help each other in the days to come, after you have gone.

Other principles for facilitating students' grief are germane for individual or group counseling or peer support groups:

- acknowledging their difficulties in a changed environment,
- helping them relocate their feelings and thoughts about the deceased,
- providing time to grieve,
- interpreting what is normal,
- acknowledging individual differences,
- offering continued support,
- examining defenses and coping styles, and
- identifying pathology for referral.

You may be called upon to help interpret these principles in terms of rules and regulations already in existence. For example, the administration may need a rationale for why a student is unable to finish the semester and may need to withdraw, if only for a short time.

The Value of Grievers as Facilitators and Educators

People in the college or university community who are grieving or who deal with grieving people can help to educate and facilitate the grief process for others. Time and again, dying students who have come to my class to talk about what they are dealing with have benefited the class as well as themselves. Parents of murdered children ask if they can return to tell another class what their experience has been. Doctors who took the class as undergraduates, make a great impression on students with their real life-and-death stories, which reinforce class readings and lecture. One faculty wife, whose husband had been murdered, talked to the class about what it was like for her and how the legal process needs improvement.

This sharing of her experience was meaningful to her in her grieving and informative and meaningful to the class.

I received a call from the father of a student six months after she had died, asking if I knew the ceramics professor with whom she had a class just before she died. I did, and I also knew that this professor's own daughter had died. The father asked if I thought there might still be a pot his daughter had been working on before she died that the university could forward to him. He said it would mean so much to the family to have something that she had created before she died. When I explained this situation to the professor he not only found the pot, he glazed it, wrote a special note from one bereaved father to another, and shipped it at his expense. The father told me how amazed he was at the university's concern for the parents of its students. While we could debate how concerned the university really was, there is little to debate about how reciprocal the process of helping the bereaved can be.

Dr. Robert L. Wrenn, PhD, has specialized in grief and loss counseling and teaching since 1976. He is on the Board of Directors of the Association for Death Education and Counseling, is a member of the International Work Group on Death, Dying and Bereavement, and is on the board of advisors for three hospices in Tucson.

When a Suicide Occurs

The suicide of a student should be taken seriously both to assist survivors and to minimize any chance of "copycat" suicides. Naturally, the best intervention is prevention. Teaching problem-solving skills, helping students to identify resources within their school and community, and building self-esteem are critical elements of suicide prevention. Review the curriculum as well. Should a suicide occur, the following guidelines may be helpful:

Develop and annually review a crisis plan. This plan should include policies for referral of a suspected suicide and the establishment of liaisons with the family of the victim, crisis teams, media, and police.

Inform the student body. It is best that students be informed as fully as is appropriate (given their developmental level, information available, and the family's wishes). Remember that accurate and factual information will minimize rumors and gossip.

Provide opportunities to review the student's life and death. Crisis teams should assist school personnel in addressing students' and staff's feelings, fears, and concerns. It is important to challenge scapegoating. People do not commit suicide because a partner ended a relationship or because they received a poor grade. Emphasize the message that suicide is a poor way to solve problems.

Provide professional assistance for any who need it. Friends, enemies, staff, and even students who did not know the person may feel vulnerable and reach out for help.

Help students shape appropriate responses. Remind them of ways they can assist survivors such as family and friends. Develop a common way of memorializing the person who committed suicide. Such memorials should emphasize prevention.

Inform parents. It may be helpful to send a letter detailing what has happened, how the school has responded, what parents should be sensitive to, and where they might obtain help.

Finally, recognize that grief takes time. Students and staff will continue to need help and support as they adapt to the loss.

Kenneth J. Doka

Practical Suggestions

Children confront illness and death regularly. It is in the news, on television, and in the movies. Children experience significant losses as well. People they know and people they love become ill, even die. Parents may divorce. Pets die. Separations occur as friendships change or families move. In all of these circumstances, children grieve.

As children grieve, the presence of understanding and supportive adults will be critical in helping them with this experience. Parents are often experiencing grief as well, and are not always available to help their children. Even if they are not experiencing their own grief, coping with their child's pain can be difficult.

Helping a Child with a Life-Threatening Illness: the School's Role

Schools can do much to ease the adjustment of a child with a life-threatening illness. As school administrators, principals and teachers work together to assist the child, these principles can guide their work:

- Understanding
- Communication
- Flexibility
- Support

Assisting the Child When a Family Member Is Ill

- Be available to the child
- Empower children to meet their own needs
- Watch for signs of distress
- Advocate for the child's needs

When a Classmate Is Ill

- Allow the class opportunities to share their own feelings and fears
- Prepare them for events
- Identify children who seem most affected
- Inform other parents, with the family's permission
- Teach children how they can show support
- Remember to take care of yourself

When a Student Dies: The School's Response

When a student dies, whether suddenly or as a result of illness, schools must respond in a sensitive manner.

- Develop and annually review a crisis plan
- Inform classes and offer help
- Inform parents
- Reach out to the grieving family
- Shape a group response
- Handle administrative details

The Grieving Child

Depending on the age, children may struggle both to understand the loss and to make spiritual sense of it. Younger children may have a difficult time sustaining strong feelings. Because of this "short feeling span" their moods may shift, and they may experience outbursts of anger or sadness. They may show grief in their own unique ways as well. Some of the ways grief may be evident include:

—acting out behavior
—regressive behavior (such as thumb sucking or clinging)
—changes in grades
—increased accidents
—sleep disturbances

While these may be manifestations of grief, it is important to monitor them. Behaviors that are illegal, dangerous or self-destructive will call for intervention.

Helping the Grieving Child in the Classroom

Sensitive teachers, administrators and counselors can do much to ease the child back into school.

- Acknowledge the loss
- Offer support
- Be sensitive to the child's sense of "different-ness"
- Refer when necessary
- Be sensitive to classmates

Getting Help

Schools do not have to handle these problems alone. Know what resources are available within your community before a crisis or problem. Hospices and funeral homes are good sources both for programs and for information. Libraries should have books and pamphlets on a variety of levels to help parents and children deal with loss and grief. You may wish to assess and develop your own school-based resources, perhaps adding print and non-print resources to your own libraries. And you may wish to plan your own staff development activities surrounding these issues and ideas.

These tips are summarized from a brochure entitled *Living With Grief: At School*, a publication of the Hospice Foundation of America. Contact HFA for more detailed information and suggestions.

Part III

Living With Grief:
At Worship

One of the places where we grieve is at worship. Here, one may think the environment is safe, because unlike schools and work-places, temples and churches are not task-oriented, but are sanctuaries—safe, holy places where one is free to ponder and where one looks to receive support. In a place dedicated to spiritual development one might expect to find the safety to explore and to express grief.

Yet the reality is more complicated than that. A recent Gallup poll found that one third of persons were likely to look to clergy for support in dealing with dying and grief. However, studies have shown that many clergy may have considerable misinformation about grief (Doka and Jendreski, 1985) and that spirituality can complicate as well as facilitate the struggles of the dying and bereaved (Doka and Morgan, 1993).

Barney's chapter addresses the essence of ministry at the end of life. To her, the center of that journey lies in companionship—a companionship not only with the patient but also with the family, community, and team. She echoes that successful hospice chaplains link dying persons and their families with spiritual resources, and she wisely cautions us that it is ultimately the patient, not the chap-lain, who determines the issues that need to be explored.

This is critical. One of the dangers involved in ministry to the dying is that one's own agenda may become primary. The goal of dying is not to reach acceptance, or achieve any other list of out-comes. Dying persons do not need to complete unfinished business or accomplish any given set of tasks. As Weisman (1992) reminds us, the only definition of an "appropriate death" is the one held by the person who is dying.

Ministry, then, involves helping a dying person address those spiritual needs. What is an appropriate death? Was my life meaningful? How can I find hope beyond the grave? Ministry lies not in answering those questions, but facilitating the exploration.

Barney's chapter notes the value of ritual. Irion's chapter discusses it further. He emphasizes that rituals are powerful interventive techniques. Van Gennep (1960) described them as *liminal*, on the threshold of consciousness. By this van Gennep means that rituals appeal to us on both a conscious and unconscious level. But Irion points out that the power of ritual is evoked only when rituals are personal and participatory. He also emphasizes the valued role that funeral rituals can have in facilitating grief. In doing so, he reinforces the idea that one useful tool of ministry, as well as other psychosocial care, is the creation of rituals that provide a sacred place and time to mark transitions, claim continued connections, affirm individuals, or finish business.

The closing chapter by Del Zoppo offers much. First, it emphasizes the concept that ministry is not a solo endeavor but a responsibility shared within a community. Second, it suggests powerful and practical ways that communities can together exercise that ministry. By doing so, communities can make "at worship" a place where persons can grieve—supported and safe.

Eleven

Ministry at the End of Life

Marilyn Barney

I was sitting with Doris just hours before her release from a long and painful illness. There were many periods of silence.

"Sing to me," she requested. So, in between the silence, I sang hymns that she loved. "Pray," she directed. The silence was now filled with my verbal prayers and those in her heart. The clock in the dining room chimed, marking the passing of time, whose meaning seemed lost in the moment. "Psalms—the 23rd." Doris knew exactly what she wanted. And after a while, she said, "Hold me, please."

I held her and stroked her as she rocked and moaned. I have never given birth, and yet I knew then the shape of my task. Doris was in labor, struggling to give birth to herself, and I was the mid-wife. Doris had chosen me to accompany her on this very important journey. After a while she fell asleep. I spent some time with her daughters, encouraging them to say goodbye, and then I left them at her bedside. When I returned to my office I received word that Doris had died, having successfully given birth to her new life.

> *All goes onward and outward,*
> *Nothing collapses*
> *And to die is different from*
> *What anyone supposes—*
> *And luckier.*
> *—Walt Whitman*

From conversations I have had with midwives and new mothers, the scene in the birthing room can be very similar. Transition into this life and out of this life need not be an emergency.

Those of us who are privileged to call ourselves ministers during this intense and intimate time in the life of an individual and family do not minister *to*, but *with*. And when we least expect it, we are ministered *to* by the life of the Transcendent, which is present in and among us throughout our lives, but in an especially palpable way in transitions such as birth and death. We are midwives on this spiritual journey, and stand as witnesses to the mystery of coming and going.

As so many other ministers have, I have often been with those who, at the end of a visit, thank me profusely for my kindness. I always wonder how I can ever communicate to them how privileged I feel by the sacred honor of sharing this part of their lives.

In a multicultural, multireligious society the challenge of this privilege of accompanying those with whom we minister is to leave our own biases and attachments for another time. We become channels for the truth that is in each of us, mirrors of the individual beauty and wisdom that is in us all. The task of a minister is to reflect this beauty and wisdom and to encourage its voice, no matter how different from our own. As the lyrics of the song go:

> *It's in every one of us to be wise.*
> *Find your heart, open up both your eyes.*
> *We can all know everything*
> *without ever knowing why;*
> *It's in every one of us to be wise.*
> —*David Pomerantz (1978)*

Dr. Ira R. Byock (1992) has complemented the work of developmental psychologists by proposing a list of developmental milestones and tasks at the end of life, among them:

> *a sense of completion with worldly affairs;*
> *a sense of completion in relationships with family, friends, and community;*
> *a sense of meaning about one's individual life;*
> *an experience of love of self;*
> *an experience of love of others;*

*an acceptance of the finality of life—of one's existence as an
individual;
a sense of a new self beyond personal loss;
a sense of meaning about life in general;
a sense of surrender to the transcendent, to the unknown—"letting go."*

The responsibility of ministry is not to take this list, or one similar to it, and devise a lesson plan for those to whom we minister,
but lists such as this can be valuable guides in knowing what might
be observed as one approaches the end of life. The definition of a
"good death" is as individual as each person. It is not our place to
decide for others how they should die, but to go with them along
the journey, supplying what provisions we can: love, compassion,
encouragement, acceptance, listening, and the support of our own
spiritual practice and prayers on their behalf. Doing is so much less
important than simply being with the person. Every life is sacred,
and the journey is a pilgrimage towards the self, towards the divine,
and towards a recognition and sense of awe in one's own place in
the universe and relationship with the Transcendent. The journey is
the voyage home.

On this journey it is natural for patients, families, and caregivers to search for meaning in their present situation. For most, the
essential character of this search is spiritual, and religious themes
often provide landmarks along the way. Such searches for meaning
are characteristic of significant landmarks in life as we seek to make
sense of and maintain control over situations in which our command seems tenuous.

For those whose spirituality is rooted in an omnipotent God or
higher being, persons providing ministry have a special invitation.
It is natural to want to ascribe responsibility for the situation, to
assess the potential for ultimate benefit or harm, and to preserve a
sense of the universe as just and fair. In other words, in situations
such as facing our own death or the death of a loved one, we need
to be assured that we have not been abandoned, that we are not
being punished for peccadilloes real or imagined, and that ultimately, we are loved and valued.

For many, a major part of achieving these goals is the telling of
one's story. Some term the telling of these stories as a *life review*—

a useful term, as long as one does not view the end of life as preparation for a test. This telling of stories can lead to so many other areas of completion. Episodes in one's life may bring forth a need for forgiveness by oneself or others, working toward the completion of past and present relationships, reconciliation with self and others, and ultimately with the individual's concept of the Transcendent. Losses not yet grieved can be mourned, accomplishments celebrated, love expressed and experienced. And an appreciation of the journey of one's life may be realized, perhaps for the first time, leaving a legacy of love and belonging. It might even be possible to see this time of coming to the closure of earthly life as being bestowed with unexpected spiritual gifts of love, forgiveness, gratitude, and peace (Kessler, 1997). This is a sacred time.

An 84-year-old woman with end-stage cancer lamented to me one day that she felt worthless and useless and didn't know why she was put on this earth. Over a cup of tea and a plate of cookies she told stories of her life, of emigrating from Eastern Europe, of building a life with her husband, of raising her children. She spoke of the love she had shared with her parents, her husband, and her children, and of her influence on her children's lives and the lives of those with whom she came in contact. And I could wholeheartedly assure her of the giftedness that she had brought to my life. By the end of the visit her suffering had abated, and she was more convinced of her place of value in the universe.

It is essential to recognize that ministry at the end of life is not with the individual alone but with the family and community as well. Facilitating the expression of emotion and saying of farewells may be useful in the journey of the individual and family, however family may be defined. Often the individual needs the permission and encouragement of loved ones before he or she can let go and proceed into the unknown.

Pathways of hope and healing can be established which will be revisited by loved ones after the death of the patient. While survivors may seek the services of bereavement professionals and support opportunities such as bereavement groups, for many the ultimate consolation and meaning reconstruction (Neimeyer, 1998) will be found in one's spiritual and religious life. A sense of benevolent fate for the dead is a significant factor in the bereavement process, and in this the minister and the faith community play key roles of encouragement and comfort. Questioning long-held teaching and dogma concerning the fate of the dead is natural as loss rearranges one's life. Often these questions are not asked in order to elicit a satisfactory answer, but in order for the questioner to receive acceptance in his or her pain. Feelings of anger and despair over the death of a loved one are difficult to verbalize, and yet verbalization may be essential in one's journey through grief. As C.S. Lewis (1961) described, following the death of his wife:

Meanwhile, where is God? This is one of the most disquieting symptoms. When you are happy, so happy that you have no sense of needing Him, you will be welcomed with open arms. But go to Him when your need is desperate, when all other help is in vain, and what do you find? A door slammed in your face, and a sound of bolting and double bolting on the inside. After that, silence.

Talk to me about the truth of religion and I'll listen gladly. Talk to me about the duty of religion and I'll listen submissively. But don't come talking to me about the consolations of religion or I shall suspect that you don't understand.

Grief lasts a long time. Ministry is for the long haul.

Rituals can be so important to providing both a sense of closure for this life and connection with the transcendence of the life to come. Encouraging family members to reconcile, to express feelings, to perform rites and rituals consonant with their religious tradition is a skillful way of encouraging closure for the dying individual and of providing memories for those who will be left behind. Often families and individuals have a historical or cultural connection with a community of faith. Connecting with that community often brings them comfort and a pathway into a spiritual construct that transcends the finality of this temporal life.

The invitation to ministry in accompanying this search for meaning at the end of life is three-fold. First, while a number of significant persons in the seeker's life will play important roles, it is often expected that the individual will turn to one who is designated as a spiritual or religious leader to provide encouragement, feedback, and direction. Second, for those who are not rooted in a religious tradition or who do not wish to see a religious leader, the person in ministry stands ready to provide guidance, encouragement, and compassion to others who may be providing ministry to the person. And third, we can work as a team with others, clergy and laity, in ministry. We cannot do this ministry alone, and we cannot answer every need placed before us.

A layperson may provide ministry in situations where clergy might not have access. Many faith communities have organized lay committees for visitation to the sick and dying. These persons need training, supervision, and support in their ministry. One well known model of this type of ministry is the Stephen Ministry, an ecumenical program that for 24 years has been preparing laypersons to provide one-on-one caring ministry to those in a variety of difficult life situations, including terminal illness and bereavement. Stephen ministers participate in a rigorous program of lay pastoral care training, followed by ongoing supervision, support, and continuing education. The program is used in thousands of congregations throughout the US, as well as in 18 countries. More than 220,000 laypeople have been trained as Stephen Ministers.

When introducing myself and my role to patients and families, I often tell them that I am the person who comes without an agenda. I am the one who just is, who keeps her mouth shut and listens, listens, listens. This is the essential task of the minister. The challenge for us as human beings and as ministers is to become compassionately involved with each other, recognizing ourselves and others as precious treasures. Every life is sacred. The sharing in that life is a sacred trust, to be lovingly and carefully maintained.

Ministry at the end of life requires courage on the part of the minister and on the part of the person undertaking this journey. There is a sense of urgency in the limitation that medical diagnosis and prognosis have placed on life. There is no time for side trips. This urgency may be expressed as a lack of tolerance on the part of the patient and loved ones for small talk and niceties. Feelings may be expressed and secrets revealed now that may be difficult or embarrassing for the individual or for those ministering with them. Dying is often messy and unattractive—emotionally and spiritually, as well as physically. The minister is called upon to accompany each individual on this journey without judgment, providing a repository for hurt, and a channel for love and acceptance.

Ultimately, this work is work on ourselves. When we accompany someone in his or her dying process, we also are witnesses to our own deaths and to the deaths of all beings who have gone before and who will come after us. In *Facing Death and Finding Hope*, Christine Longaker (1997) says that working with those who are dying not only helps us to prepare for our own deaths but also "provides us with the keys to living fully and finding meaning throughout all of the unwanted changes, losses, and painful circumstances of our lives." Those who minister not only to the dying but to those struggling across the broad spectrum of human experience will benefit from what the dying process has to teach us about suffering, healing relationships, finding meaning in life, and letting go.

We are not givers or receivers, but are in the audience of divine unfolding. Perhaps this work will lead to our emancipation from our own finite perception of reality, if only for a moment. Maybe we can encourage the freedom of others. Perhaps, one by one, all sentient beings may find healing and discover the beauty and joy of their true nature.

> *The call of death is a call of love.*
> *Death can be sweet if we answer it in the affirmative,*
> *If we accept it as one of the great eternal forms*
> *Of life and transformation.*
> —Herman Hesse

Marilyn Barney, MA, holds degrees in music, Biblical studies, and counseling psychology. She has been recognized by the Department of Health and Human Services for developing a program for HIV/AIDS-infected and affected children in foster care. She provides spiritual and bereavement care in hospice and is currently the Volunteer Coordinator at Hospice of New York.

Twelve

Ritual Responses to Death

Paul E. Irion

Cultural anthropologists have found that most cultures develop rituals for responding to profound human experiences. These have often been called *rites of passage*—rituals that surround the significant times of transition in human experience: birth, initiation into adulthood, marriage, and death. These occasions are so important that they need to be marked in special ways.

Rites of passage (van Gennep, 1960) usually have three stages: separation, transition, incorporation. They indicate that one is leaving a known circumstance in life, making a transition to a new way of life, or settling in to a changed situation. Within the context of this chapter, grieving involves profound needs that are addressed by all three of these dimensions.

Religious rituals, as well as informal personal rituals, are valuable aids to grieving. While faith communities have traditionally assisted mourners through ritual, they can do so more effectively by understanding the value of personal and participatory funerals. In this chapter we will explore the psychological, social, and religious functions of post-death rituals.

Phyllis Silverman (1987) reminds us that grief is not an illness but a response to a new situation. Life is irreversibly altered after the death of a loved one. According to Silverman one has to adjust creatively to a permanently changed life: a heavy burden, but also an opportunity.

Ritual response to a death is a drama which symbolizes that life as it was known is being left behind. It acknowledges that there will be a time of transition in which a person or group will gradually move toward a new state or a new reality. Finally, the ritual points to, but may not necessarily complete, incorporation into a new way of life, the new reality.

In contemporary American society we see the need for some sort of ritual to convey the sense of loss that is felt, and the need for the life of the group to go on without the deceased. We would find it inappropriate to pay absolutely no attention to a person's death, to act as if nothing had happened. The term *decent burial* denotes that some sort of process needs to be undertaken to significantly mark a person's death.

It is helpful for individuals or groups confronting the radical transitions necessitated by death and loss to have some familiar ritual patterns to follow in order to express their responses. But they do not have to invent channels for expression. Other people have faced similar crises of loss and have found it helpful to respond in ways that are repeated and become formal rituals. Families, faith communities, neighborhoods, and ethnic groups have established ritual patterns for confronting death and grief. Most of these are customs learned by observation and imitation, rather than some written form. They are there when needed.

Such ritual patterns need not be followed slavishly. Ritual is a resource to be offered, not imposed. Rituals should be used as signposts to communicate meaning and to guide responses to loss. People need to be free to use as much or as little established ritual as they wish.

In a mobile society it is not uncommon for people to have moved far from their hometown roots, perhaps to have drifted away from their childhood religious heritage, or to have laid aside their ethnic and cultural ties. And so they may find that many of the streams of traditional ritual have dried up for them. They may not feel that they have access to those rituals when death and loss occur. The temptation then may be to avoid *any* ritual response to mark the death of a loved one.

However, it is to be hoped that before familiar rituals are abandoned altogether, new ways of meeting the needs addressed by rituals will be explored. The alternative to traditional ritual should not be the complete absence ritual; it is far better to thoughtfully create new rituals responses, based on a solid understanding of what rituals surrounding death and loss are intended to accomplish.

Rituals is the acting out of the meanings we attach to life. Through ritual we tap into our unconscious need to be connected, to belong both to other people and to the universe. By renewing the stories of our religious community, or our family, or our ethnic heritage we demonstrate our deeply felt need not to feel alone and abandoned, especially in time of crisis. If we do not have access to such stories, we need to create new ones, to convey in our own terms that life will go on, even without the presence of the one who has died.

Rituals offer defined ways for mourners to act out their feelings. For example, in cultures that encourage people to hold in their feelings, rituals provide acceptable avenues for expression. It is all right to weep, to express pain, to describe one's loss in a ritual setting. Ritual is a way in which a social group gives permission to its members to symbolically act out their real feelings: shedding tears, kneeling before the casket, cutting their clothing or a symbolic ribbon. Because ritual permits the indirect expression of feeling, it enables people to communicate their deep feelings with others and to express what might otherwise be inexpressible.

This chapter addresses not only formal death rituals, but also informal, personal rituals designed to help a mourner cope with her or his loss. The same needs are being met in both forms of ritual. If we understand the purpose and function of ritual, we can see the value of both formal and informal ritual responses to death.

Those who belong to religious groups follow the ritual patterns of those faith communities to mark a death. Those who are not conventionally religious often develop their own formal rituals or adopt rituals from the secular community to help them cope with a death.

In addition to the traditional religious definition, as our knowledge of loss and grief has broadened through sociological and psychological study, the funeral can also be defined as the social response of any group to the death of one of its members. The funeral, apart from any religious content, is also a psychological resource for helping people to cope with the important tasks of therapeutic mourning. For religious people the funeral will always be rightly regarded as a meaningful religious service. But for those who are not committed to any religious group, the therapeutic social and psychological value of the funeral can still be experienced.

Once we understand that funerals play an important part in shaping the process of mourning, we recognize that there are ways in which we can make death rituals meaningful and effective. Mourners arranging a funeral need to be intentional in designing a ritual that will serve their needs in this time of loss. It will help them to honor the memory of the one who died and to express the dimensions of their loss. Even though the form of the religious funeral is sometimes set by church regulation or custom, mourners should work with the funeral director and clergy to shape, where possible, elements of the service to appropriately meet their needs. They should make the funeral as participatory as possible, having family and friends take part in the service, and encouraging the assembled congregation to participate by reading in unison or singing rather than being passive spectators. The funeral can give everyone attending a way of expressing his or her own sense of loss. But this kind of intentional planning will not take place unless some family members understand what death rituals are intended to accomplish and what value they have for families in grief.

Let's look rather specifically at some of the ways in which the funeral ritual can be a resource for grieving people, helping with the kinds of tasks that confront those trying to cope with loss.

The funeral has an important role in the task of confronting and accepting the new reality in which the mourner is living. This con-frontation of reality operates at two levels in most people—a thinking level and a feeling level. One does not fully take in the new reality all at once. For many, the acceptance of the reality of their new situation at the feeling level is slower and more difficult than it is in rational thought. The funeral reinforces the new reality. It is a recognition that something drastic has taken place. There are cer-tain things we do only when a person has died: notifying relatives to gather, making funeral arrangements, participating in the view-ing and the funeral, burying or cremating the body. All these activities begin to underscore the new emerging reality.

The funeral, because it is a group experience, provides what psychologists refer to as *consensual validation*. Friends and relatives gather for the funeral because they acknowledge the loss. The funeral communicates that a number of people, each in her or his own way, are experiencing the new reality. It is not just a bad dream. The presence of the deceased's body also reinforces the new reality and is a powerful reminder that the person has really died.

It is important, therefore, that the funeral be realistic. It should not sugarcoat the experience of death and loss. It is best to use the words *dead* and *died*, not euphemisms. As hospice models a realistic approach to death for the families it serves, the funeral must also be a model for helping people understand that a death has taken place, that feelings of profound loss are perfectly natural, and that there are many resources for helping people to cope with their new reality. The reality-confirming function of the funeral ritual helps construct a foundation upon which the extended struggle to live within a new reality is based.

The funeral helps people relate to their old reality by encouraging recollection of the person who died. Memory is a dimension in which we know we can continue to relate to the deceased. Remembering can be encouraged in many ways. A pastor I know asks to meet with all available members of the family, including children, on an evening before the funeral. He leads them in a time of remembering the deceased, telling stories, and looking at pictures. Then he concludes this time of remembering with a prayer of thanksgiving for memories of the life that has been lived. Some funeral homes encourage families to bring in mementos of the deceased, which are displayed during the viewing and the funeral.

The funeral ritual also helps mourners review their memories of the deceased, an important part of therapeutic mourning. The funeral can support the remembering process through the traditional use of an obituary, a practice which unfortunately is not always followed. We need to be reminded that the funeral marks the end of the life of a real person who occupied space, who was part of a network of family and friends, who worked, who loved. I am not talking about some sort of extravagant eulogy that bears little relationship with reality; I am talking about the factual description of the person's life as a catalyst to help people remember experiences they shard on that person's journey. It is perhaps helpful to introduce an obituary with that suggestion. Some funerals have a time in which those attending are encouraged to share a memory of the deceased. The funeral sermon may also contain some appropriate and genuine personal recollections of the deceased.

The rituals surrounding a death set the stage for grieving processes that will be repeated. Mourners need ways to express how much the person meant to them through stories of shared experiences. Statements by family or friends can describe the legacies of the spirit, ways the person who died has gifted others.

The funeral enables mourners to express their feelings. When rightly conducted, it gives people permission to be themselves. One of the functions of the ritual is to provide ways for putting into actions and words the deep feelings connected with the experience of profound loss. It explicitly acknowledges their feeling level. Often we accept behavior at a funeral that would not be as readily welcomed in other settings.

It can be helpful for mourners to act out the pain of separation. The observance of ritual dramatizes the loss—turning to others for support, shedding tears, talking about the one who has died and the gap that has been left in the mourners' lives. A public ritual is a first step in encouraging grieving persons to reach out to others for comfort and security rather than huddling in isolated privacy. It encourages the family to take the initiative in conversations about the deceased and the death, and encourages friends to share their expressions of loss.

An effective death ritual allows mourners to express their deep feelings, their hopes and regrets, because the ritual openly confronts and articulates such feelings. We often assume that sadness is the major feeling associated with grief, but there are many more, varying from individual to individual. Some feel intense gratitude (*She was a wonderful mother*), some feel anger (*How could he die and leave me like this?*), some feel fear (*How am I ever going to go on alone?*), some feel guilt (*Why didn't I make him go to the doctor?*), some feel despair (*I don't have anything to live for anymore*).

All feelings need not be expressed in the public setting of the funeral; some are more appropriately expressed in personal conversation with a close friend or clergyperson. But it is important for the funeral to provide a context for indicating that it is all right to have these feelings, even strong feelings. Clergy can acknowledge the pain of this loss, the changes it brings about, the difficult adjustments it requires. It is important for the ritual to recognize such negative expressions of pain and loss, rather than concentrating only on the positive dimension of hope.

Giving permission to feel grief is not manipulation, either by making people control their feelings or by trying to stir up feelings. The context conveyed by the funeral should be one of acceptance, not prescription. People need to hear, "We can handle your expressions of hurt or fear or regret." They do not need to hear, "Be brave, he wouldn't want you to be crying."

In the religious community we need to be reminded often that faith is not a substitute for grief, but a resource. Too often people are enjoined to "have faith," as if that were going to free them from the need to grieve. Comfort literally means *to make strong*. A person's faith is a source of strength to cope, rather than an easy out.

The funeral ritual provides support because it involves a community, a congregation, a circle of family and friends. Mourners are reminded that they are not alone in this painful experience. Funeral rituals, wakes, and viewings gather family and friends to support the grieving, and are ways of helping people know that they are still part of a living family. Death rituals often indicate kinship patterns; people most closely related to the deceased are given special seating, close relatives are notified first of the death. For religious people funeral rituals respond to feelings of being alone by affirming that God is with them in their pain. Members of their religious community gather with them to memorialize the one who has died and to support the mourners.

I am concerned about the trend to privatize the grief experience, to offer no occasion in which a community can express its shared loss. Because the funeral can be painful, some people are tempted to dodge it. A friend once said to me, "When I die, just take me out and plant me. I don't want anything but that done." I responded, "I know you are a modest guy, but I've been your friend for more than 25 years. If you died, I, as well as a lot of your friends, would feel a real sense of loss. I would like to have a chance to express with the rest of the community what we feel we have lost."

The funeral as a ritual response offers a turning point between the old reality and the new. It is natural following the death of a loved one to be quite preoccupied with thoughts of the person. But mourners have to separate themselves gradually from the body of the deceased, the physical presence. The funeral allows for that separation to occur with the service of committal at the graveside or crematory, providing an important sense of finality. A chapter of their lives has closed, and the bereaved must go on in new ways.

At the same time, as mourners realize that they are being supported by the people who have gathered around them for the funeral, they see that their new reality involves the living. They learn to reinvest emotional capital. The emotional energy that they have put into their relationship with the deceased can now be invested in strengthening relationships with the living. This is not immediate but a process that happens over time.

The funeral offers a structure of meaning for experiencing death and loss. This is most clearly seen in the religious dimension of the funeral, but it can also be found in a funeral that is understood socially or psychologically rather than theologically. Funeral rituals are occasions in which people try to express what they believe it means, most clearly illustrated in religious funerals in which a faith community presents its beliefs about death and the gifts of new life after death. Secular rituals might express the understanding of the ongoing nature of life in the community following the death of one of its members.

Rituals are ways in which meaning is sought and affirmed. Death is a great mystery. As long as humans have had the capacity to think they have pondered what death is and what its consequences might be. Death raises profound questions: *What does it all mean? Why did the person have to die? What are we to make of a universe in which all living things die? Is there justice in death? What happens after a person dies?*

If we are truly honest, we have to say we don't know. So human beings have responded to these kinds of questions in the realm of belief. In the religious funeral a faith community shares its beliefs about death. Ideally it does not promulgate dogma but communicates that "This is the way in which generations of people who believe as we do have tried to understand the meaning of death."

The funeral does not have to provide all the answers, but should encourage people to reflect in faith on the critical event that has taken place. This process is only beginning and usually cannot get very far until the emotional stress of the loss diminishes. Then, often some months after the funeral, the reflective process begins to make some sense. The funeral is not the destination in the quest for meaning but a signpost that points people in that direction.

We need to be reminded that loss and death are cumulative. In the same way, funerals are cumulative. Of course, a funeral is focused on the death of a particular person. But a man over here may be thinking of the death of his wife years ago and mourning her. And here sits a woman who has an aging mother with cancer, anticipating her death and mourning a loss that has not yet happened. A funeral may well serve the needs of a number of very different people.

Families may organize some of their activities following a death into informal rituals. Visits to the cemetery begin to develop into a pattern. They become special times for putting flowers on the grave: birthday, the date of the death, Memorial Day. Families are encouraged to use simple rituals at holiday gatherings. Some families will light a candle in memory of the one who has died, or they may share memories to mark the anniversary of the death.

People do not usually consciously set out to develop a personal or family ritual. They simply act in response to a need to deal with their loss. They find satisfaction because their action symbolizes the deep sense of loss they feel. Rather than just talking about it, they act it out, privately or publicly. It may be a one-time ritual or may be repeated from time to time.

By understanding the ways in which rituals can help mourners to cope with their grief, individuals and families can benefit by participating in traditional rituals or in devising new ritual responses to their loss. Effective use of such rituals makes movement from the former reality to the new reality not only possible but empowering.

Paul E. Irion is Professor Emeritus of Pastoral Theology at Lancaster Theological Seminary of the United Church of Christ in Lancaster, Pennsylvania. He was founding president and Pastoral Care Coordinator of Hospice of Lancaster County. He was honored by the Association for Death Education and Counseling as one of the pioneers in the field of serving the dying and grieving.

Programs That Work

Evergreen Community Hospice

Evergreen Community Hospice (ECH) is part of Evergreen Community Health Care (ECHC). ECHC provides acute care and care for the chronically ill throughout the life span. ECHC's community-based programs offer care and education in a wide range of settings, such as patients' homes, skilled nursing facilities, schools, and senior citizen centers.

Death and grief are not comfortable topics for most people. We wanted to change this by empowering people with the tools and information that will help them be open to quality care at the end of life. Our desire is to make end-of-life care as integral a part of the fabric of the community as prenatal care has become.

We developed a plan for working in partnership with faith communities to raise public awareness of end-of-life issues and to expand support for families facing grief and life-limiting illness. Our goal was the greation of a flexible, multi-level training and support system for faith communities to draw on to meet their own goals.

A steering committee began to look for ways to bring faith communities and other segments of the population together. We began making connections to local clergy associations, such as the Parish Nurses Association and the Interfaith Council of Washington, by holding informal talks, seminars, and panel presentations on end-of-life topics.

Some communities have well-established care ministries and are interested in support of their ongoing work, while others want help setting up, training, and supporting care teams. Our project director works with the group to provide assistance in program development. Volunteer caregivers present workshops from our own training curriculum or curricula designed to meet a particular situation. Resources are shared among participating organizations.

We rely heavily on existing resources such as our training manual, and materials published by social service agencies and regional funeral directors. Nurses or social workers explain technical details.

Many congregations offered Sunday morning religious education classes devoted to end-of-life concerns. End-of-life subjects came out in the open. Groups that initially just wanted information began to formulate care plans. They wanted to help.

Congregations that had existing care teams used our resources to enhance their training models. These resources helped them to be more comfortable in end-of-life situations where they could not "fix" things. Some volunteer caregivers reported that their faith deepened as a result of the new perspectives gained in the process.

Congregations were invited to join together in interfaith training sessions. New alliances offered care support to faith communities that had few resources. A sense of community developed among the diverse groups participating in the Faith in Action–Compassionate Care Partnership.

We began to open the conversation on end-of-life topics to the general public by inviting guest speakers to give "non-threatening" presentations on topics such as *Cultural Diversity—A Look at Death From Other Perspectives*, *When a Member of the Community Dies—Grief as Group Experience*, *Advance Directives*, and *Funeral Planning*. These presentations have been well received, and several were repeated to accommodate demand.

Some people who attended these public programs became interested in volunteering at hospice. Others asked for information on Faith In Action to take to their place of worship. Through word of mouth the reputation of the Faith In Action–Compassionate Care Partnership spread to other faith communities and organizations.

We continue to nurture our existing relationships and integrate newly participating faith communities by hosting events such as breakfast seminars for clergy. Staff is available to give ongoing support to lay caregivers. We have invited congregations to join the planning process for upcoming events. By having personnel whose primary task is to work with faith communities on caregiving and life-limiting illness concerns, we are becoming as a clearinghouse for information, a connection to other services, and a bridge across differences that joins the community in the common human experiences of dying and grief.

Rev. Karen Modell
Program Coordinator and Chaplain
Evergreen Community Hospice

Thirteen

The Religious Community in Times of Loss: Strong, Loving, and Wise

Patrick M. Del Zoppo

LORD, hear my prayer, and let my cry come to you.
Hide not your face from me in the day of my distress.
Incline your ear to me; in the day when I call, answer me speedily.
For my days vanish like smoke, and my bones burn with fire.
Withered and dried up like grass is my heart;
I forget to eat my bread.
Because of my insistent sighing I am reduced to skin and bone.
I am like a desert owl; I am like an owl among the ruins.
I am sleepless and I moan;
I am like a sparrow alone on a housetop.
—Psalm 105

The psalmist is one of our ancestors in faith. Calling up thoughts and feelings both personal and communal, he brings us into a mourning journey. It is the mourning journey experienced by most people. Grief does not discriminate. It affects those in faith fullness and those in faith crisis, those in the large urban congregation and in the small rural parish.

The mourning plea is a call to be recognized and a call to be saved. The psalmist wants us to hear the stark reality of grief—grief that affects body, mind, and spirit. Many of the speakers in the Old

Testament paint vividly descriptive pictures for us. There is a freedom and generosity in their words, a cry for mercy and a desire to be understood. The psalmist seeks companionship during his grief journey. He begs us to understand the depth of the wounds that need healing.

We are the daughters and sons of the psalmist. We move throughout our own history seeking justice, mercy, and healing.

Yet the psalmist does not end this cry in despair and hopelessness. In the midst of mourning the language presents a glimpse of readiness for transformation, a readiness to be lifted up from that which weighs the psalmist down:

> *But you, O Lord, abide forever,*
> *and your name through all generations.*
> *You will arise and have mercy on Zion for it is time to pity her,*
> *for the appointed time has come.*

It appears that the psalmist has been comforted by the ability of the community to receive this expression of pain, and now there is a request to move to another phase: healing, the transformation beyond the pain. This sufferer asks the community to legitimize and approve this new desire for healing.

In the New Testament, the Gospel of Mark records more instances of Christ's physical healings than any other Gospel. In many of these cases, Mark reports, Christ asked the person not to tell anyone of the healing. One possible reason for this strange command is that Jesus did not want the broadcast of these healings to give a distorted message that the needs of the body transcend the needs of the mind, emotions, and spirit. Rather than have this vision projected, he requested, to no avail, that these healings not be mentioned at all. That concern has largely come true in our time as we urgently wage war against death and disease and yet casually seek to meet the needs of the spirit.

All healing ministries, then—and this includes ministry to the bereaved—may best be understood as holistic healing. Holistic healing recognizes that a member of the congregation is a biologically, psychosocially, and spiritually integrated being and that providers of physical care, along with the religious and spiritual community, need to participate in a total healing process. The religious community offers more than a "nice extra." It is a vital factor promoting physical and emotional well-being. Because the human individual was created to live in harmony with other people and with God, a bereaved person's religious community has an important responsibility within the healing dynamic.

Illness disrupts the continuity of community interaction and often alters relationships. This fact affects the entire congregation, bereaved and otherwise. A spiritual community can hear the needs of its members and feel compelled to respond. There is a need for direction in spiritual leadership to mobilize an initial response that can later be continued by the congregation without a hands-on clergy presence.

The spiritual dimension is not a frill; it is basic to good health care. The living relationship of extended spiritual care calls a community to be strong, loving, and wise. An initial response of practical theology by the leadership in a congregation sets the tone for the support that will come in the near future. Strong leadership can motivate the aftercare available in the religious congregation in the aftermath of grief. In some cases the community can continue the spiritual tone set by leadership; in other cases it may provide a style beyond what the leadership can offer. Clergy may be helpful during the shock and disbelief that follow the first acknowledgment of death, but other bereaved members of the congregation may best be utilized as ongoing resources during later adjustment periods in mourning.

Good care invites healed people to walk with sufferers until a sufferer can stand alone. This requires more art than science, yet the technical training and personal attributes of a caregiver will certainly affect the quality and type of healing that he or she will provide. It is a living relationship more than a theoretical discipline, a perspective more than a category of work, a way of being more than a way of doing. It is here, in this first relational aspect of care, that a partial antidote to suffering is offered and pain alleviated.

The potential of healthcare professionals for providing spiritual care must not be overlooked. Writing as ministers and psychiatrists, the staff at Saint Christopher's Hospice in Sydenham, England, defends the role of religious values and spirituality in a combined treatment plan for survivors of hospice loss. In many American models of hospice care, the entire family, as well as the patient, is discussed in each team meeting. Not only is the team of aftercare professionals who attend the weekly team meetings updated about current patient status, but the entire interdisciplinary team is also updated as to how family and significant others are coping at this time both socially and spiritually. It is in this meeting that preliminary plans of aftercare are discussed and a future plan of action designed to meet the needs of this family is considered.

The interdisciplinary team of medical and psychosocial caregivers could also consider arranging a current or future relationship with local religious leadership. Asking a family about such an integration of care is often a first step toward a future aftercare team. In addition, the future survivors of this loss will realize that the team will not abandon them after this death. The introduction of this team approach can be successfully integrated by religious leadership of the family's choice as the time of death approaches. This continuity-of-care approach has been known to dispel fears of abandonment by family and significant others.

Proper professional skills are the first prerequisite for any provider of physical and emotional care. Yet, when encountering the transcendent, the ministry of allied believers allows for connections on the deepest of levels—levels that words and medicine cannot convey.

It is essential that the religious community offer homecoming to the bereaved. Homecoming is the communal soul responding to the individual soul. It is the essence of being fully alive and fully connected to a larger and healed group of believers. In itself, sharing religious rituals and symbols is a healing factor during a time of bereavement. Consider breathing the same incense, standing in the same candlelight, reciting a spoken prayer, and bonding within silence as a gift to the bereaved from the spiritual community. These signs and symbols resonate to the core of a sufferer's being and offer hope beyond the spoken word.

It is important that the bereaved who are isolated at home be able to hear the support of the spiritual community who remember them. Some congregations provide a cassette recording of worship services for use by those who may be homebound due to illness and grief. Congregations that provide weekly or monthly newsletters for their members could carry a corner asking for prayers for those who have died and for the bereaved. The knowledge of being remembered within a sacred space provides solidarity and restoration of security.

The Jewish community's transference of support from clergy to congregation during the year following the loss is a natural mechanism for moving along on the journey of grief. Responding to the loss in the context of a year-long life of prayer and ritual has been a healing factor in many religious communities. Other faith traditions might do well to explore or return to their own various opportunities of memorialization during the community's seasons of worship. Many communities have neglected or even abandoned helpful traditions of memorialization. Grieving people often expect this activity, but secularization of the death event has removed the major death and bereavement tasks from the communities responsible for the restoration of their members' spiritual and emotional health.

Many in the Roman Catholic tradition will remember the month's-mind Mass, in which the family and the worshipping community gathered one month after the death to celebrate a Mass in remembrance of the one who had died. The month's pause between the first and second assembly of the community allowed the bereaved to experience support after the first period of shock and disbelief. This custom has all but disappeared during the last three decades, probably a victim of the negation of many mourning patterns that have changed since urbanization.

The funeral industry has shortened the times for calling hours and visitation in the last two decades, ostensibly to provide ample time for a meal and rest between visits to the funeral home. I am not in favor of this. Catharsis through expression of grief and reality testing is an initial phase of the healing process. The time given to the reality of death, as well as a space in which to receive support in the initial aftermath of grief, are essential to the first phases of recovery and transformation. I believe it would be helpful if the funeral industry would encourage a family to do as much as they need to do in the initial days after a death.

On the other side, some helpful funeral directors have designed their facilities to be a real place for the gathering of family and friends, even to the extent of providing tables for family pictures and keepsakes, and play areas for children. Some houses of worship have a special place for the pictures of those who have died and provide a condolence book for messages from members of the congregation who want to show solidarity with the bereaved.

During a residency in a local nursing home, I often wondered about the lack of mourning by the residents after the death of a long-time friend. My question was answered in part when the residents commented that the medical staff did not encourage nursing home memorial services, even though most long-time companions were nonambulatory and could not attend planned funerals. Perhaps there weren't even funerals. A discussion with the administration produced quarterly services of remembrance in which former residents, family members, and friends could be honored for a life that was lived. Later on during the residency I was given permission for some creativity, and we established a quiet room available to all for meditation.

Included in this room was our nursing home "wailing wall," an attractive bulletin board on which we remembered the special needs of the residents. We began by putting on the board pictures of those who had died and allowed room for messages from the residents to the deceased and their families. A week later we mailed the picture and messages to the surviving family members. Later on, the board displayed the needs of the residents and their families. The residents were proud of their wailing wall and always asked guests if they had any needs that the residents could pray for. Most days you could find the residents stopping by the wailing wall to remember quietly, or just to give a quick touch of the hand onto the petitions that were left for all to see. It was a connection to the outside world of the living.

When a religious tradition does not allow for these displays of ongoing memorialization, some communities successfully borrow from other faith traditions, primarily those that manifest the beauty and support of ongoing ritualization. It is not uncommon at this time for some Christian communities to find great support in the religious traditions of the Jewish heritage, especially the rites and rituals of commemoration during the first week, month, and year after death.

Several years ago the members of my hospice team in New York City realized that as the coordinator of bereavement care I would probably take little time away for reflection after my father's sudden death. Their gift to me was to cover my patient schedule and help me to stay at home for a week. They made it possible for my immigrant Italian family to receive the support of friends, food, storytelling, and prayer in the safety of our home. In fact, in the first few days we needed to be coached in how to sit and simply receive love and support. In our circumstances we needed more than our usual two-day wake and funeral Mass. It was a life-saving gift and decision made for us by colleagues of a different faith, who allowed the caregiver to be cared for. They did for me what they believed I would not be able to do for myself. They were correct—it saved us.

It is essential that those involved in caregiving alliances provide extra support for colleagues and peers who are in grief. We may be the more fragile in the community because of the lack of support that we may afford to ourselves.

Bereavement Ministry

While accompanying my pastor on various sick calls during graduate internship, I was amazed to find that the dying person confronting us spoke as if he were a part of the internal history of the pastor. His personality took on the voice of the pastor, who had preached many a Sunday sermon on helpful ways that one could encounter death. In reality, he was dying according to the death education provided in subtle and not so subtle suggestions from pastoral leadership. In this case, the pastor's theology on the subject was an integrated approach to the whole person who would be dying. This individual wanted to have some control over his dying and not feel obliged to die at the moment suggested by others. In the end, when his family could no longer hold onto the sight and sounds of imminent death, it was the community of elders who became the midwife in his dying process—sharing meals, card games, bingo games, and traditional devotions. According to his family he did, in the end, die well. The family transferred caretaking to another community—his peers and friends. They also recovered well by their active decision to share responsibilities with their faith community.

Bereavement ministry is a ministry of presence that reestablishes trust and represents hope. It satisfies the inner cravings for a safe and secure opportunity to be incorporated into a new and changed world. An ending has occurred that demands a new beginning. Entering into the world of the bereaved is a sacred task for a community. Sensitivity, empathy, connectedness, and reconciliation are key spiritual moments for recovery after death. The religious community can honor the relationship that existed between the deceased and the survivor by providing a host of ongoing relationships for those suffering loss. Some of the roots of faith, such as the commandment to "honor thy father and thy mother," provide an opportunity for helpful relationships that can easily be provided by the senior elders in faith in most communities. They have survived and they are here to tell about it.

The strength of the community elders can be a first place to turn when a congregation cares about outreach to the bereaved. In building the ministry to the bereaved in the Archdiocese of New York some 15 years ago, I presented to 50 senior groups a year-long series of activities on loss, change, recovery, and healing. While the subjects ranged from crime to grandparenting, we established a comfort zone for an eventual no-holds-barred discussion about loss. It took time and coaching, but it was able to happen over a period of seasons.

A year later a core group of 75 took our first bereavement training program. Those who had retired early from many different walks of life had found the common denominator of faith to be their foundation. They worked in teams and recognized that, while they all read and studied various professional resources, they would eventually need to incorporate their own personalities, strengths, and talents into a team approach. They were wounded at some point in their life, and they began a foundation that now serves 7,500 people a year in pastoral bereavement counseling. Relationships from various corners of the faith community have the power to heal.

Mercy for the deceased and comfort for the bereaved are essential for all involved in this spiritual affirmation of grief and growth. The first permission to live again is bestowed by the community and embraced by the sufferer of loss. Religious communities are testing places for first solo experiences without one's lifetime partner. It is important for these communities to welcome the newly single person into social as well as religious events. Interactions between the congregation and the bereaved allow for healing because members of the community hold out hope and belief even when there is no relief in sight. Can one survive with the hopes of another? Are these spiritual connections real? Can they satisfy the human hunger for connectedness after loss? The answer is yes.

The human desire for the transcendent is greater than ever as we enter a new millennium. Bereavement care calls a community to an adventure in faith.

The transition from closeness to time alone must be negotiated delicately by the caregiver and the bereaved. It requires great patience from the caregiver and great tolerance by the bereaved. If a major loss is perceived as precipitating an identity crisis in which the cycles of life are disrupted, the spiritual community can provide an environment for natural re-entry into life and retreat from the uncertainty of the new and changed world.

Through careful listening we are able to enter, as far as possible, into the collapsed world of the bereaved. Sensitivity to the restructuring of the physical, mental, emotional, and social dimensions of humanness can help the caregiver make appropriate and meaningful responses to the bereaved person's choices. The promise of presence even in the valley of the shadow of death is fulfilled through the presence of spiritual people, ordained and lay, who incarnate the trustworthiness of that promise. It begins the restoration of safety, security, true recognition of a new world, and a response that both sufferer and community believe.

Empowering the Laity for Bereavement Ministry

Several methods exist for developing a group of lay specialists in order to call a religious community into action at the death of one of its members. There are numerous advantages in having a group of trained and supervised lay bereavement caregivers. First, it can bypass a potential clergy—laity barrier within a given community and may ease a lapsed member's return to the community by eliminating the need to become reacquainted first with clergy. This initial return to the community is often a testing of the waters for future connections. Second, it invites members of the congregation who have experienced a death in the family to reinvest some of their energy into service. Third, it can prevent the congregation from withdrawing from suffering people out of feelings of inadequacy. Such a loss of support from the community may cause the bereaved to conclude wrongly that this loss is too much to bear and too difficult to share. Depression or chronic grief, if present, could intensify the reasons for further withdrawal and isolation, thus increasing the possibility of chronic and complicated mourning. And last, there is a stabilizing and healing effect on the grieving person when the community of faith reinforces religious hope and meaning. The New Testament advises us to "call upon the elders and to pray for healing."

Know the People of Your Community

Many wonderful bereavement groups have developed in the United States. Some have been created by the wounded who have now moved on to healing and restoration, some have sprung forth from allied professions (medical, nursing, hospice, and funeral affiliates), and some have developed because a caring community of religious leadership and membership believed that more must be done for those who grieve.

Many successful efforts begin by observing the people you already know in your congregation and in the larger community. The age of the community, at either extreme, might reveal the types of death losses sustained by a community. Later widowhood is at one extreme and perinatal loss is at the other. Mobile and urban communities might serve these needs but may also want to consider parental loss suffered by middle-aged and older adults. Children, of course, need adequate care at many stages of development.

The present and future make-up of the community will suggest the kinds of resources that you may want to develop. Touching base with local school personnel, visiting nurse associations, geriatric physicians, and funeral service providers will give you good information along the planning stages. The initial efforts of a small or even larger community should take into account the needs that should be addressed immediately. Start at a point where you can be effective and in a framework in which the community will be able to view your initial effectiveness. Relationships with the local press will be very important at this time. Those who are in the initial leadership positions for planning bereavement ministries should observe other local and national models that work in communities similar to your home congregation or community.

Foster Allied Relationships

Try to get as many community leaders on board as possible. Write an initial letter to allied professionals. Get permission to duplicate articles from professional bereavement organizations or brochures from other communities that address the need for aftercare or describe successful models. If you are in a church or synagogue, seek permission to gather data from the congregation about their own loss, recovery, and bereavement concerns. Share this information with the wider community of professionals. Ask the local press to reprint some bereavement materials at important seasons of the year. Seek sponsorships to help launch your program.

Educate the Community

An initial sponsorship may provide the funds for a local evening of community education. Ask members of the community to aid you in a special presentation. Most would welcome such an opportunity to be allied with your positive ideas. Consider seasonal presentations around holiday times and religious traditions. Collaborate with neighboring places of worship and service agencies to add to your potential audience. A shorter professional presentation with follow-up discussion groups led by prepared facilitators might be an appropriate opportunity to hear the needs of the community. A brief evaluation, such as the following, could be helpful for future programming:

- First Name
- Type of loss experience and when
- How did you learn about this program?
- What is the most difficult part of grief for you?
- Would you be willing to spend an hour a week for eight weeks to help your recovery?
- Who can provide ongoing leadership for this community?

Once you have touched the awareness of the community and gathered some data about the nature of the loss experiences of your community, the type of outreach needed should become clear. With evaluations in hand and with a positive tone set by the initial community presentation, consider the available community resources that would best be able to respond with existing programs. Share the information you have gathered at the meeting. If there are no existing programs to meet the needs that surfaced in your community assessment, approach some professionals who may now wish to volunteer some time or perhaps provide an initial group session for a fee that would be appropriate for the community. If it seems that a fee would discourage the community from responding to a program, consider sponsorship from allied organizations or a cluster of local religious communities. The most important thing is that you begin with a follow-up.

Let's consider the possibility that you are the only one available with the interest in providing this outreach and the time to do so. Don't give up—start smaller. Perhaps you may not yet feel comfortable about leading a bereavement support group, but you know that you will one day move in that direction. Again, consider another type of offering, perhaps an informal gathering to read one of the many introductory books on grief and loss followed by three weeks of discussion led by a compassionate friend—you! This format can last for a year and perhaps put six books into circulation, with each member paying for his or her own materials. During this initial time of your leadership, consider the next phase for yourself and the bereaved community.

Ongoing Education and Training for You

If this is your first experience but you feel the call and motivation to provide community care, then make a bold acknowledgment: There is something bigger than you that is calling you to this outreach activity. And if you can make that statement, honor it and believe it. Trust your instincts. You are about to begin one of the most rewarding outreach services that a community and its membership can provide—community bereavement care.

Begin by reading everything about loss and bereavement that you can get your hands on, and by attending various one-day workshops. Choose programs carefully. Ask others in the community about the organizations that advertise locally and regionally.

Make sure that advertising materials don't promise too much. Inquire about personal as well as technical skills addressed by the programming. While lectures are important for the gathering of initial information, attend programs that will also answer your questions. Call the program facilitators and tell them what you are doing. If they take time to speak with you, then you may consider that training program. If they are too busy or promise too much, stay away. Give some caution to certification specialists who are all about their certificate and offer no follow-up or ongoing supervision for you. You may want to consider programs that offer you ongoing affiliation with them and those who have some connection to national leadership presenters.

One area for self-supervision in the ongoing educational process is to journal for yourself. Journal entries should be made each day. What does loss mean to you? How have you responded to dying, death, and healing in your own history? After a discussion with a bereavement group, go home and write a few notes about what transpired during the session. Reflect upon any themes that continue to surface for the group as well as some of the individual members. These are your private notes, not a diagnosis. They are for your eyes only and should not be shared with anyone, even with the group members.

Consider Bereavement Connections

As someone seeking to be a bereavement caregiver in the context of a religious congregation, you will want a training program that integrates a spiritual dimension. If you are confronted with training that avoids spiritual concerns for fear of imposing religious or spiritual beliefs upon a group, it is safe to say that you will not be happy with this kind of training. It will probably not provide you with an integration of your own personal orientation and technical skills. If grief affects the body, mind, and spirit, then a caregiver will give careful attention to the integrated skills that are part of a training program.

I first discovered a nondenominational approach to bereavement resources and spiritual connections in the work of Rev. Richard Gilbert of Indiana. He built a bereavement network for spiritual caregivers called *Connections*. This national outreach attracts callers in faith crisis and in faith fullness. Many are women and men who are standing still in their grief due to their long-term separation from their religious community. The reasons for this separation are not important in the first telephone call. The acceptance of the receiver on the other end is often their first vehicle in the resolution of grief. Sight unseen, they experience non-abandonment. Perhaps it is called grace, perhaps *mitzvah*.

It begins with the shaky dialing of an unfamiliar telephone number, and the response of an unseen believer in the healing process on the other end of the line. The call may eventually lead to a local support group, or referral to a book or tape, or perhaps to an impressive article or bibliography. You have connected with the World Pastoral Care Center and their bereavement network. It is a grassroots spiritual center that provides national resources for the local participant who needs to be integrated with bereavement training, as well as the veteran who needs to be refreshed and nourished during a time of caregiver frustration.

Your call to the World Pastoral Care Center won't provide a miracle, but it will restore your belief in yourself and affirm your talents and desire to pursue bereavement care. It is a quiet restoration of hope through a telephone or fax link. It is not a miracle. It is a marvelous connection.

The initial therapeutic alliance in healing therapies throughout various programs of aftercare begins with the person of the caregiver. It continues in the congregation's membership. It is silent and it is active. It continues on each day of worship.

Concentration on the rites of passage in times of joy and in sorrow calls forth a theology of liberation, of freedom to accept God and one another. Most religious communities can incorporate teachings about dying and rising into ceremonies that mark faith at different stages of the life cycle. A public marking of rites of passage is a wholesome spirituality that can decrease fear and increase hope within a local community. It is a gentle surrender to the seasons of life.

Opportunities for a discussion of life issues will present themselves many times in the life of a religious community. These opportunities will occur during key social and religious moments. In a recent marriage preparation session, a pastor asked the young couple what they thought the last phase of marriage would be.

After some silence, the pastor reminded the two vivacious aspirants to marriage that one day—even if very far away—one of them will experience widowhood. One will survive the other. It was not a morbid subject but, rather, a natural inclusion of a reference to the transitions of life within the seasons of religious commitment—in this case, a sacred marriage covenant.

Good spiritual care demands that we fully develop our gifts to counsel and comfort the brokenhearted and to rejoice in the transformation contained in the legitimate season of mourning. Mourning is the healing process. The tools of medicine and psychology make us better practitioners of a discipline. Mourning is a call to liberate the brokenhearted, to bind up those who are in sorrow, and to call those in prison to freedom. It is a call to healing in the reflection of the face of the God of Abraham, Isaac, and Jacob.

These reflections are an attempt to reinforce what is already available in the religious community. They represent a longing to see a liberation for healing that is inherent in every man, woman, and child. Can it be found in the secular? The answer is on the front page of every town newspaper. Consider where the journey will begin.

How important is the task of the religious leadership in times of loss? How vital is this function? Let us borrow from a description often quoted by Rabbi Jacob Goldberg, an elder in bereavement caregiving in the US. He asked me if I, as a psychologist, would give at least one hour to hearing the story of those who mourn. "Why an hour?" I asked. Rabbi Goldberg replied: "To leave enough time to help them to praise the Lord, for he is good; to sing praise to our God, for he is gracious; to help them to rebuild Jerusalem in the midst of their dying and living." Bereavement caregivers are called and gifted. They are formed, not born. They are people who are strong, loving, and wise.

Patrick M. Del Zoppo, PhD, CAS, is a Clinical/Pastoral Psychologist and director of Family Ministry for the Catholic Diocese of Rockville Centre, New York. His clinical associations in hospice care are with Visiting Nurse Hospice Care of New York and the Catholic Medical Centers of New York.

Practical Suggestions

What Faith Communities Can Do to Help

Grief affects us everywhere—at work, at school, at worship. Grief involves spiritual issues as one struggles to ask and to explore the meaning of loss. In this way, support from one's faith community can be a critical resource for persons who are struggling with grief and loss—whether the loss involves illness, death, or any significant change.

Acknowledge the Loss, Accept Grief

- Listen as grieving persons struggle with their beliefs
- Remember grievers at different points in their struggle—holidays, birthdays, anniversaries
- Use ritual

Provide Tangible Help by:

- Offering respite care
- Helping with meals or child care
- Assisting with housing or transporting out-of-town relatives or friends
- Helping to prepare food for the funeral
- Assisting with other tasks such as lawn or home care
- Being aware of other community resources, such as hospice
- Training ministry teams to visit the ill and bereaved
- Offering programs for the bereaved, such as a program on how to cope with the holidays
- Sponsoring self-help groups for the bereaved
- Creating a library of books, tapes, and videos that can assist grieving individuals

Getting Help

While it is difficult to deal with situations involving illness and loss, you do not have to face these situations alone. Your local hospice or mental health agency can be of help. Professional organizations such as Hospice Foundation of America are available to assist in finding local resources.

These tips are summarized from a brochure entitled *Living With Grief: At Worship*, a publication of the Hospice Foundation of America. Contact HFA for more detailed information and suggestions.

Part IV

Living With Grief:
At Home

Of course, one of the places where we grieve is at home. There we grieve with our intimate network, a group composed of those people—both kin and others—with whom we most regularly interact and on whom we depend for support. A future book will need to explore the many ways in which family and friends facilitate or complicate grief. The goal of this section is more modest. Primarily, it seeks to emphasize the powerful role that caregiving can have—both for those receiving and giving.

MacPherson's chapter, which begins this section, is distilled from her book *She Came To Live Out Loud*. It is the inspiring story of Anna Johannessen, who struggled with breast cancer, and of her family's reflections on her illness and subsequent death. Anna, like many of us, created her community, one that sustained her throughout her illness and supports her family afterward.

Lund's chapter emphasizes a similar point. He notes that in retirement communities, and other communities where elderly live, many individuals are touched by loss. Yet it is often these bereaved spouses who are best able to offer support. Lund's report is the first research that has validated the folk wisdom that by reaching out to support others in their grief, one helps oneself as well.

Finally, Miller's wise and poetic chapter closes this book near where it began. While caregiving does offer benefits to the caregiver, it also takes a toll. Effective self-care remains essential.

Fourteen

Caregiving Communities

Myra MacPherson

A journalist in the nation's capital once commented on the condition of people who migrate to urban areas to pursue careers. "In Washington, there are few families," he said; "therefore friends become family." Even in rural areas today it is common for some members of the family to be separated by miles. And so, increasingly, friends and the families who live close by form a community of essential companions, especially in times of need during illness and dying. This community of friends joins in an intense and complex intimacy during this process. Afterward, they share the same deep mourning as the family, often accompanied by uplifting, and sometimes haunting, memories of the death process.

These friendships, which become crucial elements in one's life, often begin in a larger community context—through churches or PTA meetings, at work or in the house next door, at the gym or on the golf course. If one is lucky—perhaps "loving" is a better word than lucky—a handful of these friends will grow into cherished members of one's special, private world.

Anna Johannessen, a feisty, wise, and witty baby boomer who battled breast cancer for years, is a classic example of a person for whom love given is love returned. In the years and months and weeks and days before she died, Anna was sustained by not only her family but also a phalanx of friends gleaned over decades through her various careers or community activities such as acting and ballet, softball and school functions. Anna was deeply moved by friends she met through her daughter's ballet school, Patty Williams and Jane Bittner, who took a hospice volunteer course in order to be better caregivers.

This article details a small part of the story of Anna and her friends and family—those moments when they became caregivers during her dying days. But before one can understand the level of synergy and deep commitment to Anna by her community of friends and family, one has to know a bit about Anna and the magical gift of life she gave to others. Anna's personality was electrifying; the bottle was always half full. She came into this world to live out loud and did so all the way to the end. Her compassion was matched by her honesty, which allowed—almost forced—those around her to treat her illness realistically, thus easing everyone's awkwardness. Friends comment on how Anna sustained them during her illness as much as they sustained her. She was able to redefine her life in positive ways, shifting her goals to accommodate each medical development; because she had hope for so long, friends and family felt the same and were able to enjoy her fully. As her mother-in-law Phoebe Johannessen said, "It is impossible to be depressed around Anna."

Her closest friend for nearly 20 years, Lockie Fuller, met Anna in Richmond, Virginia, when they were both teachers and then became next door neighbors. When Anna developed breast cancer in her late thirties, her candid approach melted the stigma of illness and trauma for her children ("I explained everything," she said) and for friends like Lockie. "When Anna's mastectomy happened, my impression was that everyone has fear of the unknown," recalls Lockie. "We think, 'What should I say; how should I react; am I saying the right thing; how do I talk to her?' My advice is don't act any other way than you would naturally. Just be there. Don't be afraid of it."

When Anna's breast cancer metastasized, Lockie recalls, "It's one thing to talk about illness, but when someone starts talking about 'How are my kids going to grow up without me?' and 'What my funeral plans are. . . .'" Lockie's eyes watered and she halted, then started again. "The first time Anna started saying those things, I thought it was a little weird. But if she wanted to talk about it, that was fine. I didn't exactly know what to say because no one had shared these thoughts with me before, but I felt it was terrific that she could. And I learned from that."

Anna cherished Lockie for her reaction to her illness. "You crave that! We have normal conversations, but if I want to talk about the disease and what it is doing to me, I can," she once said. "Some people aren't accepting and shy away from listening to a person talk about illness, disfigurement, or dying. It's not easy to listen to someone deal with it and talk about it. Lockie's always been able to listen to this straight on. And I know she's always paying attention." Anna touched Lockie's arm. "People who aren't as comfortable with letting me deal with this illness on that personal a level, shut down. They want to hear that everything's okay." Anna's thoughts echo those of bereavement counselors: The art of listening—really listening—to a sick or dying friend is a key element of caregiving. One doesn't have to act as if one has all the answers. The most insensitive form of conversing is to compare illnesses or immediately to spin off into some story of one's own.

Years went by as a determined Anna battled her spreading cancer. In the opinion of her oncologist, her positive attitude and need for involvement, to know all she could about her illness and treatment, prolonged her life. Anna was an inspiration to her family, perhaps even more because she was no plaster saint, dutifully accepting her fate. There were despairing moods and sometimes rages. More often, however, Anna's optimism took over. "Hey, I'm living with cancer, not dying from it—yet. I may beat this sucker!" she said. "I'm a fast one to put regrets behind me. Mine is not a 'coulda, woulda, shoulda' life. I don't live in the past and I can't see the future." Anna could not always keep to this maxim; emotional "nose dives" occurred when she obsessed about what would happen to her children, Ellery and Lindsay (who grew from toddlers to adolescents during her illness), or when she reflected on a lost career or not living to an old age with Jan, the husband she had loved since she was 16.

Anger, such a natural companion for those who are dying and for their caregiving friends and family, was no stranger to Anna. She raged at officials regarding the incompetence of the medical profession and the breakdown of the health and insurance system. During one of her blue days, Anna sobbed about leaving her children, then called her sister Ro (her closest relative next to Jan), who had had breast cancer more than 20 years before. Ro had undergone drastic surgery, the removal of all estrogen sources including her adrenal glands, and lives to talk about it. Anna screamed to her sister, "God dammit, why were you the lucky one? You don't have kids. Why am I not the lucky one?"

For the person who is dying, anger is validated by the professionals who instruct caregivers that it can take the form of unpleasant ferocity at everything and everyone around her, or it can be a more compassionate venting that seeks no target. "They are angry because of the losses they are experiencing, and they are angry because others—apparently for no justifiable reason—are enjoying happy, healthy, and satisfying lives," write Charles Corr, Donna Corr, and Clyde Nabe (1997) in *Death and Dying, Life and Living*. They instruct caregivers in understanding that it is reasonable to expect such strong feelings will be expressed and for them to learn to listen empathetically.

Like many who are ill, Anna used humor to vent her anger in a non–confrontational fashion. Recognized for its healing and pain-killing power, humor can make life more bearable. "It distances us from the indignities of diagnosis and treatment. It helps restore our common humanity. It dispels fear" (Jevne and Levitan, 1989, p. 136). During a time of remission Anna felt so good that she joked about the book in progress about her life; the former ad copy writer cracked, "This may be the first time that I have missed a deadline."

Anger and macabre humor, of course, are not reserved for patients alone. Caregivers and family members can experience plenty of both. Often their anger is compounded by a sense of helplessness. It is not uncommon for them to rail at doctors, hospitals, insurance companies, hospices, or any one else in the medical system who is not curing the person they love. Anna watched sadly as her sister's anger and anguish over what she termed inadequate medical treatment embittered her.

Anna said, "You cannot dwell on it or you'll go crazy." Her suggestion to the seriously ill to keep from obsessing about their plight is, "Think about other people. Do things for other people. Involve yourself with others. I've done that all my life. I have friends who say to me, 'I can't believe it, here you are in your situation, and I've just spent two hours complaining about some trivial matter and you're listening and giving me support and advice.'" Little do they know that they are giving Anna a gift by treating her as one of them. "Find things to do that make you feel good," says Anna. "You can still have a very fulfilling life and a very good time."

And so the Johannessens continued to live a life of abnormal normalcy—a life lived, with varying degrees of success, by hundreds of thousands daily in a world where medical advances have made prolonged illness common. The daily minutiae continued, except for moments of panic or sorrow or pain: groceries to buy, dinner to fix, dogs to walk, laundry and homework and house repairs to do, bills to pay, school and jobs to attend, PTA and school athletics or ballet. Abnormal normalcy.

Every one of her friends and family learned to savor the precious time they had with Anna. Jan and Anna were childhood sweethearts and their love remained strong, a wonderful source of comfort for them both. There were months of remission, then months of painful chemotherapy treatments. The roller coaster existence ended when finally there came the time when nothing further could be done to prolong her life.

Anna made the decision to go off chemo when it no longer halted the rapid growth of tumors in her liver: "Why am I poisoning myself to the point that I can't function anymore? I'm puking my guts out. I want a drug holiday. I feel that while I'm alive, I'm alive, dammit. I'm not a piece of chemical crap running around."

For weeks Anna felt better; her energy increased, she could even go to lunch with friends. Four swift months later she was dead. In those months, Anna's fierce independence gave way slowly; now it was time for her community of friends and family to do for this woman who usually did for others.

Anna's major decision was whether to die at home. Because she feared it would traumatize her children, Anna's instinct was, "don't die at home." Anna had wisely found a bereavement counselor who worked with her children for more than a year before she died. Dottie Ward-Wimmer became another warm friend in Anna's community and proved invaluable for the children. She made Anna realize that it was important not to shut the children out of this crucial decision ("Write it in pencil so that any one can change their minds if they feel like it") and that Ellery and Lindsay, now 12 and 11, needed to continue their caregiving roles; helping her eat, fetching items, letting her lean on them as she walked. "Kids are traumatized by things that they don't understand, by things that they can't participate in, and by things that they don't have a place to process afterwards. It's an open wound and it never has a chance to heal. Children are not necessarily traumatized [by witnessing dying]," said Ward-Wimmer. "Because one of the things that's going to comfort them afterward is knowing that they did everything they could do for you. It's not really where [one dies], it's how we deal with it." She disabuses Anna of the notion that the changes in her appearance will be too much for them. "They're looking at you every day. They're not looking at you physically. They're looking in your eyes. They're cuddling up to you. They don't know whether they're lying on a boob or a rib. They're lying on Mommy. Allowing them to help is very important. It's a terrible feeling to be shut out. It's much better for you, too, to be around them even if being around them is hard, because it allows you to be included and not isolated and it allows you to be able to participate and to give something. And later they will have that enormous comfort—'I gave, I tried. We did everything we could do.'"

Freed from her fears, and with the consent of her immediate family, Anna elected to die at home. Her husband says he never wavered. "I never would have forgiven myself if I had let her go to some institution." One night toward the end, Anna broke into a wild fury with such strength that it took four people to restrain her. Later Jan said, "Can you imagine how scared she'd be waking up [in that state] in a hospital room with no one she knows around her? If she can get this agitated even with us? Last night was very difficult for Lindsay, but I still don't think she'd want her mother to go anywhere."

One is struck by the absolute naturalness of Anna's dying at home, surrounded by her family and a cadre of friends, so many in fact that Jan had to ask them to come early and leave before Ellery and Lindsay returned from school. The inundation left them with no privacy, necessary for the coping process of adolescents.

The Johannessen house took on the appearance of a command post, with Jan, unfailingly polite as always, scheduling shifts of Anna's volunteer friends. Roseann, Anna's sister, would return from her New York home soon to stay indefinitely. Jan had not shaved and a dazed look occasionally overtook him, but he experienced an amazing adrenaline high, juggling detail after detail—up with Anna in the middle of night, up at 5:30 to get the children ready for school, racing to the office if he felt Anna was well covered, hugging everyone who came into the house, spending time with Anna and the children after everyone left, then on the phone with Ro. The kitchen was filled with comfort food: donuts and carrot cake, spaghetti and pizza, deli sandwiches, soups, and salads brought by the gang. Jan's uniform was shorts, flip flops, and a t-shirt. He took to putting the constantly ringing cellular phone in his shorts pocket as he moved energetically around the house. His customary, "Hi there," greeted everyone. Members of another community, the place where he worked as a scientist, also contributed—bosses and co-workers assured him that he should take all the time he needed to be with Anna. Many attended her memorial service.

For as long as possible Anna lay curled up in her special corner of the living room sofa, joining in with friends, or walking around the block with the designated caregiver of the moment. Then, with shocking speed, cancer consumed Anna and she spent the rest of her days in bed. The ravages of malignancy, the fluids in the liver, had so swollen her stomach that Anna looked five months pregnant. Roseann cut out her shorts and sweat pants at the waist for comfort. No matter how prepared Anna was to die, no one was ready for the quickness. She never got the chance to write letters to her children to be read at various milestones in their lives. Anna had planned a video, but the progression was so fast that she did not want to be immortalized as she looked then.

The contrast between a sterile hospital and her home was vivid. On her first day, a hospice nurse crisply urged a hospital bed after she noticed Jan putting Vaseline on Anna's lips. "Her mouth gets dry, sometimes she breathes with her mouth open," he explained. "Raising her head up will help with her breathing," insisted the nurse. "The hospice likes twin beds that you can raise and lower. If there is only one aide or caregiver you can turn her much easier. It's more comfortable."

But Jan would not hear of it. He and Anna had made a pact: For the children's sake Anna wanted the bedroom to look as natural as possible. And they wished to be able to sleep together to the end. The king size bed with its green down comforter became a magic carpet for friends and family. Anna was not in pain as they sprawled around her, hugging, stroking her arm, leaning close to have intimate conversations. When she grimaced slightly or moaned, they were ready with morphine. Unencumbered by visiting hours, they came and went at will; Anna was almost never alone. Without bed rails, they could hold her hand with ease, sitting on a chair next to the bed. The ubiquitous fare of hospitals—loud, intrusive TV shows complete with cackling laugh tracks—was absent in Anna's room; classical music flowed soothingly on tape.

The cruelest blow was that Anna lost her ability to voice her thoughts. She had so hoped to tell it all, up to the end. This horrible irony, the loss of Anna's talent for expressive verbalization, was not caused by medication, experts feel. "Morphine just doesn't do that," says William Lamers, a physician and psychiatrist and premier hospice consultant who in 40 years has witnessed close to 3,000 patients and families go through the death process. "I've seen people on massive doses of morphine whose speech remains lucid. It is more likely lesions in the brain. Almost all kinds of tumors are little cellular factories that can produce complicated chemicals. We know for instance that lung tumors can produce neurotransmitters that influence brain activity. Breast tumors can do the same. There's a state of confusion, agitation, delirium that results purely from the products of the cancer cells themselves. It's not terribly well examined because it is usually seen in the extreme circumstance when the patient is nearing death and the focus of those treating them is to keep them comfortable. I've seen this so many times."

Still, watching her friends and family commune with Anna, one could see that the tie was unbroken. When Anna awoke, her gibberish was often indecipherable, but her calm face, the upraised eyebrows greeting reassured everyone that Anna knew she was surrounded by friends. Everyone was convinced that Anna could hear them, aware that hearing is the last sense to go. One of the best at this one-way communicating was Anna's long time friend, Wayne Westbrook. The phone was held to Anna's ear when he called from Richmond, carrying on in an effortless manner that some people find so easy, and others envy, when dealing with the dying. Wayne did his monologue, his laughter coursing through the phone.

"Remember when we did this?" He sang snatches of favorite songs. "I know you can't talk so I'll just talk, and I know you can hear me. Love you, Anna." Anna's eyes would open at times, then close. Later that night, Lindsay came in to kiss her mother good night, then went to the piano. As the lyrical piece wafted through the house, Anna tried to sit up. Leaning on friends, she rocked slowly. As she listened to her daughter playing, tears ran down her cheeks.

One afternoon, four old Richmond friends arrived, by happenstance, at the same time. Tina McCarthy and Lockie drove up together and whooped when they saw the two others, whom they had not seen in ages. Red wine was uncorked as they sat on the bed, talking to Anna constantly, singing, joking. When Tina and Lockie said, "Anna, let's party," Anna smiled with her eyes closed. She also cried with happiness when Tina and Lockie told her they had made up and had driven up together. They had quarreled earlier in the year, and their rift had deeply troubled Anna. Their reunion made her dying days happier.

Reconciliation—either the patient dealing with discord in his or her life or a reuniting of others within the circle—can be most important. Often the dying will hang on until this resolution is achieved.

The next morning Anna awoke with a smile on her face and said to her friends, with astonishing clarity, "Let's party!" The nurse checking her vital signs said, "She's very happy this morning." Tina responded, "She partied last night." Lockie laughed. "It's a happiness hangover."

By noon that day, an assembly line of friends was with Anna. She complied when they began to roll her slightly to change her diapers but emitted a slight moan. Morphine was dripped into her mouth. Anna did not protest as her old friend bathed her bottom, an indignity she would have fought a few weeks before. Others reached for ointment and efficiently diapered Anna. All the while they kept murmuring endearingly. "It's okay, babe," said Lockie, leaning close to her, "You're worn out from partying." Tina hugged and kissed her. Speaking into Anna's ear, Lockie said, "We love you. We're going back to Richmond now. See ya soon."

As Jan and the children left one night, to celebrate Ellery's 13th birthday with tickets to a Bill Cosby concert that Anna had purchased months ago, four women friends tended to Anna. Scrubbed, hair brushed smooth, wearing Walt Disney pajamas, Anna looked like a docile child. At soft commands, she opened her mouth to drink water one sip at a time, took drops of morphine, swallowed tiny spoonfuls of sherbet (hospice nurses informed them that ice cream can create mucus which makes breathing more difficult). Human bodies, instead of a cranked up bed, supported Anna. Anna sucked on a mix of crushed ice cubes and Gatorade. When asked if she wanted Jell-O, Anna's eyebrows went up. At times, Anna seemed agitated, moving her head with slight grimaces, spreading a curled hand over her face.

Although Anna's friends and family were comforted in the knowledge that she was getting the best care possible—theirs—it is important not to romanticize caregiving. It can be trying under the best of circumstances and brutal at worst, depending on the patient or the situation. Yet for many who care for loved ones at home, the benefits can be enormous. Despite sadness, emotional and physical exhaustion, and disagreeable chores, the gratification, even joy, of helping relieve pain and suffering can be manifold. Many remember with pride that Anna was kept mostly pain free, that she did not get one bedsore, and that she never lay in dirty diapers. They kept the bedroom spotless, did mountains of laundry. Caregiving cama-raderie, a raw closeness seldom found in day-to-day living, can be a blessed memory for the rest of one's life.

In some situations, rivalries and disagreements among care-givers over treatment can be ruinous, as everyone fights for his or her moment with the dying. When Ro came to take over, along with Jan, it was natural that friends took a back seat. But everything worked smoothly. Ro recognized their need to spend private time with Anna and stepped out of the room accordingly. She also rec-ognized and was grateful for their enormous help.

The local hospice was slow to act when first called and Jan felt that he needed more instructions about what to do or what to expect. However, Jan, who seldom left Anna's side, learned much from the friends who had taken hospice courses. He felt he never could have succeeded with hospice alone, without Ro and Anna's friends.

There were rough moments when Anna went into a high agita-tion that lasted for hours; not an unusual phenomenon. The ambivalence that the dying can experience was evident in Anna's last days. On one hand, she had accepted her death; but on the other, she fought its swiftness, anguishing over her unfinished life with her children. Friends and family reassured her that she had done a fine job and that everything was in order. Anna had handled everything from wills, to the telephone tree to alert friends of her death, to funeral arrangements. She had always said that it was perfectly selfish for anyone with a prolonged illness to leave this work to loved ones. Now they told her that she could go, giving her a vitally important gift—permission to die.

Being with Anna to the last helped ease the grief of the caregivers. They had been with her at every step. There were few illusions left. A friend who was with Anna just hours before she died noticed that she looked peaceful, as if she were between worlds. Her friend did not cry; the Anna she had known was no longer in that frail body. She hoped the end would be soon. Death came early one morning when just Ro and Jan were with her, after the children had left for school. It is not unreasonable to assume that Anna had waited until they were away to die.

No matter how prepared a family is, no matter how thorough a patient is in pre-arranging the "unpleasant details," as Jan calls them, survivors can be overwhelmed by the cold technicalities that intrude on their grief at its rawest. Arranging for the body to be taken away; picking out caskets or urns; signing paperwork with funeral homes, hospitals or hospice; notifying newspapers and writing obituaries; alerting friends; and planning funerals or memorial services are some of the emotion-fraught decisions that must be made.

One of Jan's hardest tasks was going to school to pick up the children and telling them their mother had died. The bereavement counselor had stressed that Lindsay and Ellery should be given the chance to see her if they wanted. Anna lay peacefully in a fresh gown when the children arrived to say goodbye to their mother, sobbing as they hugged all the caregiving friends and family. When Jan took them for a trip to a nearby mountain for the rest of the day, the duties for Ro and Anna's friends were just beginning.

Funeral home attendants arrived and took Anna's body. Jane and Dottie stripped and changed the bed. Roseann and Margaret, the hospice nurse, took care of hospice papers, and then Margaret hugged everyone as she left. Earlier disagreements with hospice were history; Margaret was praised by everyone. Jane and Patty stayed with Roseann to keep her company. Ann Wylie house-sat until equipment was picked up. Jane drove Roseann to the funeral home.

Anna, typically, had picked a small independent funeral home where the owner actually gave them advice on how to save money. One final act was pure Anna. Anyone who knew her even slightly smiled when they learned of it. Tucked under Roseann's arm on the way to the funeral home was a container for Anna's ashes, an old cookie jar that Ro had given Anna and Jan when they were first married. It is a white ceramic Cheshire cat, with a wonderful black bow of a grin, whiskers, and mischievous shiny eyes. No one who knew Anna could think of a better final resting place.

The owner suggested that the memorial be held somewhere other than the funeral home, which can leave a negative, lasting effect on the children. Ro added, "She also felt that it's not a good idea to display the urn—and that is done in a funeral home. She was very gracious and helpful. She stressed some place that the kids could accept. Children seldom get the opportunity to hear how people feel about their parents and it would be a lasting, positive memory." Jan settled on a Quaker-style memorial service. Anna's father was too ill and depressed to attend, so the service was videotaped to take to him in Florida.

A sentiment that Roseann repeated often and with urgency was her desire to "get everything back to normal," and that the house be "as normal as possible" when Jan and the children returned from the mountain on Wednesday. This quest for normalcy is a common reminder of how little time we allow for grieving. Yet being disoriented, numb, distracted, relieved, anguished is normal at this stage. Lindsay chose to return to school the next day; it seemed to be her haven. Ellery stayed home and kept to himself. Roseann's pain was deep. "I had gone through this with my mother, and now with Anna, and it left me with the feeling of being left to bury everybody, and this is very hard on me." Some of Roseann's tears were for herself and for the heavy weight that life's circumstances had placed on her. "I feel that's what I'm being left to do—to take care of everybody at the end." She doesn't mention that she may feel, as some designated family caregivers do, that no one understands what a task this is. She is grateful for every friend of Anna's who thought of her during this time—particularly Jane and Patty, who stayed with her on the day Anna died. "It makes you feel very good when you witness such unconditional giving."

Memorial services, often termed "Celebrations of Life," have become increasingly a substitute for the traditional funeral. Certainly that was Anna's preference. More than 300 friends and family gathered in the social hall of a church, looking much like a picnic brought inside: men in sports shirts, women in flowing summer dresses, babes in arms, friends of all colors and creeds. They waited in a long line to reach the front, where a casket or urn might have been. Instead, there were two large display boards, filled with snap shots and enlargements of pictures of Anna, the glamorous mixed with the clowning. Friends came prepared, some with brand new Kleenex boxes placed by their chairs, but the many grinning faces of Anna before them produced smiles rather than tears.

In this Family Life Building, children's rainbow pictures decorated rather than stained glass. Instead of pews, folding chairs lined the room and faced the "altar" of Anna's pictures, a comforting, encircling configuration of friends. Patty Williams, who had held Anna against her chest so many times in those days when she was fed water or morphine, was in red and white polka dots. "I picked out the brightest dress I could find for Anna."

Jan had opted for no music, just uninterrupted expressions of bearing witness. There were no prayers, no dignitaries, no official speakers, no clergy, no flowers. Anna had requested that donations be sent to favorite causes. Mixed in with the many humorous memories were expressions of love and acknowledgment of loss, a necessary component in bringing closure. Much later, Jan recalls, "I had a difficult time getting through the memorial, but was helped by looking at the sea of friends and relatives. Many of the kids' teachers and friends came as well." Feeling surrounded by their own friends helped Ellery and Lindsay immensely; they smiled more than they cried.

Although well-meaning friends often say, "If there is anything I can do, please call me," Anna's friend Jane Bittner warns that most people in grief don't call. It is important to anticipate, then do it. One group that has been forced through horrific experience into becoming professionals when it comes to grief are members of the gay community. Don Wilder Plett, who lost his lover and partner, Alan Wilder, said, "Everything has become so very well rehearsed that everyone knows how to react and to help. They just do it. The food just comes. Some clients sent over a team of maids who cleaned the whole house. Instead of flowers, people send things that can live—like potted plants. All of a sudden I heard the lawn mower—someone had come over to cut the lawn for me."

Unfortunately, after the first three months, friends and family often return to their lives and real mourning and loneliness set in. The first year following Anna's death was very hard on Jan. The children chose to keep their thoughts to themselves. When grades fell, Jan consulted a bereavement counselor, but the children seemed to need few sessions. Their adjustment seemed a positive example of how grief work in advance can cushion the blow. Jan, though harried with his grief and role as a single parent, did find time to give vent to his feelings. Like many men, Jan had been conditioned to hold back his feelings but, "I have definitely found the therapeutic effects of crying. Afterward you feel like you have run the marathon." Then, slowly, he began getting on with his life, knowing it would never again be the same, never be as it was with Anna.

But he and Anna's caregiving friends remain comforted, knowing they were able to give Anna a good life to the very end. As time went by, their more vivid memories were of Anna the friend of boundless energy and unpredictable fun. Smiles replaced tears. One commented that the emptiness of life without Anna is considerable. "But just think how terrible it would be never to have known her. That's what sustains me."

Following a long career covering politics, journalist Myra MacPherson has moved into the realm of grief and dying. MacPherson is the author of two previously acclaimed best-selling works of nonfiction. MacPherson specialized in politics and social issues for many years with the Washington Post.

Fifteen

Giving and Receiving Help During Later Life Spousal Bereavement

Dale A. Lund

There is no single way to cope with grief that will be effective for everyone. No shortcuts or guarantees exist. The spontaneous ups and downs of the grief roller coaster are unavoidable. Fortunately, however, many bereaved persons, including older adults, are quite resourceful and resilient in finding ways to live with their grief and continuing to function within their families and communities (Lund, 1996; 1998). Over the past 20 years research has helped to discover and confirm many ways to ease the pain, facilitate adjustment, and make the process more tolerable. Although no one wants to ride the grief roller coaster, there are many who have learned new skills and experienced a sense of personal growth as they adapt to a new life without their deceased loved ones (Lund, 1998).

This chapter focuses primarily on the benefits to bereaved spouses when they receive help from and give help to others. There is considerable evidence indicating the importance of receiving social, emotional, and practical support from others in order to make the adjustment from being married to being single. Much less, however, is known and discussed about bereaved persons helping others, including other bereaved persons, and the value these actions have for facilitating the grieving process. In many communities, seniors, and especially widows, often voluntarily provide assistance to one another. Both forms of helping behaviors, incoming and outgoing, are discussed in this chapter, because help frequently occurs in a reciprocal manner and is better understood as a two-wayinteraction. When someone helps another he or she may have a favor returned by that person, but it is equally likely that the benefit returns as the result of helping another person. As one widow said, "When I reach out to others, I heal myself."

Most of the information in this chapter is based upon research completed at the University of Utah Gerontology Center. One longitudinal study described the bereavement coping process of 192 widows and widowers, and another tested the effectiveness of bereavement support groups with 339 participants (Lund, Caserta, and Dimond, 1993). Both projects examined bereaved spouses aged 50 and over, and included many questions regarding the kind of help most needed, what help was received, the importance of reciprocal help in support groups, and other types of help that the bereaved provided to others. While findings from these studies have been published in professional journals and books, much of the information in this chapter has not been published elsewhere.

The first section of this chapter deals with the kind of help these bereaved spouses most wanted and received from others. The next section describes the help that these bereaved spouses provided to others and some of the resulting benefits. The final section reviews some of the ways in which the bereaved help each other, usually in the form of support group participation or one-on-one interaction.

Help Most Wanted and Received

Perhaps the greatest difficulty for bereaved persons in receiving help from other people is asking for it. Nearly all bereaved persons will be told by their family members or friends to call them if they need help. Others will say, "Don't hesitate to call me if you need anything. I would like to help you if you will let me know how I can." Unfortunately, 37 percent of the bereaved in one study reported having great difficulty in asking for help, even when it was offered (Rigdon, 1985). The following statements from two widows reveal their personal reluctance to ask for help and their concern that others might be too busy. "I would rather have it [help] offered than have to ask for it. It's hard for me to ask for things, even if I know they don't mind. . . . I realize that they don't think of it and they're willing if I ask. But it's so hard to ask." "I'm very independent and I don't like to intrude on their lives. I would rather do it myself."

Another study found that 67 percent of bereaved men learned new skills on their own by trial and error, compared with 43 percent of the bereaved women (Lund, Caserta, Dimond, and Shaffer, 1989). These relatively high percentages might reflect their reluctance to ask others for help. For example, one widow admitted that she was too embarrassed to ask her son or daughter how to use the VCR, and another widow reluctantly acknowledged that she did not know how to balance her checking account. Several widowers reluctantly asked a female interviewer to show them how to use their dishwashers.

The reluctance to ask for help is only one obstacle to receiving assistance. The bereaved also need to know what it is they most want, and others need to be available and willing to help. Bereaved spouses in the longitudinal study were asked the following open-ended question six times over the first two years of bereavement: "What kinds of help from others would you appreciate the most?" The responses of 30 persons were content analyzed over the course of the study, and four patterns emerged. (These patterns are discussed in much greater detail in an unpublished doctoral dissertation (1985) by Imogene Rigdon.)

Keep in touch. About 70 percent of the respondents reported that they would most appreciate others keeping in touch with them. This was especially common after the first year, when friends and relatives typically focus more attention on their own lives. Visits and phone calls are highly desired. One woman said she was "hungry for conversation." Two other bereaved spouses described their wishes for more contact with others: "Just to be friends. Be able to say hello and visit with them and have them come and see me. Just be friendly, that's all the help I want." "I just wish the phone would ring sometimes when it doesn't."

Express concern. Many bereaved people (53 percent in the study) appreciate expressions of concern about their well-being. They prefer not being told how to live their lives, but they do want to know that others are thinking about them. One widower said very simply, "There's not much they can do except just let me know they're thinking about me."

Help with physical tasks. Forty-three percent of the bereaved spouses gave answers indicating their need for help with tasks that require physical strength. The average age of the participants was 67 years, so their need for this kind of help is not surprising. These tasks included shopping, housecleaning, repairs, and shoveling snow. Requests of this kind were also more common at the two-year period following the death of a spouse.

Receiving social invitations. About 36 percent of the spouses said that they would appreciate having others invite them out. This type of help is quite similar to the first two mentioned above, because the focus is on social interaction. One of the bereaved spouses said that she wanted "invitations out once in a while, just an afternoon shopping or a luncheon or something like that."

In addition to these four patterns some respondents reported having transportation and financial needs that were unmet.

We also learned about the help that bereaved persons had already received. Analysis revealed similar findings: apparently, many of these bereaved spouses eventually received the help they most wanted (Rigdon, 1985). Also, all of the respondents included in the content analysis indicated that others had been helpful to them. The four most common ways that friends and relatives were helpful related to emotional and social support. These bereaved spouses indicated that others had been helpful by keeping in touch, expressing concern, being available, and extending social invitations.

Again, all four of these patterns of behavior that were judged to be very helpful reflect the importance of social relationships. When someone is suddenly alone after many years of marriage, relationships with family and friends often become increasingly more important. Expressing concern, keeping in touch, being available, and offering social invitations are relatively easy ways to help, and bereaved spouses place these expressions at the top of their wish lists. This thoughtful kind of help is most appreciated when it is consistent and continues over time. These actions remind the bereaved that they are not forgotten, that they are important and valued as individuals, not just for being part of a couple, and that they have a friendship and relationship to offer others. These feelings can be internalized and used to enhance their self-esteem and serve as motivation to cope with difficult situations.

In addition to social and emotional help, bereaved spouses reported that physical and practical help were needed and appreciated. Many reported needing help with household chores such as cleaning and making repairs and maintaining yards. Some said that legal and financial assistance were helpful, along with transportation and gifts of food. There are many ways to be helpful that are not difficult to provide.

It is interesting to note that no one in this study reported that they were helped by advice concerning how to cope with the death of their husband or wife. Simple acts of giving time, expressing sincere concern and doing practical favors are most helpful.

Bereaved Spouses Helping Others

We know more about the kind of help bereaved persons want and need than we do about the help they provide to others. Discussions of grief often assume that support travels in only one direction because those in grief are the ones who need help. This assumption fails to recognize two important considerations.

First, everyone can benefit from receiving help from others. Help does not necessarily imply dependence or even need. Help and social relationships require interdependence (Rigdon, 1985). Acts of kindness and thoughtfulness can be helpful because they remind us of our social relationships and connections with others. The fact that someone is grieving the loss of a loved one does not mean that he or she no longer has relationships with others. These continuing interdependencies require reciprocity, which means that even the bereaved are expected to help others. Second, the assumption ignores the benefits of helping others. We need to better understand how helping others can facilitate the coping process of the bereaved.

We often asked what advice the bereaved spouses would give to others. For the most part they were reluctant to give advice, due to the individual nature of their experiences. After this initial hesitancy, they most often said it is important to "take one day at a time." Some even suggested that it is less overwhelming to simply "take one part of the day at a time." Breaking the day up into parts can make mornings, afternoons, and evenings more manageable.

The next most common type of advice was to keep busy (Lund, et al., 1985; Caserta, Van Pelt, and Lund, 1989). This is not meant to suggest avoiding the situation or loss. The bereaved spouses who recommended this did so because they recognized the value of maintaining social contact, doing something meaningful, and not dwelling exclusively on what they had lost.

Being active resulted in improved coping abilities and outcomes for many bereaved spouses (Lund et al., 1985), and the bereaved frequently recommend that helping others is one of the best ways to keep busy (Rigdon, 1985). This process has been referred to as the "helper-therapy" principle, that people help themselves when they help others (Riessman, 1965).

The following statements reflect the value in keeping busy and doing things for others: "Trying to do things for other people is a comfort. If you're doing for somebody else, it brings you a measure of joy and helps you to get over some rough spots." "Look around and see how you might help somebody close to you. I can't sit around and have everything myself and not be doing something for somebody else." "If you stop considering and loving people. . . then you might just as well die." "Keep busy and try to maintain an interest in doing things and socializing with other people. You need that" (Rigdon, 1985).

The longitudinal study asked a sub-sample of 51 bereaved spouses if they had helped other people during the past year and, if so, to indicate what type of help they had provided. Detailed findings are presented in an unpublished thesis (Juretich, 1984), but some of the most relevant results are highlighted here. Four categories of help were identified, and most of the bereaved provided all four kinds of help to others. The most common type of help was social support or activity: dining out, recreational travel, entertainment, and parties or celebrations. The second most common type of help provided to others was described as service: visiting someone in a hospital, providing transportation, preparing meals, babysitting, sewing, doing volunteer work, and running errands.

Giving emotional support to others was the third most common type of help provided. This type of help was most often related to letting someone else know that they were remembered or to give them specific advice related to social relationships. The fourth type of help was providing economic or financial support. This kind of support was usually provided to children and was found to be the least satisfying to the bereaved. It is interesting to note that the spouses who had most frequently given economic support to others later experienced more difficulty with depression, lower coping ability, and perceived health (Juretich, 1984). It is not clear why these relationships existed but it is possible that giving financial help was less rewarding because it involved money rather than time and emotion. Support of a more personal nature appeared to be associated with greater life satisfaction and lower depression.

By helping others, bereaved persons can find meaningful ways to remain socially connected and ultimately facilitate their own coping. This is particularly true of those for whom it represents the continuation of an important part of their own identity.

Bereaved Persons Helping Each Other

One of the most effective behaviors for bereaved persons is helping one another. There is a unique bond between bereaved persons that can facilitate communication and empathy. The reciprocal sharing of feelings, experiences, difficulties, and accomplishments provides a recognition that they have something in common with others and are not alone. In her book on widows helping other widows, Phyllis Silverman (1986) quotes a 40-year-old widow as saying, "You need to talk with someone else who is a widow—who really knows what it is like. I thought I was the only one in the world who felt this lonely and was so afraid" (p.vii).

A great deal of learning results from the exchange of ideas, coping strategies, and life experiences. Bereaved persons often find one another through informal channels such as meeting at church, employment relationships, and through mutual friends. Once they discover their common situation they begin to provide mutual self-help. These informal relationships are especially common and valuable to older widows and widowers, because many of them are retired and have time available to form and benefit from new relationships. They also have accumulated many practical skills that they can teach or exchange with others who need them.

Other more formal and systematic strategies and programs are available in most communities, however, which deliberately bring together bereaved persons so that the "helper-therapy" principle can be facilitated. Variations on the "widow to widow" concept (Silverman, 1986) have been applied to specific situations of bereaved persons: bereaved parents helping other bereaved parents, grieving children can help other grieving children (Hill, Lund, and Packard, 1996). The primary purpose of this concept is one-on-one interaction between two people who share a common grief situation. This interaction allows in-depth and personal conversations, and facilitates the development of a personal relationship. Over time, the relationship often becomes part of the coping process. In many cases, one of the bereaved plays the role of an experienced guide. It is important, however, for the more experienced griever not to play the role of therapist. The value in this approach is in the informality and shared grief; professional counselors and therapists are needed to deal with traumatic and complicated cases.

Another common way for bereaved persons to help one another is through participation in self-help groups, which, like the one-to-one approach, emphasizes the value of bringing together people who share common experiences so that they may help one another. The major difference is that the sharing occurs in groups where there are greater opportunities for discovering helpful ideas, connecting with more people, and feeling strength in numbers. Self-help groups offer bereaved persons excellent opportunities to help others and, in return, help themselves.

Many bereaved persons are reluctant to participate in these groups, however, and some may not even need the help (Lund, Dimond, and Juretich, 1985; Lund, Redburn, Juretich, and Caserta, 1989; Caserta and Lund, 1993). Some people have never been personally expressive in group situations, and feeling coerced into doing so is not likely to result in positive experiences. Others find their own unique ways to cope with grief without self-help groups.

Two studies showed that bereaved spouses most likely to participate in self-help groups were those experiencing high stress and loneliness (Lund, Dimond, and Juretich, 1985; Caserta and Lund, 1996). Many of those who wanted to participate in self-help groups reported that they had a confidant in whom they could confide, but who was not readily available, resulting in considerable frustration on the part of the bereaved person. Surprisingly, no significant demographic differences were found between bereaved spouses who were invited but refused to participate and those who did participate. Men were not less likely than women to participate; nor did income or education make a difference.

Bereaved spouses who participated in one of the self-help groups in our study reported extremely positive experiences (Lund and Caserta, 1992). When participants were asked to identify the need they hoped most would be met by being in a group, the most common response (nearly 62 percent) was "to receive emotional support from others."

The next most common response (18 percent) was "a desire to help others," another example of the potential benefits when a bereaved person wants to help others. The desire to interact with others was evident among the 10 percent who said their greatest need was "to meet others." Together these last two answers indicate that 28 percent of these study participants most wanted to be in self-help groups for social reasons. They either wanted to help others or simply have an opportunity to meet people. About 5 percent of the participants said they most wanted to be in the group to obtain information. Fortunately, most of the bereaved spouses who participated in these groups reported that their needs were well met (Lund and Caserta, 1992).

One of the reasons self-help groups worked well for bereaved persons was that the members felt they were part of a group. When asked what they liked the most about their sessions many gave answers using plural pronouns, indicating that they were part of a group and benefited from the group experiences. "It caused us to talk about our problems and we were able to release some of our pent-up feelings." "We felt that we had somewhat the same problems of grief." "We had something in common and had an understanding for each other."

Another example of the importance of social interaction during bereavement was the large percentage (64 percent) of self-help group participants who met with other members outside group meetings, even though they were not encouraged do so (Caserta and Lund, 1996). Those who continued to meet with others outside the scheduled sessions reported being less lonely at the end of the study.

Many bereaved spouses wanted more social interaction with other bereaved persons, and they found ways to make it happen. Two widows who became friends during their group sessions said they decided to take turns organizing additional group meetings at their homes because they simply wanted to socialize more. Others who had outside meetings mentioned that they did not always discuss grief and coping at those gatherings but spent considerable amounts of time talking about regular daily life. Informal activities included group dinners, walks, shopping, and entertainment. One widow said, "I'm sure glad that I met Florence. We have so much in common. We go to lunch a lot, talk on the phone and enjoy each other's company." These kinds of outcomes from self-help groups cannot be guaranteed, but they are not unusual either.

Summary

Bereaved persons can benefit not only from receiving help, but from providing help as well. There is considerable research to document what kinds of help bereaved persons most want and need, how they can be of assistance to others, and how they can help one another. Research also has identified some of the benefits that result from both receiving and giving help during bereavement.

Most of the emotional, social, and practical forms of help discussed in this chapter reflect the importance of social relationships during very difficult life transitions. Losing a loved one, especially a spouse after many years of marriage, leaves a huge void in social activity for most widows and widowers. The lost relationship and associated activities and identity cannot be replaced, but new relationships based upon reciprocal helpfulness and interdependency are valuable because they can provide meaningful use of time, make people feel more valued, and give additional purpose to life. Older widows and widowers can and do find ways to live with their grief through opportunities that exist in their daily lives in their own neighborhoods, churches, volunteer groups, and communities.

Dale A. Lund, PhD, is a professor and Director of the University of Utah Gerontology Center in Salt Lake City. He founded the Death, Dying & Bereavement Interest Group within the Gerontological Society of America. Dr. Lund was a recipient of the Outstanding Research Award from the Association for Death Education and Counseling, and the Utah Hospice Person of the Year Award.

Sixteen

If I Am Not for Myself: Caring for Yourself as a Caregiver for Those Who Grieve

James E. Miller

If I am not for myself, who will be for me?
But if I am only for myself, what am I?
And if not now, when?

These words were written over a thousand years ago by a man of wisdom named Rabbi Hillel. He was known for his gentleness, his kindness, and his concern for people from all walks of life. He was a caregiver. It's appropriate, then, that his words reach across the centuries to address those who are caregivers today—particularly those who care for the bereaved. For the purposes of this chapter, we will reverse the order of his questions so they can be dealt with in the order in which many caregivers naturally address them.

"If I am only for myself, what am I?"

Every professional who works with those who grieve has asked that question in one way or another, at one time or another, either consciously or unconsciously. It's the basic issue that must be resolved before anyone can become comfortable caring for those whose needs are great. "Am I supposed to take care of myself, or is my purpose on earth larger than that? Am I a person who can reach out to those who hurt, or am I one who is inclined to hold back from such a role? In other words, do I have what it takes to be a caregiver?"

Some of us answered that question at a very early age, when circumstances in life thrust the decision upon us. Some of us answered it when we chose a major field of study, when we selected a career, or when we followed our hearts and pursued a new career. Some of us answered that question without realizing it, when we took on the tasks of caregiving out of expediency or necessity later in life and found that the role fit us well. Some of us have had our own hearts broken and somehow we have grown through that experience and we have quietly pledged, "I will offer what I have learned so that others can benefit, so that what has happened to me will come to have value."

"But if I am not for myself, who will be for me?"

Sooner or later another question enters our consciousness, or maybe it's a series of questions. "Now that I am a caregiver, am I only and always a caregiver? Can I be a good caregiver and still get tired of caregiving? Can I genuinely care for others and still carve out time for myself even when other people's needs are so evident and so pressing? Is it selfish if I sometimes want someone to care for me in the same way I care for others?"

Our responses to Rabbi Hillel's two basic questions may appear to contradict one another: "Yes, I truly care for others," and "Yes, unquestionably I care for myself." But in reality a person can make both statements and still be an excellent caregiver. In fact, it's only in being able to make both statements equally, simultaneously, and unequivocally that one can be a vital, committed caregiver. Given that, what can be said about caring for oneself as a dedicated volunteer or as a trained professional who works regularly with those who are mourning?

Accept the fact you cannot do this work alone and still do it well.

It's a demanding task to work with people who grieve. It can tire and tax you to stay available to them through the entire painful process. You can become weighed down yourself if you're dealing with too many grieving people at once, or if other people's losses are particularly traumatic or tragic, or if you feel bewildered about the work you're doing, and how you're doing it, and how you're supposed to do it.

Sometimes you need to decompress. Rather than hold it all in, you can experience a reassuring release when you speak in confidence with someone you trust, while maintaining the confidentiality of those in your care. At other times you need perspective, either with individual situations or with your work as a whole. "What's happening here that I don't see? What are the options I haven't yet considered?" Sometimes it's more than a broader perspective or impartial feedback you desire—it's a whole different approach to your situation which may shed new light on what's happening or not happening, on what's possible or probable. If you're a psychologist, for instance, and you're dealing with a grieving person who's very religious, might a clergy person help you better understand the unique dynamics of their faith as it relates to grief? If you're a clergy person, funeral director, or bereavement coordinator, might a psychologist help you see how you can best relate when a bereaved person first seeks you out?

Sometimes you simply need encouragement—someone who says in one way or another, "I believe you can do this." Maybe there is someone with whom you consult on a regular basis. Maybe you choose to participate in a peer support group. You may ask a more experienced professional to provide supervision of your work. Perhaps you simply get together informally over a cup of coffee with people who work in related fields, where the knowing laughter may flow as easily as serious conversation.

Connecting with those who grieve is not a job for mavericks. Too much is at stake. Too much can be missed. There's too much for one person to know. When you turn to others in your professional role, you give yourself the opportunity to grow. You make your job more manageable. You can see yourself more objectively. But most of all, you can help create a healthier environment and a richer experience for those who turn to you as they grieve. And that's what your role is all about.

Understand you cannot do this work without letup.

You're likely to tell someone who is mourning that they need and deserve respite from his or her grief. Depending upon who they are and where they are in their process, breaking away from their grief for brief periods of time can facilitate their healing in the long run. The advice you give others also applies to you: You need and deserve respite from the grief work you do as well. That work can be exhausting. Its relentlessness can seem forbidding. Being so often confronted with other people's losses can stir up your own issues with loss too. Being so close to others' pain can put you in touch with your own pain as well, whether from the past, the present, or the future.

So take time away. Claim your right to do something different, something you enjoy. Make sure you have respites daily, weekly, yearly. Follow your own natural rhythm in doing this. Develop your own respite activities, whether you go someplace different or stay at home, whether you do something active or you do very little at all. Remember what you would say to those in your care: "Don't feel guilty—respites are good for you. They can help you." Listen to your own words.

Make sure you have a life apart from your work. Set clear boundaries about how much you'll do for others and how much you'll do for yourself. Save time to do those things that help you feel happy or relaxed or contented. Engage your creative side. Remind yourself that you're not forgetting or deserting those who are in your care. You're simply practicing ways to gather your energy and refresh your vitality.

In certain circumstances you may need longer times away. Experiences in your own life may dictate that. I speak often with a friend who is a grief counselor. She specializes in dealing with parents whose children have died. Several weeks ago her own teenage son was killed in an auto accident. She has wisely stopped working with others for awhile, both for her sake and her clients'. She knows the truth: She cannot do this work without letup. Neither can you.

Practice what you preach: wholeness.

You're aware, of course, that grief manifests itself in a full complement of ways within any individual. It shows up in one's body, mind, heart, and soul, as well as in one's relationships with others. As a concerned caregiver, one of your tasks is to remain open to all those avenues of expression in that other person. You're likely to encourage that person to include all aspects of his or her self on that journey through grief. Chances are you'll include your own whole self as you seek to build a relationship with such people.

It is only logical, therefore, for you to take your whole self into account when you consider any caregiving you do for yourself. What forms might this take? An entire variety, as complete as you are.

Pay attention to your body and what it's telling you. Get plenty of exercise, on the one hand, and enough rest, on the other. You can learn and practice techniques for managing stress. Eat and drink healthfully and wisely. You can find ways to stretch your mind. You can honor, explore, and give expression to your feelings. You can strive to develop mutually satisfying relationships with others.

The list is practically endless. You can open yourself in your own best ways to that which is divine. You can give yourself time alone as well as time with others. You can make room for remembering as well as dreaming, for inwardly reflecting as well as outwardly responding.

Caring for yourself requires intentionality and discipline. It calls for maintaining a sense of balance so that no single aspect of yourself overshadows any other aspects to their detriment. It calls especially for you to find ways to remain the person you already are.

Model what you stand for: healing and growth.

You have committed yourself to the possibilities that the grieving process holds. You believe in—indeed, you have witnessed—how people can return to fullness of life again, how they can integrate their losses into who they become as changed and expanded human beings. You understand that grief helps people adapt to what cannot be altered, while at the same time it helps them explore what can be altered. Without question, grieving is all about healing.

As a caregiver you cannot avoid your own losses any more than anyone else can. So as you live and lose and grieve and adapt, you open yourself to those identical possibilities of healing and growth. You're given that same opportunity through any of those experiences that contain an element of dying: separation and divorce, job loss and career change, illness and incapacitation, addiction and recovery, family shifts and personal transitions. Like those you counsel, you can place yourself in situations that foster your own healing and growth as you go through such times. You can build a pleasing physical environment around you, no matter how small. You can seek out people who bring you life and avoid those who hurt you. You can strive to keep your self-expectations reasonable and affirming. You can adopt attitudes that lead you to search for positive learning from life's heartaches. You can take a sustained introspective look and refuse to gloss over what deserves your attention. You can be willing to take risks for the sake of reaching toward something greater in life.

Henri Nouwen once described people like this as "wounded healers." They're often among the most effective caregivers of all, for they understand. They have been there. As a wounded healer, you can be especially effective when the one in your care is yourself, whether you provide that caring directly or you place yourself in another's capable hands.

In the midst of heaviness, you can find ways to be light.

Companioning those who grieve can be unavoidably saddening. When a beloved spouse dies tragically, when a family member is killed, when someone chooses suicide—these and others are serious losses that cannot be taken lightly, either by those left with their grief or by you as a caregiver. Sometimes the sheer number of upsetting deaths can make it difficult for you to move out from under their dampening influence. It's important that you are alert for such a development, and should it occur, experiment with ways to boost your outlook as a caregiver. One such way is through the use of joy and humor.

Placing to one side how this might take place in the course of your relationship with a grieving person (that's another chapter), you can fashion your own means to grapple with your heavier experiences as a professional. This is not a matter of downplaying or neglecting the seriousness of these events in people's lives. Rather, it's a matter of realizing your limits and protecting your spirits. When done consciously and appropriately, this method of self-care can help you keep your perspective, validate the other person, and lighten your emotional load at the same time.

How you choose to do this will reflect your individuality. You may wish to brighten your days, or at least parts of your days, with what brings you joy or contentment—perhaps your favorite art or music, inspiring books or videos, or simply surrounding yourself with the cleansing beauty of the created world. Some people turn to humor, whether that means watching what's funny, listening to what's witty, or reading what's light-hearted. You can let yourself be amused by cartoons, jokes, stories. You can be funny yourself. You can find amusement in the people you choose to be around or the kinds of entertainment you select. Sometimes your black humor can help you cope. At other times a professional friend may help you see the lighter side in a way that others might not understand. Done sensitively, you can find humor both in your work as a caregiver and away from that role, without being any less responsible or responsive to those who entrust themselves to your care.

Befriend your helplessness.

Almost to a person, caregivers do not like to feel helpless, at least early on as they learn that role. They are inclined to want to make a difference in people's lives. They like to believe they can decidedly influence outcomes. But caregiving does not always work that way. And grief caregivers often experience a unique kind of helplessness, as explained by Colin Parkes (1972, 163):

> *Pain is inevitable and cannot be avoided. It stems from the awareness of both parties that neither can give the other what he wants. The helper cannot bring back the person who is dead and the bereaved cannot gratify the helper by seeming helped.*

That's helplessness! Yet in addition to your inability as a grief professional to make a measurable difference in all you do, there is another truth to take to heart: You ought not always be intent on making that difference. When you do too much, those in your care do not do enough. The only way they will ultimately develop the determination, strength, and resilience to go and grow through their grief is by your letting them do just that. You can advise, but you dare not dictate. You can walk beside, but you dare not always walk ahead, nor dare you carry the other person.

How does this relate to caring for yourself as a caregiver? Awkward as you may initially feel in accepting your helplessness, you can experience a wonderful freedom in taking that stance. You are clearly not the center of responsibility. Your role is more limited, though your influence is no less important. You free yourself to do what you do best: help create a healthy, supportive environment in which the power of natural healing can begin to take place of its own accord.

Practice letting go.

While accepting your helplessness is one form of letting go, there are other forms, too. In letting go of steering the process, you allow yourself to be a participant, perhaps even a catalyst, but not the absolute authority. In letting go of any drive to serve everyone's needs—whoever they are, whatever has happened to them, whatever is going on in your life—you free yourself to concentrate on the kind of caregiving at which you're most effective in this period of your life. You also make room for other caregivers to be effective in their own ways. In letting go of always needing to have the answers, you become an inveterate beginner and learner. In letting go of only filling a particular role, you can become more human, more open, more available. And that's more enjoyable for everyone involved. In letting go of any inclination to play God, you allow the Real McCoy to fill the part.

You care for yourself when you practice letting go in small and large ways in your personal life, too. You can practice letting go of unnecessary controls, unhelpful illusions, and unhealthy thinking. You can practice letting go as it's appropriate when you go through your own life transitions, all of which will include endings and deaths in one form or another. You can even practice letting go of the work you do, the caregiving you offer, and, when it's time, the people you care for. Ultimately it comes to this: in some significant way, letting go of yourself.

Treat your work for what it is: a calling.

Not many can do what you do as a grief professional. No doubt you have heard comments like this before: "How can you relate to so many grieving people all the time? Isn't it depressing?" What such people do not understand is what you have learned from experience: It is a privilege to be granted entree into the deep parts of people's lives. It is an inspiration to see the changes that can occur, the hope that can blossom. It is a blessing to witness the ways in which love can be given and received following the death of someone close, even across the boundaries of life and death itself.

As a rule, people like you don't enter school and plan for a career by saying, "I'm going to learn how to work with the bereaved." Usually that inclination comes later. Often it's an impulse that somehow gradually beckons, invites, and guides. You don't ask so much as answer. It is often less a searching than it is an act of being found. Whatever else is going on, it is more than you that is involved.

Those who are really in tune with their work often speak of its being "the right match" for them. A friend who is a psychologist but works full-time as a college professor spoke to me recently about a counseling session she had just had with a person experiencing a life-threatening illness. "After such sessions," she reported, "I know that's what I am supposed to be doing. That's where my energy lies." She was experiencing a call.

When your work is your calling, you approach it with a kind of humble pride. Yes, you want to be an able caregiver. Yes, you want your strengths and abilities to be put to good use. But you also realize that this work is much larger than you. In an important way, you are also merely a vehicle, a conduit. But there is another way of stating that: You are *undoubtedly* a vehicle. You are a channel by which something marvelous can unfold. The most natural response you can make in such a situation is one of gratitude.

What if your caregiving work with the bereaved is not your calling? You will do well to reflect upon why that may be the case. Are you being called to do something else? Are you tired and therefore deserving of time away? Do you need more support? More tools? More training? More vision? Life is too short for you to keep doing what is not right for you. And if your work isn't right for you, it isn't right for those in your care either. Sometimes taking care of yourself as an effective caregiver means finding another way to be a channel.

Gather the lessons from your work with those in grief and live. Just live.

You draw close to others at a critical juncture of their lives. Death has taken a toll. Brokenness, loneliness, and sadness, among other experiences, are often the order of the day. But that is not all. You can also witness the overcoming of devastation, the bridging of love, the mending of relationships, and the finding of meaning. It is a noteworthy time, rich with possibility.

The lessons that come through grief are often expressed as paradoxes. People who genuinely grieve do more than just lose in the process—they also gain. People who face realistically the loss they have experienced can do more than just let go—they can also hold on. People who open themselves to death's mysteries discover that more than death awaits them—so does life, and even a whole new sense of life. There are many more lessons to be gleaned in addition to these. These lessons will be as unique as you are, as unique as all those who turn to you as a companion.

These lessons are too valuable to be ignored. You can tease them out and highlight them when you see them illustrated in the lives of others. You can pass along their message to those who will benefit, at a time when they're ready to hear. But especially you can internalize what those in your care have taught you and continue to teach yourself. You can carry those lessons to other parts of your life—indeed, to all parts of your life. Then you can do more than remember such lessons—you can live them. You can do that confidently, knowing you're on solid ground, for this is no mere second-hand information. You've been taught by those who know. You've learned it from the pros.

Emily Dickinson spoke the truth of a grief caregiver's work as well as anyone:

> *A Death blow is a Life blow to Some*
> *Who till they died, did not alive become—*
> *Who had they lived, had died but when*
> *They died, Vitality begun.*
> *(Dickinson, 1976)*

When you are a caregiver to those who grieve, their death blows can become life blows—to an extent—to you as well as to themselves. Your own death blows—to a much greater extent—can work the same purpose. The result is the same: in Dickinson's words, "vitality begun." May you know that to be true in your own life, as one who provides wonderful caring for others by caring for yourself.

James E. Miller, DMin, is a clergyman, counselor, writer, and photographer who lives and works in Fort Wayne, Indiana. Through Willowgreen Productions and Willowgreen Publishing, he has produced videotapes and books in the areas of loss and grief, managing transition, illness and dying, caregiving, and spirituality, and conducts workshops and multi-media presentations throughout North America.

Resource Organizations

AIDS National Interfaith Network

1400 I Street NW, Suite 1220, Washington, DC 20005
(202) 842-0010 Fax: (202) 842-3323
http://www.anin.org
e-mail: aninscott@aol.com or aninken@aol.com

AIDS National Interfaith Network is a not-for-profit organization created in 1988 to ensure that individuals with HIV and AIDS receive compassionate and nonjudgmental rapport, care, and assistance. ANIN coordinates a network of nearly 2,000 AIDS ministries and convenes the Council of National Religious AIDS Networks.

ALS Association National Office

27001 Agoura Road, Calabasas Hills, CA 91301-5104
(818) 880-9007 Fax: (818) 880-9006
Information and Referral Service: (800) 782-4747
http://www.alsa.org

The Amyotrophic Lateral Sclerosis (ALS) Association is dedicated to the fight against ALS, commonly referred to as Lou Gehrig's disease. The Association is a national information resource on ALS, funding research and providing referrals for counseling, training, and support.

Alzheimer's Association

919 N. Michigan Avenue, Suite 1000, Chicago, IL 60611-1676
(800) 272-3900

The Alzheimer's Association is the only national voluntary organization dedicated to conquering Alzheimer's disease through research, and through providing education and support to people with Alzheimer's disease, their families, and caregivers. The association sends out general information about the disease and caregiving responsibilities and refers callers to their local chapter, where they can get support group information and find out about resources in their area.

American Association of Pastoral Counselors

9504A Lee Highway, Fairfax, VA 22031-2303
(703) 385-6967
e-mail: info@aapc.org

> The American Association of Pastoral Counselors (AAPC) was organized in 1963 to promote, support, and credential the ministry of pastoral counseling within religious communities and the field of mental health in the United States and Canada.

American Association of Retired Persons

AARP Grief and Loss Programs
601 E Street, NW, Washington, DC 20049
(202) 434-2266
http://www.aarp.org/griefandloss
e-mail: griefandloss@aarp.org

> American Association of Retired Persons offers a variety of bereavement programming, sponsored in affiliation with local community organizations, aimed to provide support to widows and widowers of all ages and to persons grieving the death of a parent, sibling, or other loved one. AARP provides resources and materials on starting and maintaining self-help programs and support groups and facilitates two online bereavement support groups on AOL. In addition, AARP publishes a selection of bereavement-related booklets and brochures.

Americans for Better Care of the Dying

2175 K Street, NW, Suite 820, Washington, DC 20037
(202) 530-9864
http://www.abcd-caring.com
e-mail: caring@erols.com

> Americans for Better Care of the Dying (ABCD) is a not-for-profit charity dedicated to development of service systems that meet the special needs of the last phase of life. ABCD aims to: enhance the experience of the last phase of life for all Americans; advocate for the interests of patients and families; improve communication between providers and patients; involve society in end-of-life care; control pain and other symptoms; demand continuity in service systems for the seriously ill; limit the emotional and financial toll on families; and support quality improvement initiatives by front-line providers.

American Brain Tumor Association

2720 River Road, Suite 146, Des Plaines, IL 60018
(800) 886-2282
http://pubweb.acns.nwu.edu/~lberko/abta_html/abta1.htm

> The American Brain Tumor Association is a not-for-profit organization offering over 20 publications which address brain tumors,

their treatment, and coping with the disease; nationwide listing of support groups and physicians offering investigative treatments; regional Town Hall meetings; and a pen-pal program.

American Cancer Society

1599 Clifton Road, NE, Atlanta, GA 30329-4251
(800) ACS-2345
http://www.cancer.org

The American Cancer Society is the nationwide, community-based voluntary health organization dedicated to eliminating cancer as a major health problem by preventing cancer, saving lives, and diminishing suffering from cancer through research, education, advocacy, and service.

American Heart Association

7272 Greenville Avenue, Dallas, TX 75231
(214) 373-6300 or
(800)AHA-USA1 to be connected to closest affiliate in area
http://www.americanheart.org

The American Heart Association is one of the world's premier health organizations committed to reducing disability and death from cardiovascular diseases and stroke.

American Liver Foundation

75 Maiden Lane #603, New York, NY 10038
(800) GO-LIVER
http://www.liverfoundation.org

The American Liver Foundation is a national not-for-profit organization dedicated to preventing, treating, and curing hepatitis and other liver and gallbladder diseases through research and education.

American Parkinson's Disease Association

1250 Hylan Boulevard, Suite 4B, Staten Island, NY 10305-1946
(800)223-2732 or (718) 981-8001
http://www.apdaparkinson.com
e-mail: apda@admin.con2.com

The American Parkinson's Disease Association is a not-for-profit voluntary health agency committed to serving the Parkinson's community through a comprehensive program of research, education, and support, offering educational booklets and supplements, symposiums, and referrals to support groups, local chapters, and physicians specializing in Parkinson's disease throughout the United States.

American School Counselors Association

801 N. Fairfax Street, Suite 310, Alexandria, VA 22314
(800) 306-4722 Fax: (703) 683-1619
http://www.schoolcounselor.org
e-mail: asca@erols.com

American School Counselors Association, with a membership of over 13,000 school counseling professionals, focuses on providing professional development, enhancing school counseling programs, and researching effective school counseling practices. ASCA's mission is to help to ensure excellence in school counseling. Since its founding in 1952, ASCA has provided publications, educational programs and conferences, professional development workshops, and other programs for school counselors at all levels of public and private educational systems.

Association for Clinical Pastoral Education

1549 Clairmont Road, Suite 103, Decatur, GA 30033
(404) 320-1472
http://www.acpe-edu.org
e-mail: acpe@acpe-edu.org

The ACPE mission is to foster experienced-based theological education which combines the practice of pastoral care with qualified supervision and peer group reflection, and which is grounded in a person-centered approach to religious ministry.

Association for Death Education and Counseling

342 N. Main Street, West Hartford, CT 06117-2507
(860) 586-7503
http://www.adec.org
e-mail: info@adec.org

Association for Death Education and Counseling is dedicated to improving the quality of death education and death-related counseling and caregiving; to promoting the development and interchange of related theory and research; and to providing support, stimulation, and encouragement to its members and those studying and working in death-related fields.

Association for Professional Chaplains

1701 E. Woodfield Road, Suite 311, Schaumburg, IL 60173
(847) 240-1014 Fax: (847) 240-1015
http://www.professionalchaplains.org
e-mail: info@professionalchaplains.org

The Association of Professional Chaplains is an interfaith, professional pastoral care association advocating quality spiritual care of all persons in healthcare facilities, correctional institutions, long-term care units, rehabilitation centers, hospice, the military, and other specialized settings. Its purpose is to promote and develop pastoral care and professional chaplaincy as an essential dimension of total care and services provided by public and private institutions and organizations. The APC provides professional certification and standards, and serves its members with networking, resources, and educational opportunities.

Candlelighters Childhood Cancer Foundation

7910 Woodmont Avenue, Suite 460, Bethesda, MD 20814-3015
(800) 366-2223 or (301) 657-8401
http://www.candlelighters.org

Candlelighters Childhood Cancer Foundation provides support, information, and advocacy to families of children with cancer (at any stage of the illness or who are bereaved), to professionals in the field, and to adult survivors, through local groups, newsletters, and other services.

The Center to Improve Care of the Dying

2175 K Street, NW, Suite 820, Washington, DC 20037
(202) 467-2222
http://www.gwu.edu/~cicd
e-mail: cicd@gwis2.circ.gwu.edu

The Center to Improve Care of the Dying is a unique, interdisciplinary organization founded in the belief that life under the shadow of death can be rewarding, comfortable, and meaningful for almost all persons. The Center is committed to research and professional education. To improve the care of dying patients and those suffering with severely disabling diseases, the Center aims to encourage real changes in the healthcare system. Among the goals of the Center are: to understand current practice and outcomes; to measure quality and develop accountability; to educate practitioners, managers and the public; to improve service through innovation and evaluation; and to change the practice environment to enable quality services.

The Compassionate Friends

P.O. Box 3696, Oak Brook, IL 60522-3696
(630) 990-0010
http://www.compassionatefriends.org

The Compassionate Friends is a self-help organization whose purpose is to offer friendship and understanding to families following the death of a child. They have 580 chapters nationwide which provide monthly meetings, phone contacts, lending libraries and a local newsletter. The national organization provides a quarterly magazine, distributes grief-related materials, hosts an annual national conference, provides training programs and resources for local chapters and answers requests for referrals and information.

Concerns of Police Survivors

P.O. Box 230, Camdenton, MO 65020
(573) 246-4911 Fax: (573) 346-1414
http://www.nationalcops.org
e-mail: cops@nationalcops.org

Concerns of Police Survivors, Inc., is a national not-for-profit, grief-support organization that comprises nearly 9,000 surviving families of America's fallen law enforcement officers. COPS sponsors grief seminars for adults and children, holds a summer camp for grieving families, challenges young adult survivors at wilderness activities, and trains law enforcement agencies on support issues for surviving families. COPS is a hands-on organization that also provides support to newly bereaved families at the grassroots level through 31 chapter organizations. Quarterly newsletters, information to help agencies develop general orders addressing the loss of an officer, and benefits information are available through COPS.

Cystic Fibrosis Foundation

6931 Arlington Road, Bethesda, MD 20814
(800) 344-4823

The mission of the Cystic Fibrosis Foundation is to assure the development of the means to cure and control cystic fibrosis and to improve the quality of life for those with the disease.

The Dougy Center

P.O. Box 86582, Portland, OR 97286
(503) 775-5683
http://www.dougy.org
e-mail: help@dougy.org

The Dougy Center provides support groups for grieving children that are age-specific (3-5, 6-12, teens) and loss-specific (parent death, sibling death, survivors of homicide/violent death, survivors of suicide). Additional services include national trainings, consultations to schools and organizations, crisis-line information, and referrals. The Dougy Center's National Center for Grieving Children and Families is in the process of publishing a series of guidebooks based on what they've learned from the children they've served.

Employee Assistance Professional Association

2101 Wilson Boulevard, Suite 500, Arlington, VA 22201
(703) 522-6272 Fax: (703) 522-4585
http://www.eap-association.com

The Employee Assistance Professionals Association was established in 1971. EAPA provides members with the resources they need to enhance performance and ensure continued growth and success.

EAPA is the recognized voice of the employee assistance field. EAPA has more than 100 chapters in the United States, Canada, and worldwide. They provide numerous training programs for employee assistance professionals and others in the workplace.

Growth House

http://www.growthhouse.org
e-mail: info@growthhouse.org

The mission of Growth House, Inc., is to improve the quality of compassionate care for people who are dying, through public education about hospice and home care, palliative care, pain management, death with dignity, bereavement, and related issues. This award-winning web site offers the net's most extensive directory of reviewed resources for life-threatening illness and end-of-life care. Growth House offers a free monthly e-mail newsletter covering new and noteworthy net resources for terminal care, life-threatening illness, and bereavement. Growth House provides the Inter-Institutional Collaborative Network on End Of Life Care, which links major professional organizations internationally.

Hospice Foundation of America

2001 S Street, NW, Suite 300, Washington, DC 20009
(202) 638-5419 Fax (202) 638-5312
777 17th Street, Suite 401, Miami Beach, FL 33139
(800) 854-3402
http://www.hospicefoundation.org
e-mail: hfa@hospicefoundation.org

Hospice Foundation of America is a not-for-profit organization that provides leadership in the development and application of hospice and its philosophy of care. The Foundation produces an annual National Bereavement Teleconference and publishes the *Living With Grief* book series in conjunction with the teleconference. In addition to the annual teleconference, HFA offers a number of other resources. *A Guide to Recalling and Telling Your Life Story* is a tool to assist people in writing their autobiographies. *Clergy to Clergy: Ministering to Those Facing Illness, Death and Grief* is an audiotape series developed to help clergy members of all faiths minister to their communities and see to their own needs as caregivers. HFA publishes *Journeys*, a monthly newsletter to help in bereavement; has published a series of educational ads; and provides a number of free informational brochures to hospices, military service centers, and other organizations. HFA is a member of the Combined Federal Campaign through Health Charities of America.

Last Acts Campaign

c/o Barksdale Ballard, 1915 Kidwell Dr. Suite 205, Vienna, VA 22182
(703) 827-8771 Fax: (703) 827-0783
http://www.lastacts.org
e-mail: lastacts@aol.com

Last Acts is a national campaign to engage both health professionals and the public in efforts to improve care at the end of life. Last
Acts is made up of 275 partner organizations that believe that
every segment of society-employers, clergy, voluntary health organization leaders, medical and nursing professionals, counselors,
among others-has a role to play as a part of a larger movement
that addresses end-of-life concerns at the national, state and community levels. The three guiding principles of Last Acts are to
identify models that improve end-of-life care, to examine systems
of end-of-life care that may be improved, and to improve the culture of dying in America.

Leukemia Society of America

600 Third Avenue, New York, NY 10016
(800) 955-4LSA
http://www.leukemia.org

The Leukemia Society of America is a voluntary not-for-profit
health organization to cure leukemia and its related cancers—lym-
phoma, myeloma, and Hodgkin's disease—and improve the quality
of life for patients and their families.

MADD: Mothers Against Drunk Driving

511 E. John Carpenter Freeway, Suite 700, Irving, TX 75062
(800) 438-6233 Fax: (972) 869-2206
http://www.madd.org
e-mail: info@madd.org

MADD's mission is to stop drunk driving and help victims of this
violent crime.

Multiple Sclerosis Association of America

706 Haddonfield Road, Cherry Hill, NJ 08002
(800) 833-4672
http://www.msaa.com

The Multiple Sclerosis Association of America is a national not-for-
profit healthcare agency providing direct care services to those with
MS. These services include a national toll free hotline, peer counseling, support groups, therapeutic equipment loan program,
educational literature, symptom management therapies, and other
vital services.

National AIDS Fund

1400 I Street, NW, Suite 1220, Washington, DC 20005
(202) 408-4848 Fax: (202) 408-1818
http://www.aidsfund.org
e-mail: info@aidsfund.org

Now in its tenth year, the National AIDS Fund is a grantmaking organization dedicated to eliminating HIV/AIDS as a major health and social problem. It provides program and technical assistance for hundreds of local educational, direct service, and other HIV/AIDS programs.

The Fund also works with the nation's employers to manage AIDS in the workplace and educate employees about HIV/AIDS prevention. The Fund provides businesses a national network of leading experts who deal with HIV/AIDS policy issues, and publishes a broad range of HIV/AIDS publications. It also offers onsite problem solving and manager/employee training programs, as well as access to its Workplace Resource Center, which contains information, publications, and other resources for dealing with AIDS in the workplace.

National Brain Tumor Foundation

785 Market Street, Suite 1600, San Francisco, CA 94103
(800) 934-CURE or (415) 284-0208 Fax: (415) 284-0209
http://www.braintumor.org
e-mail: nbtf@braintumor.org

The National Brain Tumor Foundation provides a variety of support and educational services for patients and their families, including booklets, newsletters, support group listings and assistance in starting new groups, a toll free brain tumor information line, the Support Line patient/giver network, and national and regional conferences.

National Family Caregiving Association

10605 Concord St., Suite 501, Kensington, MD 20895-2504
(301) 942-6430 Fax: (301) 942-2302
http://www.nfcacares.org
e-mail: info@nfcacares.org

The National Family Caregivers Association provides information, education, support and validation, public awareness and advocacy for America's family caregivers. It is the only organization reaching across the life span and the boundaries of relationship and diagnoses to address the common needs of all caregivers. NFCA has a bereavement program for former caregivers that addresses their special grief.

National Federation of Interfaith Volunteer Caregivers

368 Broadway, Suite 103, Kingston, NY 12401
(914) 331-1358
http://www.nfivc.org
e-mail: nfivc@aol.com

The purpose of the National Federation of Interfaith Volunteer Caregivers, Inc. is to promote, in all congregations throughout the United States, the ministry of caregiving to persons and their families without reference to age, gender, race, or religious affiliation. NFIVC provides support and training to start and operate Interfaith Volunteer Caregiving Projects (IVCPs). Through IVCPs, Volunteer Caregivers provide compassionate one-on-one care to those in need.

National Kidney Foundation

30 East 33rd Street, New York, NY 10016
(800) 622-9010 or (212) 889-2210
http://www.kidney.org

The National Kidney Foundation, a major voluntary health organization, is dedicated to preventing kidney and urinary tract diseases, improving the health and well-being of individuals and families affected by these diseases and increasing the availability of all organs for transplantation. The foundation conducts programs in research, professional education, patient and community services, public education and donation. It publishes a number of materials about the grieving process.

National Hospice Organization

1901 N. Moore Street, Suite 901, Arlington, VA 22209
(703) 243-5900
http://www.nho.org
e-mail: drsnho@cais.com

The National Hospice Organization (NHO) is the oldest and largest public benefit organization in the US devoted exclusively to hospice care. NHO operates the Hospice Helpline (1-800-658-8898) to provide the general public and healthcare professionals with information about hospice care, reimbursement sources, as well as referrals to local hospice programs throughout the US. NHO publishes a variety of brochures on hospice care, grief in the workplace, and bereavement.

Office of Minority Health Resource Center

P.O. Box 37337, Washington, DC 20013-7337
(800) 444-6472 Fax: (301) 589-0884 TTY: (301) 589-0951
http://www.omhrc.gov

The Office of Minority Health Resource Center (OMH-RC) was established to facilitate the exchange of information and strategies to improve the health status of racial and ethnic minorities. The center's mission is to collect and distribute information on the health of Blacks, Hispanics, Asians and Pacific Islanders, American Indians and Alaska Natives. The Resource Persons Network of OMH-RC consists of minority health experts available to provide technical assistance, offer advice, and speak at workshops. OMH-RC publishes a bimonthly newsletter called Closing the Gap. Services are provided at no cost.

Project on Death in America

Open Society Institute
400 W. 59th Street, New York, NY 10019
http://www.soros.org/death/index.htm
e-mail: pdia@sorosny.org

Project on Death in America's goal is to understand and transform the forces that have created and now sustain the current culture of dying. The Project supports epidemiological, ethnographic, and historical research and other programs that illuminate the social and medical context of dying and grieving. PDIA's initiatives include professional education; nursing, social work, and pastoral care; arts and humanities; public policy, legal, comunity-based, and grant making.

Stephen Ministries

2045 Innerbelt Business Center Drive, St. Louis, MO 63114
(314) 428-2600 Fax: (314) 428-7888
http://www.stephenministries.org

Stephen Ministries is a not-for-profit, transdenominational, religious and educational organization founded in 1975. Stephen Ministries is a full-service ministry organization that offers a number of ministry systems and resources to enhance ministry in congregations including the Stephen Series and the ChristCare Series system of small group ministry. The Stephen Series is a complete system for training and organizing lay persons for caring ministry in and around congregations. Over 6,000 congregations from 80 different Christian denominations are enrolled over six continents.

Tragedy Assistance Program for Survivors

2001 S Street, NW, Suite 300, Washington, DC 20009
(800) 959-TAPS
http://www.taps.org
e-mail: TAPSHQ@aol.com

Tragedy Assistance Program for Survivors (TAPS) is a national not-for-profit organization made up of, and providing services at no cost to, all those who have suffered the loss of a loved one in the Armed Forces. The heart of TAPS is its national military survivor peer support network called SurvivorLINK, which links together the families, friends, and co-workers of those who are grieving. TAPS also offers bereavement counseling referral, provides case worker assistance that carries the work of the casualty assistance officers into the future, hosts the nation's only annual National Military Survivor Seminar and Kids Camp, publishes a quarterly journal mailed at no charge to survivors and caregivers, maintains a comprehensive website, and offers a 24 hour toll free crisis and information line..

Widowed Persons Service

4270 Chicago Drive, SW, Grandville, MI 49418
(616) 538-0101

Widowed Persons Service is a self-help support group for men and women who have experienced the loss of a spouse through death. They offer daytime and evening support group meetings, seminars, social activities and public education of the widowed experience. They have a directory of the 270 programs across the country. They have produced five excellent videos on the widowed experience that many hospices have purchased.

World Pastoral Care Center

1504 N. Campbell Street, Valparaiso, IN 46385-3454
888-224-7685 or (219) 464-8183 Fax: (219) 531-2230

The World Pastoral Care Center, with Connections—Spiritual Links, is a bridge builder to existing programs and services with advocacy, support, subscription series, and programs related to bereavement, spirituality, spiritual care, a consultation service, and a starting point for resource information when new needs for care are identified.

References

Where We Grieve – Doka

Corr, C. (1998, March). Enhancing the concept of disenfranchised grief. Presentation to the Annual Meeting of the Association for Death Education and Counseling, Chicago, IL.

Doka, K. (1995). Talking to children about illness. In K. Doka (Ed.), *hildren mourning, mourning children* (pp. 31-55). Washington, DC: Hospice oundation of America/Taylor and Francis.

Doka, K. (1989). *Disenfranchised grief: Recognizing hidden sorrow.* San Francisco: Jossey-Bass.

Chapter 2 – Lattanzi-Licht

Barnett, A. A. (1997). Fixing dysfunctional family leave. *Business & Health, 15,* 22-25.

Brookes, T. (1997). *Signs of life.* New York: Random House/Times Books.

Cable, D. G. (1997). Grief in the American culture. In K. J. Doka and J. D. Davidson (Eds.), *Living with grief: Who we are, how we grieve* (pp. 61-70). Philadelphia: Hospice Foundation of America/Brunner/Mazel.

Hammonds, K. H. (1996, November). Balancing work and family, *Business Week,* 74-90.

Harper, B. C. (1994). *Death: The coping mechanism of the health professional* (2nd ed.). Greensville, SC: Southeastern University Press.

Lattanzi, M. E. (1981). Coping with work-related losses. *The personnel and guidance journal, 59 (6),* 350-351.

Lattanzi-Licht. M. (1994, October). Grief in the workplace. Presentation at the National Hospice Organization Annual Symposium, Washington, DC.

Lattanzi-Licht, M. (1995a, May). Grief in the workplace: Management perspectives. Presentation at the National Hospice Organization Management and Leadership Conference, Washington, DC.

Lattanzi-Licht, M. (1995b, November). Grief and trauma in the hospice workplace. Presentation at the National Hospice Organization Annual Symposium, Phoenix, AZ.

Lattanzi-Licht, M., Mahoney, J., and Miller, G.W. (1998). *The hospice choice: In pursuit of a peaceful death.* New York: Simon & Schuster/Fireside.

National Hospice Organization (1995). Illness/death affects worker productivity, *Newsline, 7,* 20.

Rando, T. A. (1993). *Treatment of complicated mourning.* Champaign, IL: Research Press.

Raphael, B. (1983). *Anatomy of bereavement.* New York: Basic Books, Inc.

Schoenberg, B., Carr, S. C., Peretz, D. and Kutcher, A. K. (1970). *Loss and grief: Psychological management in medical practice.* New York: Columbia University Press.

Viorst, J. (1986). *Necessary losses.* New York: Simon & Schuster.

Ziegler, J. (1996). How corporations cope when death intrudes. *Business & Health, 14,* 31-42.

Chapter 3 – Kirby

D'Angelo, J. J. (1994). Alcoholism and chemical dependency in law enforcement: Its effects on the officer and the family members. In J. T. Reese and E. Scriver (Eds.), *Law enforcement families: Issues and answers* (pp. 57-66). Washington, DC: Federal Bureau of Investigation.

Doka, K. J. (1989). Disenfranchised grief. In K. J. Doka (Ed.), *Disenfranchised grief* (pp. 3-11). Lexington, MA: Lexington Books.

Everly, G. S., and Mitchell, J. T. (1997). *Critical incident stress management.* Ellicott City, MD: Chevron Publishing Corporation.

Eyetsemitan, F. (1998). Stifled grief in the workplace. *Death Studies, 22 (5),* 469-480.

Gerberth, V. J. (1992). Secondary victims of homicide. *Law and Order, 40 (9),* 91-97.

Gilbert, R., and Bolger, G. (1986). A coordinated approach to alcoholism treatment. In J. T. Reese and H. A. Goldstein (Eds.), *Psychological services for law enforcement* (pp. 115-120). Washington, DC: Federal Bureau of Investigation.

Hodgkinson, P. E. (1989). Technological disaster - survival and bereavement. *Social Science Medical, 29 (3),* 351-356.

Klyner, N. (1986). L.A.P.D.'s peer counseling program after three years. In J. T. Reese and H. A. Goldstein (Eds.), *Psychological services for law enforcement* (pp. 121-135). Washington, DC: Federal Bureau of Investigation.

Mann, J. P., and Neece, J. (1990). Workers' compensation for law enforcement related post traumatic stress disorder. *Behavioral Sciences and the Law, 8,* 447-456.

Mitchell, J., and Bray G. (1990). *Emergency services stress.* Englewood Cliffs, NJ: Prentice Hall.

Parkes, C. (1993). Psychiatric problems following bereavement by murder or manslaughter. *British Journal of Psychiatry, 162,* 49-54.

Rando, T. A. (1993). *Treatment of complicated mourning.* Champaign, IL: Research Press.

Saathoff, G. B., and Buckman, J. (1990). Diagnostic results of psychiatric evaluations of state police officers. *Hospital and community psychiatry, 41,* 429-432.

Sawyer, S.F. (1989). *Support services to surviving families of line-of-duty death* (Grant No. 89-PS- CX-0001). Rockville, MD: National Institute of Justice.

Stein, A. J., and Winokuer, R. (1989). Monday mourning: Managing employee grief. In K. J. Doka (Ed.), *Disenfranchised grief* (pp. 91-102). Lexington, MA: Lexington Books.

Stillman, F.A. (1987). *Line-of-duty deaths: Survivor and departmental responses* (Grant No. 89-PS -CX-0001). Rockville, MD: National Institute of Justice.

Sunoo, B. P., and Solomon, C. M. (1996). Facing grief: How and why to help people heal. *Personnel Journal, 75 (4),* 78-89.

Chapter 4 – Zucker

American Cancer Society (1998). When cancer strikes a co-worker. [Brochure]. Available: www.cancer.org.

Centers for Disease Control (1995). *HIV/AIDS surveillance report, 9*:2.

Doka, K. J. (1994). *Disenfranchised grief: Recognizing hidden sorrow.* Lexington, MA: Lexington Books.

Frazee, V. (1996). When grief causes employees jobs to suffer. *Workforce, 75,* (6), 165.

Frolkey, C. (1996). Trauma in the workplace. *Personnel Journal. 65,* (11), 10-14.

Henderson, J. (1997). How to support grief and loss in the workplace. *Workforce, 76,* (9), 3-6.

Kuhar, M. S. (1995). Fatality: Preventing workplace fatalities. *Occupational Hazards, 57,* (4), 44-48.

Mitchell, J. T., and Everly, G. Jr. (1995). *Critical incident stress debriefing: CISD: An operations manual for the prevention of stress among emergency and disaster workers (2nd ed.).* Ellicott City, MD: Chevron Publishing Corporation.

Ramsey, R. (1995). How to handle employee grief. *Supervision, 56,* 10, 6.

Reigel, M. (1998). *Grief at the workplace.* Unpublished article.

Slack, J. D. (1995). The Americans with disabilities act and the workplace: Management's responsibilities in AIDS-related situations. *Public Administration Review, 55,* (4), 365.

Tyler, M. (1996). A manager's handbook handling traumatic events. *United States Department of Agriculture Safety and Health Division,* HRSS-OERWP-15.

West, M. (1998, April 27). Companies learning to deal with grief in workplace. *The Arizona Republic,* pp. A1.

Chapter 5 – Carroll

Powell, C., Gen. (personal communication, Novermber, 1992).

Worden, J. W. (1991). *Grief counseling and grief therapy: A handbook for the mental health practitioner.* New York: Springer.

Chapter 6 – Coleman

Business responds to AIDS (BRTA) manager's kit. (1998). *Business Responds To AIDS Resource Service, Public Health Service.* Atlanta, GA: Centers for Disease Control and Prevention, Public Health Service.

Centers for Disease Control (1997). *HIV/AIDS surveillance   report, 9:2.

Rosenstock, I. M. (1966). Why people use health services. *Milbank Memorial Fund Quarterly 44,* 2.

World Health Organization on AIDS. (1992, March–April). *World Health.*

Chapter 7 – Brenner

Bigelo, G. and Hollinger, J. (1996). Grief and AIDS: Surviving catastrophic multiple loss. *The Hospice Journal, 11,* (4), 83-96.

Brenner, P. (1977). Managing patients and families at the end of life: Hospice assumptions, structures, and practice in response to staff stress. *Cancer Investigation 15* (3), 257-264.

Capra, F. (1966). *The web of life: A new scientific understanding of living systems.* New York: Doubleday.

Capra, F. (1982). *The turning point.* New York: Simon and Schuster.

Cassell, E. J., M. D. (1982). The nature of suffering and the goals of medicine. *New England Journal of Medicine, 306,* 639-45.

Dali Lama, H. H. (1997). *Sleeping, dreaming, and dying.* Somerville, MA: Wisdom Publications.

Kerenyi, C. (1959). *Asklepios: Archtetypal image of the physician's existence.* New Jersey: Princeton University Press, Bollinger   Series LSV-3.

Kubler-Ross, E. (1975). *Death: The final stage of growth.* New York: Simon and Schuster.

Levine, S. and O. (1982). *Who dies? An investigation of conscious living and conscious dying.* New York: Anchor Books, Doubleday.

Nouwen, H. (1979). *The wounded healer.* New York: Doubleday.

Osteseski, F. (1998, March). *Mindfulness in the practice of hospice care.* Workshop Presentation at Jacob Perlow Hospice, New York, NY.

Chapter 8 – Matthews

Allen, L. (1990). Working with bereaved teenagers. In J. D. Morgan (Ed.), *The Dying and the Bereaved Teenager* (pp. 39-41). Philadelphia: The Charles Press.

Barrett, R. K. (1995). Children and traumatic loss. In K. J.   Doka (Ed.), *Children mourning, mourning children* (pp. 85-88). Washington, DC: Hospice Foundation of America/Taylor and Francis.

Cragg, C. E. and Berman, H. A. (1990). Adolescents' reactions to the death of a parent. In J. D. Morgan (Ed.), *The dying and the bereaved teenager* (pp. 42-49). Philadelphia: The Charles Press.

Goldman, L. (1994). *Life and loss: A guide to help grieving children.* Bristol, PA: Accelerated Development/Taylor and Francis Group.

Harris, M. (1995). *The loss that is forever: The lifelong impact of the early death of a mother or father.* New York: Penguin Group.

Hayes, R. L. (1988). Coping with loss: A developmental approach to helping children and youth. In J. Carlson and J. Lewis (Eds.), *Counseling the Adolescent: Individual, Family, and School Interventions* (pp. 73-92). Denver: Love Publishing.

Peterson, S. and Straub, R. L. (1992). *School Crisis Survival Guide: Management Techniques and Materials for Counselors and Administrators.* West Nyack, NY: The Center for Applied Research in Education.

Riethmayer, J. (1997). *When trauma hits!.* Bryan, TX: BJR Enterprises.

Sims, A. (1990). Who am I now? A sibling shares her grief. In J. D. Morgan (Ed.), *The Dying and the Bereaved Teenager* (pp. 33-38). Philadelphia: The Charles Press.

Stevenson, R. G. (1995). The role of the school: Bereaved students and students facing life-threatening illnesses. In K. J. Doka (Ed.), *Children mourning, mourning children* (pp. 97-111). Washington, DC: Hospice Foundation of America/Taylor and Francis.

Whiting, P. and Matthews, J. (1997). *Responding to loss: A manual to assist educators in responding to loss in the schools.* Columbia, SC: SC-ETV.

At Worship – Doka

Doka, K. and Jendreski, M. (1985). Clergy understandings of grief, bereavement and mourning. *Research Record, 2,* 105-114.

Doka, K. and Morgan J. (1993). *Death and spirituality.* Amityville, NY: Bayword Press.

Van Gennep, A. (1960). *The rites of passage.* Chicago: University of Chicago Press.

Weisman, A. (1972). *On dying and denying: A psychiatric study of terminnity.* New York: Behavioral Publications.

Chapter 9 – Levine and Khalili

D'Costa, E. (Personal communication, August 30, 1998).

Dane, B. and Levine, C. (1994). *AIDS and the new orphans: Coping with death.* Westport, CT: Auburn House.

Donovan, P. (1998). School-based sexuality education: The issues and challenges. *Family Planning Perspectives 30,* 188-193.

Federation of Protestant Welfare Agencies. (1996). Estimated number of children and adolescents orphaned by maternal HIV/AIDS deaths in New York State. *Families in crisis: Report of the working committee on HIV, children and families* (pp. 5-11). New York: Author.

Geballe, S. and Gruendel, J. (1998). The crisis within the crisis: The growing epidemic of AIDS orphans. In S. Books (Ed.), *Invisible children in the society and its schools* (pp. 61). Mahway, NJ: Lawrence Erlbaum Associates, Publishers.

Hudis, J. (1995). Adolescents living in families with AIDS. In W. Andiman, S. Geballe, and J. Gruendel (Eds.), *Forgotten children of the AIDS epidemic* (pp. 83-94). New Haven, CT: Yale University Press.

McKelvy, L. (1998, May). Students and HIV-related bereavement: Eleven actions teachers can take. *HIV/AIDS Team Update.* New York: TA Project.

Michaels, D. and Levine, C. (1992). Estimates of the number of motherless youth orphaned by HIV in the U.S. *Journal of the American Medical Association 268*, 3456-3461.

Richardson, L. (1998). Group helps students who've lost parents to AIDS. *The New York Times*.

Rusnar, K. and Fiester, L. (1998). *Families with AIDS: Report of a conference held by Casey Family Services* (December 11-13, 1997). Baltimore, MD: Annie E. Casey Foundation.

Valleroy, L. et al. (1998). HIV infection in disadvantaged out-of-school youth: Prevalence for US Job Corps entrants, 1990 through 1996. *Journal of Acquired Immune Deficiency: Human Retrovirology, 19*, (1), 67-73.

Chapter 10 – Wrenn

Marrone, R. (1997). *Death, mourning and caring.* Pacific Grove, CA: Brooks/Cole Publishing Company.

Rickgarn, R. L. V. (1996). The need for postvention on college campuses: A rationale and case study findings. In C. A. Corr and D. E. Balk (Eds.), *Handbook of Adolescent Death and Bereavement.* New York: Springer.

Whitaker, L. C. and Slimak, R. E. (Eds.). (1990). *College Student Suicide.* New York: Haworth.

Worden, J. W. (1991). *Grief Counseling and Grief Therapy (2nd ed.).* New York: Springer.

Chapter 11 – Barney

Byock, I., (1992, November 3). Address to the Ninth International Conference on the Care of the Terminally Ill, Montreal, Canada.

Hesse, H. in Roech, R. (1996). *To die well: A holistic guide to the dying and their caregivers.* New York: Harper Collins.

Kessler, D. (1997). *The rights of the dying: A companion for life's final moments.* New York: Harper Collins.

Lewis, C. S. (1961). *A grief observed.* Boston: Faber and Faber.

Longaker, C. (1997). *Facing death and finding hope: A guide to the emotional and spiritual care of the dying.* New York: Doubleday.

Neimeyer, R. (1998). Dimensions of diversity in the reconstruction of meaning. In J. Davidson and K. Doka (Eds.) *Living with grief: Who we are, how we grieve.* Washington, DC: Hospice Foundation of America/Brunner/Mazel.

Pomerantz, D. (1973). *It's in every one of us.* Warner Brothers Music.

Whitman, W. (n.d.). Song of myself. In P. McNees (Ed.), *Dying:A book of comfort.* (Section 6, Verses 129 and 130). New York: Doubleday.

Living With Grief: At Home – Doka

MacPherson, M. (1999). *She came to live out loud.* New York: Scribner.

Chapter 12 – Irion

Marris, P. (1958). *Widows and their families.* London: Routledge and Kegan Paul.

Silverman, P. Unpublished lecture given at Lancaster Theological Seminary.

Van Gennep, A. (1960). *Rites of passage.* (M. Vizedom and G. Caffee, Trans.). Chicago: University of Chicago Press.

Chapter 14 – MacPherson

Corr, C. A., Nabe, C. M., and Corr, D. M. (1997). *Death and dying, life and living.* Pacific Grove, CA: Brooks/Cole Publishing Co.

Jevne, R. F., and Levitan, A., (1989). *No time for nonsense: Getting well against the odds.* San Diego, CA.: LuraMedia.

Chapter 15 – Lund

Caserta, M. S., and Lund, D. A. (1993). Intrapersonal resources and the effectiveness of self-help groups for bereaved older adults. *The Gerontologist, 33,* 619-629.

Caserta, M. S., and Lund, D. A. (1996). Beyond bereavement support group meetings: Exploring outside contact among the members. *Death Studies, 20,* 537-556.

Caserta, M. S., Van Pelt, J. and Lund, D. A. (1989). Advice on the adjustment to loss from bereaved older adults: An examination of resources and outcomes. In D.A. Lund (Ed.), *Older Bereaved Spouses: Research with Practical Applications.* Washington DC: Taylor Francis/Hemisphere.

Hill, R. D., Lund, D. A. and Packard, R. E. (1996). Bereavement. In J. I. Sheikh (Ed.), *Treating the Elderly.* San Francisco: Jossey-Bass.

Juretich, M. (1984). *Outgoing helping behavior as a coping strategy during the first year of bereavement among the elderly: Toward a model for nursing intervention.* Unpublished masters thesis, University of Utah College of Nursing.

Lund, D. A. (1996). Bereavement and loss. In J. E. Birren (Ed.), *Encyclopedia of Gerontology*. San Diego: Academic Press.

Lund, D. A. (1998). Bereavement. In B. Edelstein (Ed.), *Clinical Geropsychology*. (Vol. 8 of Comprehensive clinical psychology). Oxford, England: Elsevier Science.

Lund, D. A., Caserta, M. S. and Dimond, M. F. (1993). The course of spousal bereavement in later life. In M. S. Stroebe, W. Stroebe and R. O. Hansson (Eds.), *Handbook of bereavement: Theory, research and intervention*. Cambridge University Press.

Competencies, tasks of daily living and adjustments to spousal bereavement in later life. In D. A. Lund (Ed.), *Older bereaved spouses: Research with practical applications*. Washington, DC: Taylor Francis/Hemisphere.

Lund, D. A., Dimond, M. F. and Juretich, M. (1985). Bereavement support groups for the elderly: Characteristics of potential participants. *Death Studies*, *9*, 309-321.

Lund, D. A., Dimond, M. F., Caserta, M. S., Johnson, R. J., Poulton, J. L., and Connelly, R. J. (1986). Identifying elderly with coping difficulties after two years of bereavement. *Omega: Journal of Death and Dying*, *16*, 213-224.

Lund, D. A., Redburn, D., Juretich, M., and Caserta, M. S. (1989). Resolving problems in implementing bereavement self-help groups. In D. A. Lund (Ed.), *Older bereaved spouses: Research with practical applications*, Washington, DC: Taylor Francis/Hemisphere.

Riessman, F. (1965). The helper-therapy principle. *Social Work*, *10*, 27-32.

Rigdon, I. S. (1985). *Toward a theory of helpfulness for the elderly bereaved: An invitation to a new life*. Unpublished doctoral dissertation, University of Utah College of Nursing.

Silverman, P. R. (1986). *Widow to widow*, New York: Springer.

Chapter 16 – Miller

Dickinson, E. (1976). *The complete poems of Emily Dickinson*. (T. Johnson, Ed.), Boston: Little Brown and Company.

Parks, C. (1972). *Bereavement: Studies of grief in adult life*. New York: International Universities Press.